Triumph STAG
1970-1980

Compiled by
R.M. Clarke

ISBN 0 907073 26 3

Distributed by
Brooklands Book Distribution,
'Holmerise', Seven Hills Road,
Cobham, Surrey, England.

BROOKLANDS BOOKS SERIES

AC Ace & Aceca 1953-1983
AC Cobra 1962-1969
Alfa Romeo Giulia Berlinas 1962-1976
Alfa Romeo Giulia Coupés 1963-1976
Alfa Romeo Spider 1966-1981
Aston Martin Gold Portfolio 1972-1985
Austin Seven 1922-1982
Austin A30 & A35 1951-1962
Austin Healey 100 1952-1959
Austin Healey 3000 1959-1967
Austin Healey 100 & 3000 Collection No. 1
Austin Healey 'Frogeye' Sprite Collection No. 1
Austin Healey Sprite 1958-1971
Avanti 1962-1983
BMW Six Cylinder Coupés 1969-1975
BMW 1600 Collection No. 1
BMW 2002 1968-1976
Bristol Cars Gold Portfolio 1946-1985
Buick Riviera 1963-1978
Cadillac Eldorado 1967-1978
Cadillac in the Sixties No. 1
Camaro 1966-1970
Chevrolet Camaro Collection No. 1
Chevelle & SS 1964-1972
Chevy II Nova & SS 1962-1973
Chrysler 300 1955-1970
Citroen Traction Avant 1934-1957
Citroen 2CV 1949-1982
Cobras & Replicas 1962-1983
Cortina 1600E & GT 1967-1970
Corvair 1959-1968
Daimler Dart & V-8 250 1959-1969
Datsun 240z & 260z 1970-1977
De Tomaso Collection No. 1
Dodge Charger 1966-1974
Excalibur Collection No. 1
Ferrari Cars 1946-1956
Ferrari Cars 1962-1966
Ferrari Cars 1969-1973
Ferrari Dino 1965-1974
Ferrari Dino 308 1974-1979
Ferrari 308 & Mondial 1980-1984
Ferrari Collection No. 1
Fiat X1/9 1972-1980
Ford Falcon 1960-1970
Ford Mustang 1964-1967
Ford Mustang 1967-1973
Ford RS Escort 1968-1980
High Performance Escorts MkI 1968-1974
High Performance Escorts MkII 1975-1980
Hudson & Railton Cars 1936-1940
Jaguar (& S.S) Cars 1931-1937
Jaguar Cars 1957-1961
Jaguar Cars 1961-1964
Jaguar Cars 1964-1968
Jaguar E-Type 1961-1966
Jaguar E-Type 1966-1971
Jaguar XKE Collection No. 1
Jaguar XJ6 1968-1972
Jaguar XJ6 Series II 1973-1979
Jaguar XJ6 & XJ12 Series III 1979-1985
Jaguar XJ12 1972-1980
Jaguar XJS 1975-1980
Jensen Cars 1946-1967
Jensen Cars 1967-1979
Jensen Interceptor Gold Portfolio 1966-1986
Lamborghini Cars 1964-1970
Lamborghini Cars 1970-1975
Lamborghini Countach Collection No. 1
Lamborghini Countach & Urraco 1974-1980
Lamborghini Countach & Jalpa 1980-1985
Lancia Stratos 1972-1985
Land Rover 1948-1973
Land Rover Series II & IIa 1958-1971
Land Rover Series III 1971-1985
Lotus Cortina 1963-1970
Lotus Elan 1962-1973
Lotus Elan Collection No. 1
Lotus Elan Collection No. 2
Lotus Elite 1957-1964
Lotus Elite & Eclat 1974-1981
Lotus Turbo Esprit 1980-1986
Lotus Europa 1966-1975
Lotus Europa Collection No. 1
Lotus Seven 1957-1980
Lotus Seven Collection No. 1
Maserati 1965-1970
Maserati 1970-1975
Mazda RX-7 Collection No. 1
Mercedes 230/250/280SL 1963-1971
Mercedes 350/450SL & SLC 1971-1980
Mercedes Benz Cars 1949-1954
Mercedes Benz Cars 1954-1957
Mercedes Benz Cars 1957-1961
Mercedes Benz Competition Cars 1950-1957
Metropolitan 1954-1962
MG Cars 1929-1934
MG TC 1945-1949
MG TD 1949-1953
MG TF 1953-1955
MG Cars 1957-1959
MG Cars 1959-1962

MG Midget 1961-1980
MG MGA 1955-1962
MGA Collection No. 1
MGB Roadsters 1962-1980
MGB GT 1965-1980
Mini Cooper 1961-1971
Morgan Cars 1960-1970
Morgan Cars 1969-1979
Morris Minor Collection No. 1
Old's Cutlass & 4-4-2 1964-1972
Oldsmobile Toronado 1966-1978
Opel GT 1968-1973
Pantera 1970-1973
Pantera & Mangusta 1969-1974
Plymouth Barracuda 1964-1974
Pontiac GTO 1964-1970
Pontiac Firebird 1967-1973
Pontiac Tempest & GTO 1961-1965
Porsche Cars 1960-1964
Porsche Cars 1964-1968
Porsche Cars 1968-1972
Porsche Cars in the Sixties
Porsche Cars 1972-1975
Porsche 356 1952-1965
Porsche 911 Collection No. 1
Porsche 911 Collection No. 2
Porsche 911 1965-1969
Porsche 911 1970-1972
Porsche 911 1973-1977
Porsche 911 Carrera 1973-1977
Porsche 911 SC 1978-1983
Porsche 911 Turbo 1975-1984
Porsche 914 1969-1975
Porsche 914 Collection No. 1
Porsche 924 1975-1981
Porsche 928 Collection No. 1
Porsche 944 1981-1985
Porsche Turbo Collection No. 1
Reliant Scimitar 1964-1982
Rolls Royce Silver Cloud 1955-1965
Rolls Royce Silver Shadow 1965-1980
Range Rover 1970-1981
Rover 3 & 3.5 Litre 1958-1973
Rover P4 1949-1959
Rover P4 1955-1964
Rover 2000 + 2200 1963-1977
Rover 3500 1968-1977
Rover 3500 & Vitesse 1976-1986
Saab Sonett Collection No. 1
Saab Turbo 1976-1983
Singer Sports Cars 1933-1934
Studebaker Hawks & Larks 1956-1963
Sunbeam Alpine & Tiger 1959-1967
Thunderbird 1955-1957
Thunderbird 1958-1963
Triumph 2000-2.5-2500 1963-1977
Triumph Spitfire 1962-1980
Triumph Spitfire Collection No. 1
Triumph Stag 1970-1980
Triumph Stag Collection No. 1
Triumph TR2 & TR3 1952-1960
Triumph TR4.TR5.TR250 1961-1968
Triumph TR6 1969-1976
Triumph TR6 Collection No. 1
Triumph TR7 & TR8 1975-1981
Triumph GT6 1966-1974
Triumph Vitesse & Herald 1959-1971
TVR 1960-1980
Volkswagen Cars 1936-1956
VW Beetle 1956-1977
VW Beetle Collection No. 1
VW Golf GTi 1976-1986
VW Karmann Ghia 1955-1982
VW Scirocco 1974-1981
Volvo 1800 1960-1973
Volvo 120 Series 1956-1970

BROOKLANDS MUSCLE CARS SERIES

American Motors Muscle Cars 1966-1970
Buick Muscle Cars 1965-1970
Camaro Muscle Cars 1966-1972
Capri Muscle Cars 1969-1983
Chevrolet Muscle Cars 1966-1972
Dodge Muscle Cars 1967-1970
Mercury Muscle Cars 1966-1971
Mini Muscle Cars 1961-1979
Mopar Muscle Cars 1964-1967
Mopar Muscle Cars 1968-1971
Mustang Muscle Cars 1967-1971
Shelby Mustang Muscle Cars 1965-1970
Oldsmobile Muscle Cars 1964-1970
Plymouth Muscle Cars 1966-1971
Pontiac Muscle Cars 1966-1972
Muscle Cars Compared 1966-1971
Muscle Cars Compared Book 2 1965-1971

BROOKLANDS ROAD & TRACK SERIES

Road & Track on Alfa Romeo 1949-1963
Road & Track on Alfa Romeo 1964-1970
Road & Track on Alfa Romeo 1971-1976
Road & Track on Alfa Romeo 1977-1984
Road & Track on Aston Martin 1962-1984

Road & Track on Audi 1952-1980
Road & Track on Audi 1980-1986
Road & Track on Austin Healey 1953-1970
Road & Track on BMW Cars 1966-1974
Road & Track on BMW Cars 1975-1978
Road & Track on BMW Cars 1979-1983
Road & Track on Cobra, Shelby &
  Ford GT40 1962-1983
Road & Track on Corvette 1953-1967
Road & Track on Corvette 1968-1982
Road & Track on Corvette 1982-1986
Road & Track on Datsun Z 1970-1983
Road & Track on Ferrari 1950-1968
Road & Track on Ferrari 1968-1974
Road & Track on Ferrari 1975-1981
Road & Track on Ferrari 1981-1984
Road & Track on Fiat Sports Cars 1968-1981
Road & Track on Jaguar 1950-1960
Road & Track on Jaguar 1961-1968
Road & Track on Jaguar 1968-1974
Road & Track on Jaguar 1974-1982
Road & Track on Lamborghini 1964-1985
Road & Track on Lotus 1972-1981
Road & Track on Maserati 1952-1974
Road & Track on Maserati 1975-1983
Road & Track on Mazda R x 7 1978-1986
Road & Track on Mercedes Sports & GT Cars
  1970-1980
Road & Track on MG Sports Cars 1949-1961
Road & Track on MG Sports Cars 1962-1980
Road & Track on Mustang 1964-1977
Road & Track on Peugeot 1955-1986
Road & Track on Pontiac 1960-1983
Road & Track on Porsche 1951-1967
Road & Track on Porsche 1968-1971
Road & Track on Porsche 1972-1975
Road & Track on Porsche 1975-1978
Road & Track on Porsche 1979-1982
Road & Track on Porsche 1982-1985
Road & Track on Rolls Royce & Bentley 1950-1965
Road & Track on Rolls Royce & Bentley 1966-1984
Road & Track on Saab 1955-1985
Road & Track on Toyota Sports & G T Cars 1966-198
Road & Track on Triumph Sports Cars 1953-1967
Road & Track on Triumph Sports Cars 1967-1974
Road & Track on Triumph Sports Cars 1974-1982
Road & Track on Volkswagen 1951-1968
Road & Track on Volkswagen 1968-1978
Road & Track on Volkswagen 1978-1985
Road & Track on Volvo 1957-1974
Road & Track on Volvo 1975-1985

BROOKLANDS CAR AND DRIVER SERIES

Car and Driver on BMW 1955-1977
Car and Driver on BMW 1977-1985
Car and Driver on Cobra, Shelby & Ford GT40
  1963-1984
Car and Driver on Datsun Z 1600 & 2000
  1966-1984
Car and Driver on Corvette 1956-1967
Car and Driver on Corvette 1968-1977
Car and Driver on Corvette 1978-1982
Car and Driver on Ferrari 1955-1962
Car and Driver on Ferrari 1963-1975
Car and Driver on Ferrari 1976-1983
Car and Driver on Mopar 1956-1967
Car and Driver on Mopar 1968-1975
Car and Driver on Pontiac 1961-1975
Car and Driver on Porsche 1955-1962
Car and Driver on Porsche 1963-1970
Car and Driver on Porsche 1970-1976
Car and Driver on Porsche 1977-1981
Car and Driver on Porsche 1982-1986
Car and Driver on Saab 1956-1985
Car and Driver on Volvo 1955-1986

BROOKLANDS MOTOR & THOROUGHBRED & CLASSIC CAR SERIES

Motor & T & CC on Ferrari 1966-1976
Motor & T & CC on Ferrari 1976-1984
Motor & T & CC on Lotus 1979-1983
Motor & T & CC on Morris Minor 1948-1983

BROOKLANDS PRACTICAL CLASSICS SERIE.

Practical Classics on MGB Restoration
Practical Classics on Midget/Sprite Restoration
Practical Classics on Mini Cooper Restoration
Practical Classics on Morris Minor Restoration
Practical Classics on Land Rover Restoration
Practical Classics on V W Beele Restoration

BROOKLANDS MILITARY VEHICLES SERIES

Allied Military Vehicles Collection No. 1
Allied Military Vehicles Collection No. 2
Dodge Military Vehicles Collection No. 1
Military Jeeps 1941-1945
Off Road Jeeps 1944-1971
V W Kugelwagen 1940-1975

CONTENTS

ACKNOWLEDGEMENTS

When the '70s started the existence of the Stag was known to only a select few people within the Triumph organisation. When the decade ended some 25,000 had been manufactured, it had been out of production for over two years and it had already become a sought after collectors' car.

Like many writers, painters and composers, its true qualities were not recognised during its lifetime. Happily the majority are still on the road today and because luxury grand tourers are becoming somewhat of a rarity they are being well cared for and the chances are that many will survive into the next century.

Brooklands Books' aim is to make available to today's owners of interesting vehicles a comprehensive selection of out of print articles covering a particular make or model. This can only be done with the goodwill of the publishers of the world's leading motoring magazines and I am sure that Stag enthusiasts will wish to join with me in thanking the management of Autocar, Autosport, Car, Modern Motor, Motor, Motor Sport, Road & Track, Road Test, Thoroughbred & Classic Cars and Wheels for allowing their copyright works to appear in this collection. My thanks are also due to Tony Hart who kindly allowed me to photograph his beautifully preserved model which can be seen on the front cover.

R.M. Clarke

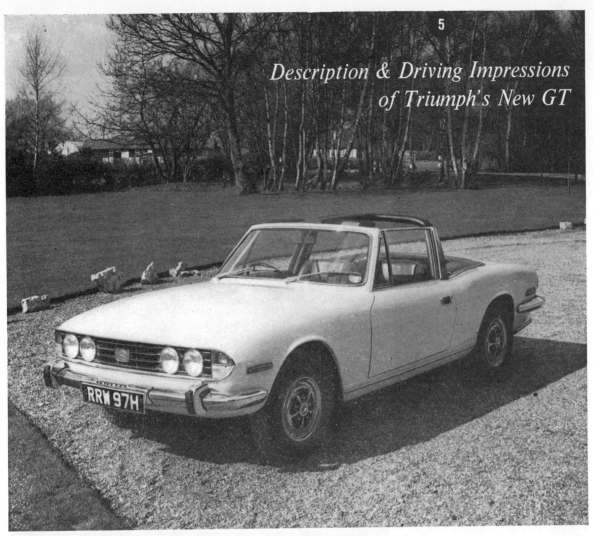

Description & Driving Impressions of Triumph's New GT

TRIUMPH STAG V-8

BY CYRIL POSTHUMUS

A HIGH-PERFORMANCE luxury grand tourer from a marque which, in its time, has produced a whining baby called the Super Seven, the knife-edged Mayflower and Renown series, and the early spartan sports TRs of the '50s, shows how far Triumph has progressed. Their new Stag is a fine, fast, exceptionally smooth performer in the currently somewhat neglected 3-liter class and its qualities should ensure a big demand for it from world markets. The U.S. version, which will come with wire wheels, stainless steel rocker panels and tinted glass as standard equipment, will have a list price of about $5300.

Its evolution is logical yet fascinating. Having designed and developed a 45-degree 1.7-liter slant-4 single overhead cam engine for Saab of Sweden to power their 99 model, what could be more inviting than to pair up two blocks at 90 degrees on a common crankcase, juggle the bore and stroke and produce a 3-liter V-8? The Saab's cylinder dimensions are 83.5 x 78 mm; the Stag has a slightly bigger bore and shorter stroke at 86 x 64.5 mm, and the 2-plane crankshaft runs in five plain bearings. Like Austin, Triumph has hedged on the toothed belt drive system which bolder makers like Fiat and Ford employ, putting their trust in time-proven single chains. There are two side-draft Stromberg carburetors

in the vee, Lucas alternator and ballasted coil ignition, and a no-loss cooling system with expansion chamber and pressure cap. Output is 145 bhp at 5500 rpm, with typical V-8 torque of 170 lb-ft at 3500 rpm, the overall result being velvet smoothness all along the line.

The excellent Triumph 2.0/2.5 PI Mk 2 sedan contributes both the independent front and rear suspension by coil spring/shock units and the all-synchromesh 4-speed gearbox to the Stag, while the front grille and twin quartz-halogen headlight units and stainless steel wheel trims also owe some allegiance to the Mk 2. The steel-panelled unitary body is a 2-plus-2, available with a soft top, a detachable hard top, or both, and the structure embodies a fully padded roll-over bar of T-form, running between the two door pillars and the center of the screen header rail and serving as an excellent safety feature. The soft top can be raised or lowered by one person in under a minute and when down lies concealed in a covered well behind the rear seats. There is a TR-6-style zip-out rear window panel for extra ventilation in hot weather and fixed quarter windows.

Electrically operated windows are standard, while the hard top has forward-hinged anti-draft quarter windows and heated rear window as standard, electrical circuits for the latter automatically connecting or dis-connecting when the top is fitted or re-moved. The standard of luxury in the Stag is indeed very high; it wouldn't be British without a bit of wood, of course, although the non-reflective walnut veneer on the facia and central console has a synthetic look about it. The facia has a matte-black padded surround and the instruments—all that a keen, conscientious driver would need—are set in a compact curved area ahead of him, as on the PI Mk 2. The controls are very well laid out; the separate, fully reclining, vinyl-trimmed seats adjust every way—fore, aft, height and rake—and the steering column is adjustable both axially and vertically. With near 120 mph and V-8 pickup, the Stag has extra large disc front brakes of 10.6-in. diameter and 9.0-in. drum brakes at the rear, with servo assistance.

Driving Impressions

SUMPTUOUS COMFORT is the first im-pression on getting into Triumph's new 3-liter V-8. You can juggle the seat and the steering column around until they suit *you* and the control lay-out is the work of serious sports car designers—handbrake in the proper place in the middle behind the gearbox hump, gear lever just right, lights and winkers through one fingertip lever, wiper and washer on the other and good, big pedals. A leather-clad igni-tion key fitting into a steering column lock is a lot less awkward than most, once one is used to it, and a tweak of it brings pleasant 8-cylinder noises, subdued save when you stab the ac-celerator hard. Acceleration is highly impressive on the Stag and when hap-py that everything was warm we got a 0 to 50 mph in 7.3 sec and 0 to 70 in 12.7 with quite a wind blowing, where-as Triumph themselves claim 7.0s and 12.5s. The gearchange, with a nice short lever, has quite a wide move-ment but is satisfyingly free and not "notchy" (a particular hate of mine after many Maxi miles); the speedome-ter is set right ahead, the tachometer next to the right, somewhat concealed by one of the steering wheel spokes. A cluster of telltale lights mollycoddle the driver with information about oil pressure, winkers, headlight beam, choke, fuel and handbrake, adding to the feeling of confident well being which the Stag imparts.

Is it churlish to complain that the power steering is, if anything, too light? It happens with other cars too, that one takes too big a bite at the wheel initially, and in reaction a few miles further I found I tended to un-der-steer for a corner, then had to take a little more. Obviously familiar-ity acclimatizes one to this, which can-not fairly be called a fault, although

TRIUMPH STAG V-8

one has to watch it when cornering really fast, and lack of feel can be a handicap. Here's where the Citroen SM's progressive power steering will come in eventually, one presumes.

My main impression of the Stag over a fine choice of Belgian roads ranging from *pavée* to pleasant tree-lined B roads and short, sharp stretches of autoroute, was of its almost soft smoothness; there was nothing taut or "sports car" about its handling, save for its precision. The ride was impeccable, the sudden tire patter over a patch of *pavée* reassuringly stable with no lurch or pitch while one could corner very fast without the tire squeal eloquent of forces in conflict. Effortlessness is a strong characteristic; at 1000

rpm, road speed in top gear was an indicated 19.9 mph, but engine flexibility enabled me to come down to 16 mph without snatch or niggle, before accelerating hard, still in top gear, with equal lack of fuss. On the other hand, a grabbed lower gear, then into top again at about 5300 rpm produced most intoxicating pick-up, and one could find oneself in the upper 90s very quickly, all without fuss other than wind noise. This gay deception caught me out at about 90 mph through a fast bend, but when I had to brake suddenly for oncoming traffic while still in the bend, the car wavered from its line not at all. Abundant power is always pleasant and passing in the Stag was a mere matter of aim and fire, with truly superb braking to look after the deceleration side of things.

It is in essence a fast, luxury grand tourer in the old meaning of the word, i.e., ideal for a rapid, comfortable drive for two or three plus luggage across France to the Riviera, or to Germany, Switzerland or Italy, without tiring its occupants. Obviously that V-8 engine has more potential, and its performance in the 2-plus-2 Stag makes one think immediately of its use in an angrier form with double-double Webers or fuel injection, in a shorter, lighter 2-seater sports car with firmer suspension—a TR-7, say—but for anything like that, we must wait and see. British Leyland has chosen for the moment to make maximum use of existing tooling and pieces from the 2.5 sedan and Saab engine for a luxury tourer. As it is, the Triumph Stag must rate highly for easy, untiring high performance with all mod cons. There are options with Laycock overdrive and Borg-Warner Type 35 automatic transmission to make driving it even easier and in such a form the Stag should appeal greatly to many Americans. The discerning few who want a real sports car must hope for a V-8 TR-7 some time in the future. ⓨ

TRIUMPH STAG SPECIFICATIONS

Engine.................sohc 90° V-8	Tires... Michelin XAS radial 185HR14
Bore x stroke, mm........86.0 x 64.5	Chassis/body...............unit steel
Equivalent in.........3.385 x 2.539	Front suspension: MacPherson struts,
Displacement, cc/cu in....2997/182.9	coil springs, tube shocks
Compression ratio..............8.8:1	Rear suspension: independent with
Bhp @ rpm...............145 @ 5500	semi-trailing arms, coil springs, tube
Torque @ rpm, lb-ft.......170 @ 3500	shocks
Transmission: 4-spd manual, 3-spd auto-	Curb weight, lb................2800
matic, 4-spd manual w/o'drive	Wheelbase, in..................100.0
Final drive ratio...............3.7:1	Track, front/rear..........52.5/52.9
Steering: power assisted rack & pinion	Length........................173.8
Turns, lock to lock.............4.0	Width.........................63.5
Brakes: 10.6-in. dia. discs front, 9.0-dia.	Height (soft top)...............49.5
drums rear, servo-assisted	Fuel tank capacity, U.S. gal.......16.8
Wheels.............steel disc 14 x 5J	Maximum speed, mph (mfr).......118

AUTOCAR 11 June 1970

TRIUMPH STAG

Vee-8 power and a sporting image

By Jeffrey Daniels

"Why the Stag?" is not an easy question to answer. It is not a replacement for anything, and falls in the middle of a range already well-endowed with sporting vehicles. If anything, it is a classic gap-filler in the Triumph tradition, without any direct competition.

THE Stag had its origins four years ago (in other words, well before British Leyland came into being). Michelotti, who had done most of Triumph's styling under contract for a long time, was asked to produce a design study for a sports coupé using the existing Triumph 2000 floor pan and mechanical units.

This original study was progressively developed, with one major mechanical change when the in-line engine was abandoned in favour of the new vee-8 unit, and several changes in the body concept, including a shortening of the wheelbase. A new nose and tail treatment was devised, which was thought so successful that it was adapted to the 2000 saloon when it emerged in Mark 2 form. It is interesting to note, when looking at the undoubted family resemblance between the Stag and the saloons, that the Stag was first on the drawing board.

Engine

The vee-8 engine is of course the real centre of interest in the Stag. It is by no means entirely new, for Saab have been using half of it in the 99 for some time. It was a simple matter (in mind from the earliest days of the design) to take two of the 45deg canted, single overhead cam Saab engines and make a vee of them.

The Stag engine is not, however, twice the capacity. When siamesing two four-cylinder engines in this way, one runs into trouble with balance weights fouling pistons unless the stroke is shortened. Originally, indeed, the vee-8 had a capacity of 2.5 litres, but was stretched to three litres rather more than a year ago. It now has a slightly larger bore than the Saab unit, but a much shorter stroke, giving a bore/stroke ratio of 1.33. There is still a little stretch potential left in the engine, but not a great deal.

The large bore makes it possible to achieve very respectable valve sizes within the limits of the in-line layout, and the combustion chamber shape is an efficient wedge, reminiscent of that used by Fiat in the highly successful 128 engine. Power output is modest at 145bhp (net), but tuning at the moment is for flexibility, as the 8.8 compression ratio and 16-56-56-16 timing bear witness. Even so, there is more power here than comes from the 2.5PI in-line unit, and rather more torque as well.

Chrome-iron is used for the block, and aluminium alloy for the heads (and inlet manifold). The installed weight of the engine comes very close to that of the smaller 2.5PI. The head design itself is ingenious. The use of slanted bolts to secure it, allows the camshafts to be taken off without disturbing anything else.

This is just one aspect of the design which shows how much thought has gone into making the whole unit easy to service. The camshafts are chain-driven, and the drive sprockets can be undone and left *in situ* while the camshafts are removed, avoiding the necessity to reset the timing afterwards. Incidentally, the choice of chain drive was taken quite deliberately, despite the availability of toothed belts, in the interests of reduced engine length and better oil-tightness.

Another neat feature is the ease with which the entire inlet manifold assembly can be removed. The two Strombergs sit facing towards one another, in the manner of the SUs in the Rover 3500. Their good anti-pollution characteristics mean that the 1971 California regulations can be met with the aid of an inlet hot-spot and a thermostatically controlled air inlet valve. This was one reason why carburettors rather than fuel injection were chosen for the Stag. Triumph make no secret of the fact that they are looking at the possibility of injection, but stress that any system they use will have to be capable of meeting the American pollution requirements.

The crankshaft is a two-plane, forged-steel unit running in five main bearings. Engines have been run with single-plane cranks, but their vibration characteristics are inevitably far worse. Each crankshaft throw accommodates two big ends, with their own oil supplies from the adjacent main bearing.

Triumph quite rightly stress that the tremendous amount of work done on the Saab engine, especially in the reliability and durability fields, can in large measure be read across to the vee-8. Since Saab are now apparently satisfied that the four is the most durable engine in Europe, this bodes well for the life of the Stag.

All the most important features of the smaller engine are retained, including the distributor and water pump drive from a jackshaft (driven by one of the camshaft drive chains) running the length of the engine in the vee. This has enabled the layout of the front end of the engine to be kept very simple.

A viscous-drive fan of no less than 16.5in. dia. is used, thus reducing power losses and noise generation at high engine speeds. Electric fan operation was seriously considered, but it was felt that a unit able to produce an adequate output in the most difficult cooling conditions would be bulky and difficult to install. There are separate vee-belt drives to the alternator and power steering pump and, when fitted, to the air conditioning pump. This use of separate belts means that belt length and width can be kept to a minimum, at the expense of having a rather wide, multi-channel pulley at the front of the crankshaft.

Vic Berris' cutaway drawing of the Stag engine takes the form of a rear three-quarter view, and is complemented by the cross-section above, where the view is from the front. Points to note are the shortness not only of the stroke, but also of the connecting rods, leading to a very compact unit; the slanting cylinder head retaining bolts; and the central jackshaft which drives the water pump, distributor and oil pump

Below: the arrangement of the camshaft drive chains shows clearly the way the slant-four Saab engine (effectively the right-hand bank) has been duplicated. The extra tensioner has been added close to the first, and the second chain is shorter because there is no jackshaft for it to drive

Autocar COPYRIGHT

VIC BERRIS

AUTOCAR, 11 June 1970

TRIUMPH STAG...

Body

There are two points to bear in mind where the Stag body is concerned. One is that it bears a resemblance to the 2000 saloon, especially in the nose and tail; the other is that it is open.

Because it is open (neglecting for the time being the optional hard top), there is clearly a torsional stiffness problem. This has been got over partly by conventional stiffening of the floor area—a glance at our cut-away drawing shows the massive sills and two large transverse stiffeners—and also by using a 'Targa-bar' arrangement. This is a very strong, permanent structural member which absorbs a good deal of torsional strain between the front and rear halves of the car (the doors, of course, being the basic sources of weakness), and also adds to the beam-stiffness of the body shell as a whole. Apart from this, it acts as a valuable safety feature should the car be involved in a roll-over accident.

Compared with the 2000 saloon, the Stag sits on a wheelbase which is 6in. less. The overall length is 8in. less, which underlines the fact that the front and rear overhangs are very similar to those of the saloons. The vee-8 engine sits neatly under the bonnet, and not too far back, despite the encroachment of the MacPherson strut housings into the available width. Not surprisingly, the engine will fit the saloons with equal ease and, in fact, much of the development running was done with saloons so equipped, for obvious reasons.

The back end of the body follows conventional lines, with both the spare wheel and the large (14-gallon) fuel tank housed beneath the boot floor. A complex tank-venting system will be installed in cars for the American market, to comply with the latest regulations. Most of the rear suspension loads are taken out into the area of the rear bulkhead.

Usable length in the interior of the car is naturally limited by the shorter wheelbase to considerably less than that in the saloon. A few more inches are subtracted by the need to accommodate a folding hood. This is very neatly stowed in a well beside and behind the rear seats, covered by a padded, rear-hinged panel. A good deal of effort was expended trying to arrive at some means of making the hood power-operated, which was thought important for the American market, but this proved not to be possible. However, raising and lowering the hood is a very simple, single-handed operation.

There is an alternative hard top; the car can be had with this *and* the soft top, or with either on its own, although if it is bought with the hard top only, the well behind the rear seats remains, so it is not a way of coming by some more room in the back. The hard top can be removed readily, and carries little stress (other than those involved with its own aerodynamic loads). Sealing is by rubber beading, resulting in the edges standing clear of the bodywork, so that there is no risk to the paint. Both the soft and hard tops are glazed at the sides and the back, preserving a good field of view for the driver. The rear window of the hard top is electrically heated as standard, and its rear quarter windows are hinged at the front, so that they can be opened to provide through-flow ventilation (saloon-type face level ventilation is provided).

A good deal of the body interior has been borrowed from the saloon, including the excellent dashboard and minor control layout. An innovation for Triumph is the use of electrically operated side windows, the switches for which are mounted on the massive central console.

Common features between the Stag and the saloons are emphasized by the fact that 23 of the body panels (not all external, of course) are interchangeable. In a way, it is surprising that the final result can have such different dimensions, one of the most significant being the Stag's much reduced height—it is over 6in. lower. Some of this is accounted for in reduced ground clearance, but the rest is a matter of body design.

Suspension

Suspension design closely follows that of the 2000 saloon (or, more strictly, of the 2.5PI), with the same MacPherson struts at the front and semi-trailing arms at the back. Again, it is interesting to note that the wider rear wheel track introduced with the Mark 2 saloons last October was first mooted for the Stag.

At the front, there are a number of changes for the Stag. The front spring rates have been softened to 110 lb/in. in the interests of ride comfort, and the roll stiffness brought back up to the mark with the aid of an anti-roll bar. Front suspension travel between full bump and full rebound is 6.47in. Suspension loads are fed into the body in the conventional way, making use of the widely-spaced attachment points of this suspension layout. Braking loads are absorbed by semi-leading lower links, straight into the front bulkhead.

Rear suspension design follows that of the saloons very closely indeed, using the same principle of a massive sub-frame attached to the body by four widely spaced, rubber-insulated attachment points. The coil springs, with a rate of 322 lb./in., are placed well forward of the axle line, the mechanical advantage of roughly two-to-one reducing the equivalent stiffness at the wheel. The telescopic dampers are mounted aft of the axle line. Full travel between bump and rebound is slightly larger than at the front, at 6.55in.

Transmission

There are no surprises here. The gearbox is taken from the 2.5PI, save for a higher first gear, and overdrive is an option (as is Borg-Warner 35 automatic transmission). Final drive ratio is 3.7-to-1, midway between the 4.1 of the 2000 and the 3.45 of the 2.5PI, clearly intended to match the potential performance as closely as possible. Gearbox and final drive are joined by a single-piece propeller shaft; the length involved is short enough to ensure that no whirling problems occur. Clutch diameter is 9in., which is half an inch more than that in the 2.5PI.

Brakes

The Stag's brakes are the biggest yet from Triumph, notably larger than the 2.5PI brakes, even though these were uprated considerably last October. The front discs are no less than 10.6in. in diameter, and while the rear drums are still 9in. diameter,

continued

SPECIFICATION
FRONT ENGINE, REAR-WHEEL DRIVE

ENGINE

Cylinders	. .	8, in 90 deg vee
Main bearings	.	5
Cooling system		Water, pump, fan and thermostat
Bore	. .	86.0mm (3.39in.)
Stroke	. .	64.5mm (2.54in.)
Displacement	.	2,997cc (182.9cu.in.)
Valve gear	.	Single overhead camshaft per bank
Compression ratio		8.8 to 1 Min. octane rating: 97RM
Carburettors	.	2 Zenith-Stromberg 1.75CD
Fuel pump	.	SU electric
Oil filter	.	Full flow, replaceable element
Max. power	.	145 bhp (net) at 5,500 rpm
Max. torque	.	170 lb.ft (net) at 3,500 rpm
Max. bmep	.	140 psi at 3,500 rpm

TRANSMISSION

Clutch	.	Laycock diaphragm spring, 9.0in. dia
Gearbox	.	4-speed, all synchromesh or Borg-Warner 35 three speed automatic with torque converter
Gear ratios	.	Top 1.0
		OD top 0.82
		Top (Auto) 1.0
		Third 1.386 Inter 1.45
		Second 2.10
		First 2.995 Low 2.39
		Reverse 3.369 Reverse 2.09
Final drive	.	Hypoid bevel, 3.7 to 1

CHASSIS AND BODY

Construction	.	Integral, with steel body

SUSPENSION

Front	. .	Independent, MacPherson struts, lower links, coil springs, telescopic dampers, anti-roll bar
Rear	. .	Independent, semi-trailing arms, coil springs, telescopic dampers

STEERING

Type	. .	Power-assisted rack and pinion
Wheel dia.	.	16.0in.

BRAKES

Make and type	.	Lockheed disc front, drum rear
Servo	. .	Lockheed vacuum
Dimensions	.	F 10.6in. dia.
		R 9.0in. dia. 2.25in. wide shoes
Swept area	.	F 220sq.in., R 127 sq.in.
		Total 347sq.in. (208sq.in./ton laden)

WHEELS

Type	. .	Pressed steel disc, 4-stud fixing 5.5in. wide rim
Tyres—make	.	Michelin
—type	.	XAS radial ply tubed
—size	.	185-14in

EQUIPMENT

Battery	.	12 volt 56 Ah
Alternator	.	Lucas 11AC, 45 amp a.c.
Headlamps	.	Lucas four-lamp tungsten-halogen 110/220 watt (total)
Reversing lamp	.	Standard
Electric fuses	.	8
Screen wipers	.	Two-speed
Screen washer	.	Standard, electric
Interior heater	.	Standard, air-mixing type
Heated backlight		Standard with hardtop
Safety belts	.	Extra, mounting points standard
Interior trim	.	pvc seats and headlining
Floor covering	.	Carpet
Jack	. .	Scissor-type
Jacking points	.	2 each side under body
Windscreen	.	Toughened
Underbody	.	Phosphor treatment prior to painting

MAINTENANCE

Fuel tank	. .	14 Imp. gallons (64 litres)
Cooling system	.	18.5 pints (including heater)
Engine sump	.	8 pints (4.5 litres) SAE 10W/40 Change oil every 6,000 miles. Change filter element every 12,000 miles.
Gearbox and OD	.	3.75 pints SAE 90EP. Check oil every 6,000 miles
Final drive	.	2 pints SAE 90EP. Check oil every 6,000 miles
Grease	. .	No points
Typre pressures	.	F 26; R 26psi (normal driving)
		F 26; R 30 psi (full load)
Max. payload	.	728 lb (330kg)

DIMENSIONS

Wheelbase	.	8ft 4in. (254cm)
Track: front	.	4ft 4.5in. (133cm)
Track: rear	.	4ft 4.9in. (134cm)
Overall length	.	14ft 5.8in. (442cm)
Overall width	.	5ft 3.5in. (161cm)
Overall height (unladen)	.	4ft 1½in. (125.8 cm)
Ground clearance (laden)	.	4in. (10cm)
Turning circle	.	30ft (1040 cm)
Kerb weight (with all optional extras)		3,020 lb (1,375 ,kg)
(basic)		2,807 lb (1,275 kg)

PERFORMANCE DATA

Top gear mph per 1,000 rpm	19.0
Overdrive top mph per 1,000 rpm	23.1
Mean piston speed at max. power	2,330 ft/min
Bhp per ton laden	86.8

The Stag's kinship with the Mark 2 saloon shows up here in the similarity of the nose treatment. Actually the Stag is a smaller car all round, with a wheelbase six inches shorter and considerably less height. Tyres on this car, as on all Stags initially, are Michelin XAS

A glance into the cockpit would convince many people that the interior was a straight transplant from the saloons. In fact there are notable differences, including the door interior trim and the provision of switches in the centre console for the electrically operated windows

TRIUMPH STAG...

*Above : Top view of the Stag emphasizes the form of
roll-bar arrangement, which plays an important part in keeping the car
rigid—always a problem with an open design of unitary
construction. The rigid, padded cover for the hood recess can also
be seen here, as can the length of the boot ;
its relative shallowness is not so apparent*

Autocar
COPYRIGHT

VIC BERRIS

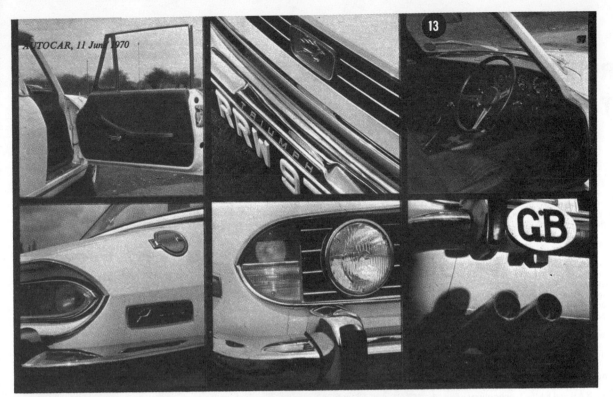

*Above : Detail views show door interior treatment, with
combined door pull armrests ; the Stag badge in the front grille centre ;
the facia, very reminiscent of the 2000 Mk2 saloon ; the other
Stag badge, on the rear wing (note the locking fuel filler cap) ; the
lamp cluster treatment at the front, again very like the saloon ;
and the twin exhaust pipes*

*Best seen in a cutaway drawing like this is the way the
vee-8 engine sits fairly well forward, with
the front mountings over the front axle line. Transmission and
suspension follow normal Triumph practice (the car is
drawn as an automatic). Note that the
propeller shaft is a single unit, and that the two exhaust
systems are separate throughout their length*

continued . . .

14

TRIUMPH STAG...

Above: The three-quarter rear view, with the hardtop in position, again betrays a relationship with the saloons. The hardtop is well endowed with window area; the rear quarter windows hinge open at their leading edges, and the rear screen is electrically heated

their width has been increased to 2.5in. Total swept area is up to 347 sq.in., which more than compensates for the fact that the Stag is rather heavier than the 2.5PI. A split-circuit safety braking system is employed, of course, and a 3:1 brake servo is standard.

Steering

Power steering is standard on the Stag. The decision that this should be so enabled the rest of the system to be designed with less regard to the need for keeping steering effort low. The pump is situated high on the right front of the engine, and powers an Adwest rack and pinion system. The steering wheel is relatively large at 16in. diameter, and the column adjusts for length and rake, as in the Triumph 1300. There is also a column lock.

Standard wheels are 5.5in. steel-discs, carrying 70-series 185-14 radials. Initially, Michelin XAS will be the tyre equipment on all cars. The effect of the lower final drive and the lower tyre profile in reducing the overall gearing is offset to some extent by the use of 14in. wheels, but the mph per 1,000rpm figure in direct top is still only 19 as compared with 20.2 for the 2.5PI.

Equipment

The aim has been to cut the number of options to a minimum by having a high basic standard of equipment. Much of this (radial-ply tyres, brake servo, power steering, electric windows) has already been discussed. The interior bears a strong resemblance to the 2.5PI, with the same instrumentation and equipment; the front seats naturally have adjustable squabs, although lack of space means that they do not recline fully.

A Lucas 11AC45-amp alternator powers the electrical system, which carries considerable loads through its fully fused circuits. The starter is of the pre-engaged type, and the battery is of 56 Ah capacity.

An air-mixing heater and comprehensive ventilation system is virtually inherited from the Mark 2 saloons.

Production

The design of the Stag engine means that it can be built on the same line as the Saab engine, and both units are now flowing off the same Coventry production line in large numbers. The body is produced in the new Triumph Merseyside plant, and sent fully finished and trimmed to Coventry for final assembly. Initial production target is 10,000 a year, with the capacity to expand if the demand proves high enough. The Mark 2 saloon production rate, for the sake of comparison, is currently about three times this figure. The first few months' production is earmarked for the home market, with introduction into overseas markets, including the all-important American and Common Market ones, when experience and stocks have been built up. □

Above: The view into the engine compartment, looking forwards. Accessibility to most components is extremely good, indeed better than the picture suggests. The fan, not visible here, is of impressive diameter, and is of the viscous-drive type

Left: The wiper system has been carefully engineered to clear the greatest possible area of screen, especially on the driver's side

Below left: The rear view looks very saloon-like with the hardtop in place. There is no Stag badge on the back panel, but the twin tailpipes are a give-away

Below: The front seats are released by a catch high up on the door side, tipping slightly sideways as well as forwards to permit access to the back seat

AUTOCAR 11 June 1970

DRIVING THE VEE 8 STAG

First impressions from a trip in Belgium

SO far, the only Stag driving we have managed was a relatively short trip in northern Belgium. This is not ideal driving country, for the road system mainly consists of fast, open straights joined by very slow corners through little villages. On the other hand the celebrated Belgian *pavè* is still very much in evidence, so that one is well placed to learn a good deal about ride and road noise.

To some extent, the visual impression of the Stag as a "cut-and-shut" 2000 Mk2 saloon disappear when one enters the car, despite the close similarity of the instrument panel and minor control layout. One sits fairly low, with the result that the most comfortable driving position involves leaning back slightly; the steering column is adjustable for rake and reach, so that it is possible to settle really comfortably. Visibility is good without being outstanding. The nose is quite long and wide, but the front corners are well defined so that it is easy enough to place the car accurately in a traffic stream. The tail is visible for reversing. One excellent feature is the use of a parallelogram system for the driver's wiper, so that it clears the largest possible area of the big, steeply raked screen without leaving any blind spots.

Thoughts of the saloon recede even farther when the engine is started. A single turn of the key produces a subdued but characteristic vee-8 rumble, with a slightly uneven idle at about 700 rpm. Throttle response is smooth and progressive. But the pedal movement feels rather long. Indeed, all the control movements are on the long side, not least those of clutch and gearbox; this seems to have been preferred in order to keep the controls as light as possible —which they certainly are.

Moving away from rest, the smoothness and urge of the new engine becomes obvious. There is no impression of the car running away with the driver, but the low-speed punch is certainly there if required. As one moves higher up the speed scale it becomes obvious that the engine is going to stay with you all the way. There is no hint of low-speed torque having been obtained at the expense of high-speed strangulation. A yellow sector on the tachometer advises one not exceed 5,500 rpm—at which maximum power is developed—for cruising; the red line is at 6,500 rpm, which is a high limit for a relatively large unit like this. The engine is perfectly willing to rev right up to the red line, and in direct top gear it is possible to cruise well into the yellow. Triumph's claimed maximum is 118 mph in either direct or overdrive top, corresponding to 4,900 and 5,960 rpm respectively: in other words, about equally spaced either side of the maximum power point.

The gearbox is adapted from the 2.5PI, using a higher first gear, both to suit the engine characteristics and to reduce the torque loading on the final drive. By modern standards it is not a particularly good change, but the synchromesh is strong and there is no baulking. In any case, the lazy driver will find that with a bit of throttle-feathering, the Stag can be trundled away from 10 mph in direct top, and selecting overdrive is simply a matter of sliding the little inset switch in the top of the gear lever. The spacing of the gears and the choice of overdrive ratio means that overdrive third falls nicely between direct third and top, so that the Stag (if thus equipped) is effectively a six-gear car.

Considerable efforts have been made to make the Stag a quiet car to ride in and in large measure this has been achieved. The viscous-drive fan undoubtedly plays its part in keeping down noise from under the bonnet. The engine itself is certainly subdued up to about 5,000 rpm, after which some induction and exhaust noise starts to intrude. Wind noise is quite low, and the suppression of road noise has been very successful, so that even on steel-braced Michelins over dreadful Belgian surfaces, little noise penetrated the interior. In keeping with the general policy, other noises seem to have been suppressed as far as possible: the heater fan, wiper motor and electric windows are all quiet in operation, as is the comprehensive ventilation system, which works extremely well. It is even possible to close the doors quietly.

If the object of taking us to Belgium was to demonstrate that the ride was good even over very poor surfaces, then it was successful. Even though the Stag is no more than a half-way approach to the classic French theory of soft, long-stroke springs and lots of damping, it copes remarkably well with all but the very worst surfaces. The suspension travel of well over 6in. is sufficient to smooth out any sort of main-road imperfection up to and including deepish potholes. At the same time it is firm enough to avoid more than the slightest suggestion of float; there is no sign of pitch, and roll angles are small. The seat springing feels as though it complements the suspension well, and the design includes enough wrap-round to support occupants against sideways forces right up to shoulder level.

It was difficult to gain a real impression of the handling. Straight-line stability is excellent, and the power steering light: almost too light to begin with, but eventually feeling well harmonized with the lightness of the other controls. Even so, it is still not really good enough to compare with the very best systems available.

Where open corners could be found, the handling appeared to be basically slight understeer, with sufficient power always on tap to push the tail wider if needed. Beyond this, judgment will have to await our full Road Test, to be published as soon as possible.

Short drives of this nature are no place to start punishing the brakes systematically; but there was nothing to indicate that the Stag's massive disc-drum system, the largest yet fitted to a Triumph, is anything but entirely adequate. Pedal pressures are kept well down with the help of a large servo. The handbrake is situated between the seats, and is light and effective in use.

On the basis of this short meeting, it seems that the Stag might be a *genuine* example of that rare breed, the GT car. From the British Leyland point of view, it plugs the gap between the MGB and the Jaguar E-type. It is rather faster, much better-equipped and more comfortable than the former, but nothing like as fast, or as expensive, as the latter. Prices were settled after the main description in our colour section went to press: they are as follows. □

PRICES

Triumph Stag
Soft top £1,995 17s 6d (£1,527 basic)
Hard top £2,041 11s 5d (£1,562 basic)
Hard + soft top £2,093 15s 10d (£1,602 basic)

The new Triumph Stag's 2 plus 2 body is available either as a soft top or with a detachable hard top.

JOHN BOLSTER tries

The new Triumph Stag

The Triumph Stag is an entirely new model for which there must be an immense demand. In brief, British Leyland have produced a 2 plus 2 GT which has all the looks, refinement and performance of continental cars like the Mercedes-Benz 280 SL at just over half the price. In fact, it can probably see off the opposition fairly comfortably in at least two of these three respects, and how Lord Stokes proposes to satisfy the potential demand one would be interested to know.

The heart of the Stag is a very interesting new engine. It is a V8 with a single overhead-camshaft for each head, with chain drive. It is, in effect, the "other half" added to the inclined four-cylinder Triumph engine used in the Saab 99. The in-line valves are operated directly through inverted bucket tappets, seating in wedge-shaped combustion chambers in aluminium cylinder heads. The cast-iron 90 deg block carries the forged alloy steel crankshaft, which has integral balance weights, on five main bearings. A bonded rubber torsion vibration damper is on the front end.

An excellent vintage feature is the positive drive to the water pump, through skew-gears from a jack-shaft which also drives the distributor. The fan is belt-driven separately and has a viscous coupling to reduce noise at high revs. The engine is very much over-square with dimensions of 86 mm by 64.5 mm (2997 cc), and on the moderate compression ratio of 8.8 to 1 it develops a net output of 145 bhp at 5500 rpm. It is interesting that fuel injection is not at present standardised, an electric fuel pump at the rear of the car delivering to two horizontal Stromberg carburetters within the vee. An inertia switch cuts off the fuel supply in the event of an accident, a valuable safety feature.

The V8 engine can be mounted in unit with a manual gearbox, similar to that of the Triumps 2.5 PI. Alternatively, a Borg-Warner automatic transmission has been developed for this power unit. The hypoid final drive housing is secured to the rubber-mounted sub-frame that also carries the rear suspension.

No separate chassis frame is employed, the body being a pressed-steel monocoque. It is a two-door 2 plus 2 and is available either as a soft-top or with a detachable hard-top. In either case, a padded roll-over bar gives the structural rigidity that a roof normally confers. It is an extension of the door pillars and has a central member that projects forward to join the screen. This overhead construction is immensely rigid and reinforces the whole body, acting like a roof in eliminating scuttle shake.

Independent front suspension of the MacPherson type is used, with semi-trailing arms behind. The rack and pinion steering has power assistance as standard. To give an idea of the size of this new GT, it has the same track a the 2.5 saloon and is 6½ ins shorter in the wheelbase, but still 1 ft longer than the TR6. The very delightful styling of the body is unmistakably the work of Giovanni Michelotti.

A brief test

I was able to try the Stag in Belgium on roads ranging from fast, smooth straights to the most appalling *pavé*, with plenty of corners thrown in, plus some heavy traffic. I chose an open car because the weather was superb, and I was not at all disappointed that it had automatic transmission. Triumph and Borg-Warner had already demonstrated such an extraordinary *rapport* over the 2.5 PI that I wanted to see if they could do it again with the 3-litre V8. They could!

The Stag is as far as it could possibly be from a hairy sports car. It is very quiet indeed and the engine is especially smooth, with hardly a suspicion of the V8 exhaust

The interior is well planned with a nicely laid out dash.

beat. There is a lot of torque in the lower and middle ranges, the car feeling very lively in consequence, and one is very seldom tempted to select the ratios manually, though there is provision for so doing. The transmission works very smoothly and there is no need to use high revs on the lower gears, though the engine spins very freely when required to do so.

The car rides astonishingly well over bad roads but does not feel excessively "soft" and is steady at its maximum speed, which appears to be just below 120 mph. The steering is extremely light, which is a little disconcerning at first, but it is found with experience to give adequate feel of the road. The insulation of road and tyre noises is of a very high standard indeed. There is enough understeer to give high-speed stability in side-winds but the Stag is well-balanced for taking fast curves; the amount of roll is rather less than one expects with such comfortable suspension.

Everything about the Stag is luxurious, but it accelerates like a sports car and seems very happy to cruise at 100 mph. The new Triumph 3-litre V8 engine is delightfully willing and plays with the relatively light 2 plus 2 body. This is a very important addition to the British Leyland range which will bring prestige to its makers and pleasure to its owners. We hope to publish a full-length road test soon.

Car Reviewed: Triumph Stag open 2 plus 2, price £1,996 or £2,042 with hard top, including tax.
Engine: Eight cylinders, 86 mm by 64.5 mm, 2997 cc. Single chain-driven overhead camshaft to each bank. Compression ratio 8.8 to 1. 145 bhp at 5,500 rpm. Two horizontal Stromberg carburetters.
Transmission: Single dry plate diaphragm-spring clutch. 4-speed all-synchromesh gearbox with central change, ratios 1.0, 1.386, 2.10, and 2.995 to 1. Chassis-mounted hypoid unit, ratio 3.7 to 1. Optional extra: Borg-Warner automatic transmission.
Chassis: Combined steel body and chassis. MacPherson independent front suspension with anti-roll bar. Power-assisted rack and pinion steering. Independent rear suspension by semi-trailing arms with coil springs and telescopic dampers. Disc front and drum rear brakes. Bolt-on steel wheels fitted Michelin 185 HR 14 radial ply tyres.
Equipment: 12-volt lighting and starting. Speedometer. Rev-counter. Water temperature, battery condition and fuel gauges. Heating, demisting and ventilation system. Two-speed windscreen wipers and washers. Flashing direction indicators. Reversing lamps. Optional extra: Refrigerated air conditioning.
Dimensions: Wheelbase 8 ft 4 ins. Track, front 4 ft 4½ ins; rear 4 ft 4⅞ ins. Overall length 14 ft 5¾ ins. Width 5 ft 3½ ins. Weight 1 ton 5 cwt.
Performance: (approximate) Maximum speed 118 mph. Speeds in gears: third 79 mph, second 52 mph, first 36 mph. Acceleration: 0-30 mph, 3.5 s; 0-50 mph, 7 s; 0-60 mph, 9.5 s; 0-80 mph, 16 s; 0-100 mph, 29 s.

The rear of the car is unmistakably Triumph (above). Cutaway drawing of the new 3-litre V8 engine, which gives 145 bhp (below).

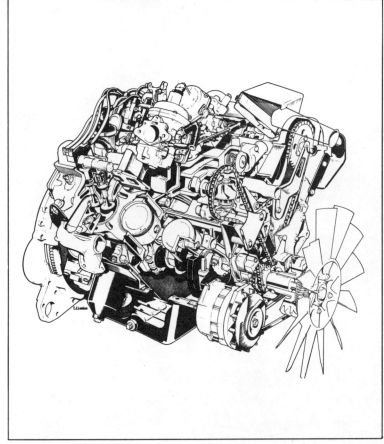

AUTOTEST

TRIUMPH STAG
(2,997 c.c.)

AT-A-GLANCE: New 2+2 sports car with vee-8 engine. Performance disappointing but above-average fuel consumption. Soft, well-damped ride and light, power-assisted steering. Good brakes. Fast, relaxed car on long journeys.

MANUFACTURER

Standard-Triumph International Ltd, Coventry, England.

PRICES (Hard-plus-soft top version)

Basic	£1,602	0s	0d
Purchase Tax	£491	15s	10d
Seat belts (approx.)	£14	0s	0d
Total (in G.B.)	£2,107	15s	10d

EXTRAS (inc. P.T.)

Automatic transmission	£104	8s	11d
Overdrive*	£65	5s	7d

*Fitted to test car

PRICE AS TESTED £2,173 1s 5d

PERFORMANCE SUMMARY

Mean maximum speed	115 mph
Standing start ¼-mile	18.2 sec
0-60 mph	11.6 sec
30-70 mph through gears	11.2 sec
Typical fuel consumption	22 mpg
Miles per tankful	310

TRIUMPH obviously looked hard at their own line up as well as those of their competitors before deciding to design a new two-plus-two sporting car. Their intention was to provide a British model to compete with such Continental names as Alfa Romeo and Mercedes-Benz. What started out as a £1,500 project due for release in 1968 has turned out to be a £2,000 car introduced only this summer.

For those who missed our description and cutaway drawing published on 11 June, the Stag is a new model based on some of the Triumph 2000 Mk. II running gear and powered by a new 3-litre overhead camshaft vee-8 engine. The power unit in fact utilizes some of the tooling set up for the Saab 99 engine, sharing much of the top-end design. It is made mainly from iron castings and develops 145 bhp (net) at 5,500 rpm.

This is not a great deal more than that of the 2.5 PI engine used in the TR6 (142 bhp net), but one assumes that there is a lot of potential in it which is being saved for future years. It develops more torque than the TR6 engine though (170 instead of 149 lb. ft.) and is inherently a smoother and less temperamental unit.

Starting is always easy and there is a manual choke control for the twin side-draught Stromberg carburettors. It was seldom needed during the warm weather of the test, except for the first cold start of the day. Carburation on the test car was smooth, although we noticed

traces of fuel starvation when making full throttle acceleration runs at MIRA. This may have accounted for the disappointing figures, which were not as good as those claimed by the manufacturers.

From a standing start 60 mph came up in 11.6sec and 100 mph in 36.9sec. These times are really no better than those measured on the 2.5 PI saloon we tested earlier this year and are 2.1sec and 7.9sec respectively more than those claimed by Triumph for the Stag. It should not be overlooked, however, that the Stag weighs about 2½cwt more than the 2.5 PI and is much higher geared, especially in bottom.

Overall gearing on the Stag is about the same as that of the 2.5 PI, a difference in final drive ratio offsetting slightly larger wheels. First gear ratio is 3.02 instead of 3.27 to 1 which permits it to run up to over 40 mph before the rev counter touches the red line at 6,500 rpm. There is an amber warning sector from 5,500 (peak power speed) to the red line. We found it best to change gear at about 6,000 rpm.

In second it is possible to reach an indicated 60 mph (true 58.5 mph) and in third over 90 mph. Unlike on other Triumphs, the optional overdrive (fitted to the test car and listed as a £65 extra) fills the gap between third and top, giving a useful maximum of about 100 mph and a theoretical one of 112 mph.

We found that the conditions affected top speed considerably, as did the trim of the car at the time. In a straight line on a French *autoroute* with quite a brisk cross wind we recorded a mean maximum in overdrive top of 115 mph with the hardtop fitted. In direct top this speed fell to 113 mph and with the roof off to only 106 mph. Overdrive top is a very high gear indeed (24.2 mph) meant mainly for easy cruising, and the Stag is an effortless car to keep above the ton, with the rev counter reading no more than 4,500 rpm most of the time.

At our present legal motorway limit of 70 mph, only 2,900 rpm is required, which is below even the peak of the torque curve. At these high speeds there is a fair amount of wind roar with the hardtop in place or the hood erect, and with the roof down the roll-over frame causes a very audible whistle. In the main, however, the Stag is a quiet car, the engine and exhaust being particularly well silenced.

Our test car was a pre-production model and its gearbox appeared to have suffered from hard use. Second and top synchromesh were weak and the lever chattered noisily when accelerating in third gear. The clutch, too, on our car was heavy to operate and the action was not smooth. These points are probably not typical and we do not expect them to crop up on the cars being sold to the public.

Anyone coming to the Stag and expecting it to be a taut little sports car like the TR6 will be disappointed. It is much more a touring car and rides and handles in the same way as the Mark II saloons with which it shares front and rear suspensions.

Initially therefore the ride feels soft and the standard power-assisted steering needs learning. With longer acquaintance one begins to appreciate that the soft springs are well damped and that they soak up large and small bumps remarkably easily. Very little road noise is transmitted through from the wheels, which are shod with Michelin XAS radial-ply tyres as standard.

Roll angles are well controlled and once the lack of feel in the steering has become familiar the Stag can be driven very fast on dry roads. With power-on, cornering is stable, initial understeer being largely disguised by the power steering and any tail-out transition being finally killed by the inside rear wheel lifting and spinning. Cutting the power in a bend causes a progressive and safe tucking-in effect at the front.

In the wet we experienced severe traction problems around country lanes as well as on greasy London streets, the tail sometimes letting go under acceleration without warning. In France also the front end slid out on very wet bends, making fast driving in these conditions a real test of skill and courage. At 100 mph the wipers lifted off the screen and above 110 mph on a badly drained *autoroute* the tyres could be felt aquaplaning.

Under better conditions the Stag is a fine touring car with a long-legged character which eats up miles very easily. On a run to the north-east and back we recorded 22.4 mpg and put 50 miles into every hour without effort.

For a 3-litre car of this weight the fuel consumption overall of 20.6 mpg is not at all

22 ☞

Michelotti's styling is elegant and well in tune with the rest of the Triumph range. The wheeltrims are dummies. The roll over frame (below) contributes a lot to scuttle stiffness and also prevents collapse of the screen, should the car turn over in an accident

ACCELERATION

SECONDS

SPEED MPH TRUE INDICATED	TIME IN SECS
30 / 30	3.9
40 / 40	5.8
50 / 50	8.1
60 / 61	11.6
70 / 73	15.1
80 / 85	19.6
90 / 97	25.7
100 / 108	36.9

SPEED RANGE, GEAR RATIOS AND TIME IN SECONDS

mph	O.D. Top (3.04)	Top (3.70)	O.D. 3rd (4.20)	3rd (5.13)	2nd (7.77)	1st (11.08)
10-30	—	9.1	8.2	6.4	4.1	3.0
20-40	10.8	8.2	7.1	5.5	3.5	3.1
30-50	11.1	8.4	7.0	5.4	3.8	—
40-60	11.3	8.4	7.1	5.6	4.9	—
50-70	11.6	8.8	7.8	6.7	—	—
60-80	13.2	9.9	9.1	8.5	—	—
70-90	16.1	12.6	11.9	13.7	—	—
80-100	21.9	18.0	17.9	—	—	—

Standing ¼-mile
18.2 sec 75 mph
Standing kilometre
33.4 sec 98 mph
Test distance
1,762 miles
Mileage recorder
1.0 per cent
over-reading

PERFORMANCE
MAXIMUM SPEEDS

Gear	mph	kph	rpm
O.D. Top (mean)	115	185	4,770
(best)	117	188	4,850
Top	113	182	5,710
O.D. 3rd	100	161	5,790
3rd	92	148	6,500
2nd	61	98	6,500
1st	42	68	6,500

BRAKES
(from 70 mph in neutral)
Pedal load for 0.5g stops in lb

1	45-35	6	30
2	45-40	7	30-35
3	40-35	8	35-40
4	35	9	35-45
5	32	10	35-45

Retardation measured with Bowmonk decelerometer

RESPONSE (from 30 mph in neutral)

Load	g	Distance
20lb	0.24	125ft
40lb	0.53	57ft
60lb	0.77	39ft
80lb	0.93	32ft
100lb	0.95	31ft
120lb	1.0	30.1ft
Handbrake	0.32	94ft

Max. Gradient 1 in 5.

CLUTCH
Pedal 40lb and 4¾in.
MOTORWAY CRUISING
Indicated speed at 70 mph	73 mph
Engine (rpm at 70 mph)	2,910 rpm
(mean piston speed)	1,230 ft/min.
Fuel (mpg at 70 mph)	26.1 mpg
Passing (50-70 mph)	8.8 sec

COMPARISONS

MAXIMUM SPEED MPH
Porsche 911 T	(£3,671)	129
Reliant Scimitar GTE	(£2,019)	117
Alfa Romeo 1750 GTV	(£2,431)	116
Triumph Stag	**(£2,042)**	**115**
Ford Capri 3000 GT	(£1,422)	113

0-60 MPH, SEC
Porsche 911 T	8.1
Ford Capri 3000 GT	10.3
Reliant Scimitar GTE	10.7
Alfa Romeo 1750 GTV	11.2
Triumph Stag	**11.6**

STANDING ¼-MILE, SEC
Porsche 911 T	16.0
Reliant Scimitar GTE	17.4
Ford Capri 3000 GT	17.6
Alfa Romeo 1750 GTV	18.0
Triumph Stag	**18.2**

OVERALL MPG
Alfa Romeo 1750 GTV	23.9
Triumph Stag	**20.6**
Ford Capri 3000 GT	19.3
Reliant Scimitar GTE	18.5
Porsche 911 T	17.9

GEARING (with 185-14in. tyres)
O.D. Top	24.1 mph per 1,000 rpm
Top	19.8 mph per 1,000 rpm
O.D. 3rd	17.3 mph per 1,000 rpm
3rd	14.2 mph per 1,000 rpm
2nd	9.3 mph per 1,000 rpm
1st	6.5 mph per 1,000 rpm

TEST CONDITIONS:
Weather: Overcast. Wind: 10-15 mph. Temperature: 13 deg. C. (56 deg. F).
Barometer: 29.35 in. hg. Humidity: 50 per cent. Surfaces: Dry concrete and asphalt.

WEIGHT:
Kerb weight: 25.1 cwt (2,805lb—1,273kg) (with oil, water and half full fuel tank).
Distribution, per cent F, 55.7; R, 44.3. Laden as tested: 28.4 cwt (3,185lb—1,445kg).

TURNING CIRCLES:
Between kerbs L, 33ft 10in.: R, 34ft 3in. Between Walls L, 36ft 1in.: R, 36ft 6in.,
steering wheel turns, lock to lock 2.8.

Figures taken at unknown mileage by our own staff at the Motor Industry Research
Association proving ground at Nuneaton and on the Continent.

TRIUMPH STAG (2,997 c.c.) *AUTOCAR* 30 July 1970

CONSUMPTION

FUEL
At constant speeds—mpg)

	Direct	Overdrive
30 mph	29.8	36.0
40 mph	30.5	34.8
50 mph	28.8	33.3
60 mph	25.8	29.4
70 mph	23.0	26.1
80 mph	20.3	22.9
90 mph	17.8	19.8
100 mph	15.6	17.0

Typical mpg 22 (12.8 litres/100km)
Calculated (DIN) mpg 23.7 (11.9 litres/100km)
Overall mpg 20.6 (13.7 litres/100km)
Grade of fuel . . . Premium, 4-star (min. 97RM)

OIL
Miles per pint (SAE 10W/40) 1,500

SPECIFICATION FRONT ENGINE, REAR WHEEL DRIVE

ENGINE
Cylinders . . . 8, in 90-deg vee
Main bearings . 5
Cooling system . Water; pump, fan and thermostat
Bore . . . . . 86.0 mm (3.39 in.)
Stroke . . . . 64.5 mm (2.54 in.)
Displacement . . 2,997 c.c. (182.9 cu. in.)
Valve gear . . . Single overhead camshaft per bank
Compression ratio 8.8-to-1. Min. octane rating: 97RM
Carburettors . . 2 Zenith-Stromberg 1.75CD
Fuel pump . . . SU electric
Oil filter . . . . Full flow, renewable element
Max. power . . . 145 bhp (net) at 5,500 rpm
Max. torque . . 170 lb.ft. (net) at 3,500 rpm
Max. bmep . . . 140 psi at 3,500 rpm

TRANSMISSION
Clutch . . . . Laycock diaphragm spring, 9.0 in. dia.
Gearbox . . . 4-speed, all-synchromesh
Gear ratios . . Top 1.0 OD Top 0.82
Third 1.386 OD Third 1.135
Second 2.100
First 2.995
Reverse 3.369
Final drive . . Hypoid bevel, ratio 3.7-to-1

CHASSIS and BODY
Construction . . Integral, with steel body

SUSPENSION
Front . . . . . Independent, MacPherson struts, lower, links, coil springs, telescopic dampers, anti-roll bar
Rear . . . . . Independent, semi-trailing arms, coil springs, telescopic dampers

STEERING
Type . . . . Power-assisted rack and pinion
Wheel dia. . . 15¾ in.

BRAKES
Make and type . Lockheed disc front, drum rear
Servo . . . . Lockheed vacuum
Dimensions . . F 10.6 in. dia. R 9.0 in. dia. 2.25in. wide shoes
Swept area. . . F 220 sq. in., R 127 sq. in. Total 347 sq. in. (245 sq. in./ton laden)

WHEELS
Type . . . . . Pressed steel disc, 4-stud fixing, 5.5in. wide rim
Tyres—make . . Michelin
—type . . XAS
—size . . 815-14in.

EQUIPMENT
Battery . . . . 12 Volt 56 Ah
Alternator . . . Lucas IIAC, 45 amp a.c.
Headlamps. . . Lucas 4-lamp tungsten-halogen, 110/220 watt (total)
Reversing lamp . Standard
Electric fuses . 8
Screen wipers . Two-speed
Screen washer . Standard, electric
Interior heater . Standard, air-mixing type
Heated backlight Standard with hardtop
Safety belts . . Extra, mounting points standard
Interior trim . . Pvc seats and headlining
Floor covering . Carpet
Jack . . . . . Scissor type
Jacking points . 2 each side under body
Windscreen . . Toughened
Underbody
protection . . Phosphate treatment prior to painting

MAINTENANCE
Fuel tank . . . 14 Imp. gallons (64 litres)
Cooling system . 18.5 pints (including heater)
Engine sump . . 8 pints (4.5 litres) SAE 10W/40. Change oil every 6,000 miles. Change filter element every 12,000 miles
Gearbox and
overdrive . . 3.75 pints SAE 90EP. Change oil every 6,000 miles
Final drive . . 2 pints SAE 90EP. Change oil every 6,000 miles
Grease . . . . No points
Tyre pressures . F 26; R 26 psi (normal driving); F 26; R 30 psi (full load)
Max. payload . . 728 lb (330 kg)

PERFORMANCE DATA
Top gear mph per 1,000 rpm 19.8
Overdrive top mph per 1,000 rpm . . . 24.1
Mean piston speed at max. power . . . 2,300 ft/min.
Bhp per ton laden 102

STANDARD GARAGE 16ft x 8ft 6in.

OVERALL LENGTH 14' 5·75"
OVERALL WIDTH 5'3·5"
OVERALL HEIGHT 4'3·5"
GROUND CLEARANCE 6"
FRONT TRACK 4' 4·5"
WHEELBASE 8'4"
REAR TRACK 4' 4·87"

SCALE 0.3in. to 1ft
Cushions uncompressed

AUTOTEST
TRIUMPH STAG . . .

bad and even when squirting the Stag about in heavy traffic we never got less than 18 mpg. At a steady 70 mph in overdrive top it will cover 26 miles on a gallon of 4-star premium, and at the same speed in direct it covers 23 miles.

Disc front brakes with servo assistance and drums at the rear worked efficiently and showed no real signs of fade either on the road or during our 10 stops in rapid succession at MIRA. Pedal effort for most check braking is reasonable, but it took a hefty 120lb shove to get the ultimate 1g stop. A large red warning light right in front of the driver warns of any fluid loss or any pressure difference between the divided front and rear hydraulic circuits.

The driving position is easy to tailor, with a neat tilt and telescope mechanism for the steering column and seatbacks adjustable for rake. There is enough legroom for a 6ft driver but we would have preferred a wheel smaller than the 15¾in. dia. one fitted. It has a nicely stitched leather rim and satin finished spokes.

In the back there is room for two adults if those in the front compromise on legroom, but it is meant for occasional use or for children. With the roof off, backseat passengers get an odd view of the roll-over frame, although it can be detached if required. We did not try taking it off because it must contribute considerably to the body stiffness.

The hardtop attachment and complete hood mechanism is a very fair copy of that used on the Mercedes-Benz 280 SL two-seater. A hinged metal tonneau panel hides the folded roof completely out of sight and putting it up is a quick and simple operation. Removing the hardtop is a two-man job as it is heavy and calls for care in avoiding the padded pvc of the roll-over frame where it rakes back behind the doors. The central rear pin is an electric connection for the standard heated backlight.

Two-speed wipers are standard and they are operated together with the powerful electric washers by a stalk on the left of the steering column. The wiper on the driver's side has a parallelogram action which drastically improves the area it sweeps. Most of the other controls are like those of the 2000, with similar rotary lighting switch, the same (ex 1300) "all systems go" combination warning dial and the same tasteful matt veneer woodwork. A battery condition voltmeter is fitted instead of an ammeter but there is not, surprisingly, an oil pressure gauge. The overdrive switch is in the top of the gearlever knob, surely the most logical place of all.

One key works the ignition and steering lock, together with both doors and the fuel filler flap. A second key is needed for the boot and yet a third key for the glove box. The boot is lined with carpet and takes a good volume of luggage although it is not very deep. Quartz iodine headlamp bulbs give bright illumination but their small diameter restricts their performance overall.

Heater controls are the same as on the 2000, with an independent cold air ventilation system and a two-speed fan which boosts both systems. Temperature control was sensitive but the swivelling eyeball nozzles at the ends of the facia did not pass enough air to be really effective in hot weather and with the roof on we noticed rather too much engine heat permeating through the bulkhead and floor for comfort in the cockpit.

The Stag is one of those cars which you appreciate the more you drive it. It has an easy and relaxing way of packing many miles into each hour and it is a satisfying and spirited car to drive fast. For a touring car it proves comfortable and we climbed out after 15 hours of travelling, tired but not fatigued and in no way stiff. Our test mileage was longer than usual because we took it abroad for maximum speed measurements and because we all enjoyed driving it. We liked it so much in fact that we shall be adding one to our long term test fleet as soon as we can get delivery. □

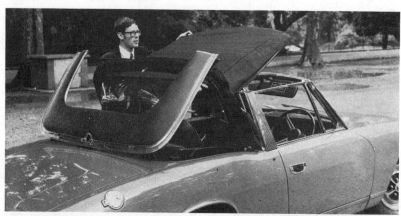

Top: The soft top folds away completely out of sight under the padded metal tonneau panel. Instructions for hood stowage are on the back of the sun vizor

Below left: Accessibility on the ohc vee-8 engine is good, with all the fillers nice and high. The battery is out of sight behind the right-hand headlamps

Below right: The rear seat room is generous for a sports car, but getting in and out is as tricky as ever

Above left: The spare wheel lies under the boot floor, which has been lifted out here together with the carpet.
Above right: There is room for a reasonable amount of luggage and the lid is self-supporting

Below: The optional hardtop suits the body shape well. It costs £98 extra including a heated backlight and opening rear quarterlights

▶ 34

runs—which also caused the Velcro seal above the passenger's window to come undone.

Fortunately, the weather was kind and we had the top down for much of the time. We loved the Stag like this. Buffetting can be kept in check, if not eliminated, by raising the side windows (rigidly held by slim frames) and, to a lesser extent, by tilting the sun visors to act as wind deflectors. With the exhaust burbling a discreetly sporting tune, we discovered in the Stag a new sort of open air motoring; nothing else at the price can do it in such style, comfort and luxury.

This, of course, is the car's special charm. But the excellence of the concept, of a versatile three-in-one car, is not quite matched by the means of achieving it. There are snags. The fully trimmed hardtop, for instance, is inordinately heavy and very much a two-man job to fit and remove—more a seasonal than a daily routine even though securing it, with five simple catches, is very easy. The contact for the heated back window is automatically made when you snap the top down.

With the soft top (which is invisibly stowed under a hinged cover that blends with the trim) the problem is one of tension rather than weight. Whichever way we arranged things the final task of securing the top rail catches proved a real strain—beyond the pull of most women—simply because there was not enough "give" in the frame initially to engage the pegs. The hood on our car was also invariably reluctant to hinge back again smoothly. It's a very substantial, elaborate and weatherproof piece of equipment—even partially trimmed on the inside—but it's by no means the easiest or quickest to erect and stow. Perhaps with further practice we'd have overcome the snags.

Open or closed it's hard to imagine anyone being uncomfortable in the front. The seats, deeply contoured for lateral, lumbar and side support, are adjustable for reach, rake and height. The steering wheel is also quickly adjustable in two planes. So except perhaps for very long legged drivers who might want an exta inch or so of rearward movement, everyone should be able to tailor themselves a perfect position.

The controls are particularly good. Within limits you can put the steering wheel where you want; and the pedals, though slightly offset to the right, are all arranged at the same comfortable height so they can easily be worked by pivoting your heel on the floor. The brake and throttle are reasonably placed for simultaneous heel and toe operation but the strong servo assistance makes the brake too flimsy a fulcrum unless you are braking hard. The handbrake is conveniently placed between the seats, the gearlever a hand's span away from the steering wheel.

The important minor controls are outstanding, a model example of how they should be arranged. The horn, dip, flasher and indicators are all controlled by the right-hand column stalk, the washers and two-speed wipers by a stalk on the left. Both are within fingertip reach, crisp in action and clearly identified with symbols. A large knurled knob just ahead of the right stalk operates the lights. Opposite on the left is the ignition key which, if you wriggle and twist, can also be enticed to lock the steering or release itself. Steering/ignition locks can be infuriating things.

The rest of the switchgear is on the central console, rather distant except for handy rocker switches in front of the gearlever operating the interior lights and the rather lethargic electric windows. Awkwardly placed behind the gearlever, and surrounded by the ash tray, are three slides. One regulates airflow to the excellent central ventilation grilles, supplemented by conventional eyeball vents at each end of the facia. The other two regulate the temperature and distribution of air from the heater—pretty effectively so far as we could judge during a warm spell—though output from the ventilation grilles is greatly reduced when the heater is on. With the powerful (but noisy) two-speed fan in operation, warm-up is quick and demisting efficient.

Good vision was obviously a design priority: the heated back window is a standard fitting and the driver's wiper has a parallelogram arm so that it sweeps with an efficient squeegee action right up to the pillar, leaving no murky wedges. With the hardtop in place you get a very good all-round view. With the soft top the side panels butting up to thick rear pillars can form an awkward blind spot. If you sit up, the back corners are just visible from the driver's seat and there's an excellent automatic reversing light. The headlights give an intense, uniform spread of light, free from spots and whirls: but their range was not particularly long on our car. Perhaps they needed raising a little.

Back seat accommodation is cramped though not impossible for six footers. Sensibly, the seat cushion is deeply troughed so that your thighs get some support even in the knees-up position forced on adults. With the front seats right back there is ample room for two or three small children.

Fittings and furniture

As in the design of its switchgear so in decor and appointments, the Stag is a front runner. The clear and comprehensive instruments are set into an unpretentious matt walnut facia, concave on the driver's side to minimize parallax error. A clock, rev counter, battery charge indicator and all-systems-go warning light cluster are standard. Rich leatherette trim luxuriously covers the doors, the seats are richly upholstered in non slip basket-weave, and well fitted carpets cover the floor. As we've observed before, Triumph are also setting the standard in seat belt design.

We liked some of the details too: red warning lights in the door edges; powerful reversing lights; anti-thief quarter light knobs; neat door release levers and locks. There was something amiss with the lockup arrangements of our car though since all the keywork—for doors, facia locker, flush petrol filler and ignition—proved a fiddly and sometimes exasperating job. Smokers also complained about the inaccessibility of the central ash tray.

Stowage space inside is generous and well planned. Apart from the locker there's a shelf beneath the facia, pouches on the doors and seat backs, and recesses in the rear sidewalls. By saloon standards, the boot is not very big—wide but rather shallow because of the spare wheel and fuel tank beneath.

Servicing and accessibility

As you'd expect, there's nothing very demanding about the servicing schedule, done on a 6000-mile cycle. All the ancillaries needing regular attention are quite easy to get at under the wide, front-hinged bonnet, supported by a self-locking stay. There's a modest tool kit in the boot. ■

1 coil. 2 distributor. 3 twin Stromberg carburetters. 4 fuel filter. 5 oil filler cap. 6 viscous coupled. 7 radiator overflow. 8 brake servo. 9 dip stick. 10 washer bottle. 11 power steering pump

MAKE: Triumph. MODEL: Stag. MAKERS: British Leyland (Triumph) Ltd., Coventry, England

TAKING THE STAG BY THE HORNS

Is Triumph's £2000 personal car
a logical upward step for
Capri and 124S owners?
L J K SETRIGHT

ANY STAG WORTHY OF attention is distinguished by brow, bez, trez and at least a three-point top, if not by a flurry on the Stock Exchange; but the creature emblazoned on the badge of Triumph's new V8 is to be noted for anatomic implausibility, if not for what Browning called Hornmadness. Never mind; from what I am told the car was named Stag (Triumph are careful to omit the article) mainly because their American salesmen thought the name just right for appealing to customers who wished or needed to have associations with masculinity, virility, and all that sort of thing. The word is an Icelandic one, referring not to the male red deer in particular but to any male animal, and it comes from *stiga* which means to mount. It is all laughably inappropriate, for there is nothing phallic or prurient about this car, none of what I recently read (in another motoring magazine and in another context) charmingly described as red-blooded foul-breathed hairy masculinity; this Stag performs with reasonable vigour, but its manner is suave and urbane, not just manly but gentlemanly.

Considering its parentage this is not surprising. Most of the car's suspension, running gear, transmission and minor assemblies come from the Triumph 2000, which is nothing if not smooth. The body is new and attractive, but has a strong flavour of current Michelotti 2000 lightly spiced with a hint of Pininfarina Fiat Dino. The engine, which is the most interesting part, is what we have been awaiting for some time—a V8 composed of two Saab slant fours.

Those slant fours are not pukka Saabs, of course, but were designed and built by Triumph in convenient time for the Swedes to buy them when they went looking for just such an engine. In fact they had asked Ricardo to do a design for them along similar lines; but Ricardo had been consulting with Triumph and knew that the British engine would suit the Swedes very well. Introductions were duly made and contracts eventually settled, and so the 1709cc Triumph engine found its way into the Saab 99. Something must have happened to it in the process, for the engine was originally designed as a 1500cc job; and it is probable though not certain that the process was reversed in making the 2997cc V8, for its bore and stroke are respectively 86 and

64.5mm, while those of the Saab engine are 83.5 and 78.

This does not quite explain how 2 × 80bhp = 145bhp. Yet the performance is quite satisfactory, brisk though not dramatic. Flexibility is beyond criticism, the transition from burble to bellow depending on throttle opening rather than on revs. Perhaps most important of all, there is little danger of the current version being superseded by a more powerful one in the near future, the fear of which often dissuades people from buying a new model lest its depreciation be artificially accelerated by planned obsolescence. For that matter there is little danger of the same engine finding its way into other cars soon (though the long-term likelihood of a V8 TR7 looks assured) for production limitations are imposed by the laziness, inefficiency and general incompetence of the British foundry trade, which has a lot to learn from its American counterpart. To put it another way, the Stag's iron block is not an easy one to cast.

Its aluminium alloy heads do not present the same problems. Much of their conformation is the product of manifolding requirements, for underbonnet space is severely limited. It is probably with the aid of non-standard heads that Triumph have experimentally run this V8 at considerably higher ratings—though they have naturally altered other things and even tried a single-plane crankshaft. Cam forms are easily changed, too: they are gentle enough at present, but there is plenty of room in the wedge-shaped combustion chambers above the mildly dished piston crowns for the valves to lift farther and faster. Alas, there is no room for making the valves and ports bigger. So the overhead camshaft makes no contribution to high performance; it is there merely as an aid to longevity, minimising the inertia loadings

throughout the valve train and keeping the noise down. Ample justification, of course—an overhead camshaft engine does not *have* to be racy. For that matter it does not have to be complex or difficult to work on, but this particular design was under way at a time when cogged belts were in their infancy, and when quick, easy tappet adjustment was just a spark of genius short-circuiting the conventions at GM, Fiat and MV Agusta. Not to put too fine a point on it, this Triumph design has been around for years.

So has the Triumph 2000, subscriber of so much to this new enterprise. When Triumph, in the persons of that polished salesman Mr Sims and that candid engineer Mr Lloyd, first presented the Stag to the motoring press and we all acted out our profundities of professed doubts and feigned enthusiasms, little was said of this background save that the suspensions were similar and that the gearbox was a stronger version

than that of the saloons. In conning the specification I later noticed that the internal ratios of the gearbox were the same as in the saloons save that bottom gear was higher, 2.995 to one instead of 3.281. Now this is not an age and Leyland's is not a business in which that sort of thing is done unless it is strictly necessary: what customer is likely to express concern, or even to notice, the fact that 5500rpm in bottom gear produces 36 mph rather than 33? What was that about making the gearbox stronger? One way of increasing the torque capacity of a gearbox (which is not quite the same thing) is to raise the bottom-gear ratio and thus reduce the torque multiplication; and this is what has been done for the Stag. It cannot be mere coincidence that the first-gear reductions in Stag and 2.5PI are inversely proportional to the maximum torque outputs of their engines. Make of this what you will: either Triumph are admirably punctilious about maintaining their safety factors, or that gearbox is teetering on the brink of expensive disaster.

While on the subject of teetering, I note with some alarm that the track of the Stag is quoted as 52.5in at the front and 52.875in at the rear, *four up*. Forsooth, is the track so very different when the car is otherwise laden? Are camber variations and tyre scrub so pronounced even within the range of normal static deflexion? Or is this new caution a product of the Trade Descriptions Act, under the provisions of which some petty monger of righteousness might sue the manufacturers because the rear track of his unladen Stag measures only 52.75in? Undoubtedly there are camber changes taking place as the suspensions flex, but there is nothing in the feel or behaviour of the car to suggest that in general driving they might be noticeable. Indeed they should be less so than in the saloons, for the Stag's bigger (14in) wheels are girt with Michelin XAs radials which have plenty of spare capacity for lopsided genuflection. The car does not, it seems, depend on these tyres for its roadworthiness, for when sold to the USA it will wear G800GP70 Goodyears, which are also good but very different. Mr Engineer Lloyd said that the tyres were chosen merely because supplies happened to be conveniently available in the Coventry vicinity.

When it is in the right place at the right time the XAs is a superb tyre, and the Stag that I drove briefly during the press preview seemed to have large reserves of roadholding and safety. It was no

epic drive, amounting to no more than 40 miles of Belgian roads (mostly major) with John Bolster navigating, followed by a further 40 as passenger while he drove. It was enough, however, to establish that the Stag is a car that can cover the ground quickly and without fuss, cruising happily at any speed up to its maximum and displaying no behavioural oddities even when cornering quite fast. The maximum speed is supposed to be 118.

I would not criticise anyone for choosing the car in this form. The Borg-Warner was very smooth in everything it did, and seemed admirably matched to the engine. It was even quicker and smoother to use the kick-down than to employ the PRND21 lever, and that is a rare experience. As for the topless order, on a fine sunny day it felt absolutely right to be driving this sort of car in wide-open trim. Aerodynamic backwash and uplift only began to affect the security of my hat at 80mph, while wind noise was actually rather nice—no roaring and buffeting but a subdued musical note, apparently generated by the roll-over hoop that is an integral and impressive feature of the design. When the Stag was being designed it seemed likely that legislation would call for roll-over protection, and having tried it the Triumph engineers were so taken with the idea that they kept it on. Apart from looking interesting and being very reassuring to the occupants, it also does sterling service as a body stiffener, restoring to the basically floppy open car some of the structural rigidity of the

saloons. The hoop is made as an extension of the door pillars, with a central tee-piece linking it to the top rail of the windscreen; with its aid the car has a torsional stiffness exceeding 5000lb ft/deg. The soft hood fits over the top of it; so can the hard top, and somebody has had the bright idea of printing the instructions for deploying and dismantling the hood on the upper surface of the driver's sun visor.

There are other good ideas in the interior, though not all of them have been well carried out: release knobs for the backs of the front seats are very difficult to grasp if the seats are well back, though if anyone were wanting to sit in the rear occasionals the front seats would have to be moved forward anyway, so little space is there behind. On the other hand there is plenty of scope for steering-wheel adjustment, two inches vertically and four axially being at the disposal of a lever that can be unclamped and reclamped while driving. The steering itself is powered as in the 2.5 PI, with the same rather big wheel and the same rather slow gearing. The result is that the steering feels too light and dead, the four turns from lock to lock being at least one and perhaps 1.5 turns more than are wanted. The steering does not feel very accurate, either; in fact my main criticism of the car's handling is that it lacks precision. There is no sensation of lost motion, nor much sensation of anything else, but the overall effect is as if there were quanitities of rubber interposed between the steering wheel and the road wheels. The rubber

mountings for the rear suspension subframe may have something to do with it. Whether they have or not, the car steers in a rubbery sort of way: in the type of fastish bend that one swings through at 60 or 70mph it does not feel possible to place the car precisely, and it may drift as much as a yard from the chosen line. On the other hand there is seldom any feeling of losing it, for the mild understeer is fairly consistent. Only once or twice did I have the suspicion that the tail might be getting a little wayward as roll angles increased or as power was poured on in a corner—and although Triumph speak of low-friction splines in the drive-shafts, I suspect that it was probably binding of these that produced slight lurching when trying a bit hard.

As I said, there was precious little opportunity for this sort of thing. Being in Belgium, we had plenty of humpy pavé that the Stag took very well at 60, and plenty of good modern roads where 110 was quite in order—though the cross-wind stability of the car (in open form, at least) is not all that it might be. Again it might be roll steering, for the suspension is quite soft, as is the whole car. It is emphatically not a sports car, but rather a good-looking sporting tourer, in the same vein as the big Peugeot coupé and convertible. It costs a mere £2000, so it should sell very well indeed, possibly taking some business from BMW and Reliant but generally creating a new demand. As the first car from Triumph with Liverpudlian parentage it augurs well for Speke's future. ●

Delightful drawing at left, done by an apprentice in Triumph's engineering department, shows salient points of the fourth but by no means the last modern V8 engine to emerge from the Leyland group in recent years. Michelotti-styled body was apparently conceived some time ago (as was the engine) but has been updated with the aid of recognition features borrowed from current 2000 saloons. There are many echoes of Pininfarina practice, exemplified by the Fiat Dino Spyder and the Peugeot 504 coupé and convertible, but the Triumph's clever price/power combination keeps it well apart from existing competition

STAG" may not be everyone's idea of a good name for a successful automobile, but this new two-plus-two from the Standard-Triumph division of British Leyland is the most exciting new model from any British factory for many a long day.

Stag is a good-looking, two-door, occasional four seater with room in the back for real people — not legless midgets.

Styling of the monocoque body is by Giovanni Michelotti who has been influencing the designs from Standard-Triumph since the days of the Herald in the late 50s. The heritage shows in the new car. The spider-coupe (and it is both) is powered by a new 90-degree

ABOVE: Interior is strongly reminiscent of Mk. 2 2000 with curved dash, walnut veneer, and padded wheel.
TOP: Stag in spider form with Targa-type roll bar in place.
RIGHT: Shapely from all angles, Stag offers space for four adults and luggage.

Triumph enters the GT lists with a Targa-type V8 with looks, comfort — and performance, reports Dev. Dvoretsky

STAG V8 BY TRIUMPH

short-stroke 3-litre V8 with chain-driven single ohc giving 145 bhp nett at 5,500 rpm.

It is nominally a 120 mph machine, which can get to 60 mph in under 10 secs, has a reasonable thirst, exceptionally long legs, and an all-independent suspension borrowed from the 2.5 PI and TR-6 models. Stag takes over where the Rover-Triumph concept (now more than seven years old) left off, and carries on into the sphere of real grand touring. The Rover/Triumph 2000's were oriented towards the family man with a sporting inclination. The Stag follows the same trend — only moreso.

It's BLMC's first real challenge in the highly competitive luxury grand touring class which has long been the domain of continental makers.

Price of only 1527 Stg. basic for the softtop version, 1562 **Stg.** for the hardtop or 1602 Stg. for the combined softtop/hardtop. This will make it one of the world's most-wanted cars. With automatic and air-conditioning, practically the only two extras, the price could rise to around 1800/1850 Stg. basic — say around $6000 - $6500 fully equipped in Australia. If it were assembled in New Zealand along with the XJ-6 and Rover 2000 the price could drop a thousand dollars. And at that price it would be a sure-fire winner in Australia.

But don't rush your dealers yet. For the first 12 months production will be restricted to the home market. A production rate of about 15,000 a year will be underway by September.

But even when exports do start, it's likely most will go Stateside.

Hammering

Already U.S. dealers are hammering on the doors of the new 11-million Stg. factory at Speke just outside Liverpool where the bodies for Stag will be produced and at Coventry where the engines will be made and the car assembled.

It seems likely that something will have to make way for Stag on the now hard-pressed Coventry lines. No one will be surprised to see the end of the 11-year old Herald/Vitesse series to make way for the stylish newcomer.

Though production is bound to rise, I reckon this is going to be the Rover 2000/3500 and Jaguar XJ-6 all over again. (The former still three to six months lag on delivery and the latter

12 months and more in some markets)!

What makes the Stag such a certainty? It's a car that combines the good looks and sleekness of sports car and limousine. It is well appointed, extremely comfortable, has a high top speed and extremely good acceleration that few will use but which means so much at the traffic light G.P. It is easy to get into and out of — which means the not-so-young who'd like to feel they aren't out of it yet and who can afford it, won't hesitate. It's an easy car to drive (it comes equipped with Adwest power steering the same as the XJ-6) and even without automatic the torque is so good gear changing can be left to a minimum.

It's safe and though I wouldn't say the suspension is infallible, it will certainly be tops to most who buy it. Combine all this with the safety of a three-point roll-over bar, the air-conditioned comfort or the open-to-the-wind appeal plus the fact it can carry four at a pinch and you have answered the problem of hundreds of thousands of motorists.

Engine

The basic design was originally dreamed up by Harry Webster (now BLMC chief engineer) and STI sales chief Lindon Mills four years ago. The design and concept hardly changed from the word go. Originally the idea was to use a vee made from two of the 1700 cc single ohc units built by Triumph for SAAB. But later this was reduced to 2.5 litres. When 'Spen' King was moved from Rover to take over from Harry Webster as STI engineer he immediately upped the

ENGINE bay is a neat installation, with access to the important ancilliaries an easy matter. V8 is made up of two Triumph fours — developed originally for Saab — siamesed.

capacity and increased the power output. The result was an engine that simply screamed "torque".

Bore and stroke of the original 1709 four cylinder unit is 83.5 by 78 mm and output 87 at 5500 rpm. The V8 has a bore of 86 and a stroke of 64.5 and an overall capacity of 2997 cc (182.9 cubic inches). Output is 145 bhp nett at 5,500 rpm. Torque is 170lb. ft. at 3500 rpm.

The single overhead camshaft on each bank is chain driven — the two-plane crankshaft has five main bearings as have the camshafts themselves.

Twin side-draught Stromberg carbs are used, though it's a pretty open secret that STI have been playing around with Bosch electronic fuel injection. This is unlikely to be seen for a couple of years, at least.

An alternator is standard equipment and there is a 'no-loss' cooling system with expansion chamber and 13 psi pressure cap. The fan has a viscous coupling which cuts down roar. Power gets down to the rear wheels through a nine inch diaphragm clutch. The four speed all-synchromesh gearbox is similar to that of the Triumph 2000/2.5 Pl Mk 2. Overdrive is available on third and top and when fitted with the standard 3.7:1 rear axle gives a road speed at 1000 rpm in overdrive top of 24.1 mph — a real loper.

Standard ratio either with four speed box or Borg Warner overdrive is 19.8 mph per 1000 rpm. Tyres are Michelin 185 HR 14 in radial XAS tubeless on 5J rims.

Suspension is the fully-independent type of the 2.5 Pl Mk. 2 with front struts with coil springs controlled by telescopic dampers and an anti-roll bar. At the rear there are semi-trailing

arms, mounted on a rubber insulated steel sub-frame, with coil spring/damper units.

The servo assisted brakes — disc front, rear drum — are operated from a dual safety hydraulic system.

The monocoque body looks prettier in the flesh than some of its pictures suggest. The front treatment is very 2.5 Pl, with quad quartz halogen headlamps — probably the first production car to be so fitted. The wraparound bumper treatment front and rear and the rear treatment with its gently sloping boot is neat and attractive.

The hard-top which — like the Mercedes 280SL type requires at least two men or a small hoist in the garage to lift — is a solid affair containing not only the two opening rear side vents but an electrically-heated rear screen as standard. The well for the soft top is neatly covered by a solid frame vinyl covered top. Putting the close-fitting soft-top up takes about two minutes. The hard-top is held in position at five points controlled by levers — two at the screen, two behind the roll over bars and one at the rear.

Rollover

And its the roll-over bars in the Stag that are going to cause a lot of conversation. They are real roll-over bars and anticipate the possible criticism, on the grounds of safety, the sports car may come up against with safety legislation in the next few years. The softly padded triangulated bar is virtually an extension of the door pillars, and offers not only protection in case of roll-over but helps keep the monocoque stiff. It also acts as a sort of grab handle for the passenger if the

Continued on page 30

CUTAWAY of 90 deg. V8 shows chain drive for camshafts, centrally-positioned Zenith carburettors, viscous-coupled cooling fan.

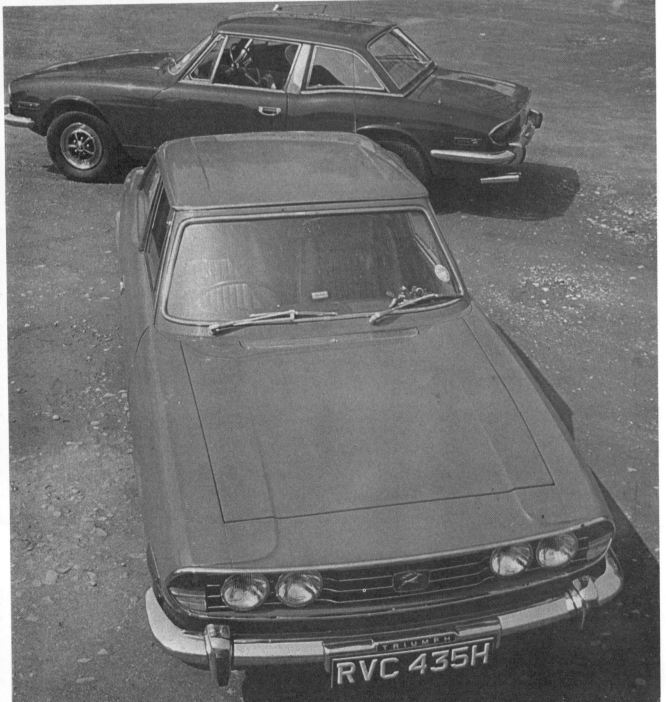

from the adjustable-for-rake steering column controls the wipers and the (right) headlamps and horn. There's a three-spoke steering wheel with big central boss and leather covered rim.

Overall length is 14ft. 5¾in. and width 5ft 3½ in., height (with soft-top erect) is 4ft 1½in., wheelbase is 8ft 4in. and track front 4ft 4½in. and rear 4ft 4in. Ground clearance fully loaded — four in., turning circle (four turns lock to lock) is 34 ft.

The Stag is full of interesting ideas as you quickly notice once you step inside. A small light lower right of the glove box throws light down on to the floor (or the passengers feet) at night to become a perfect map reading light. 'Puddle' lights come on as the door opens and shine down from the armrests and form door warning lights for oncoming traffic. Stag has rear seat attachments for safety belts as well as the single attachment inertia-type lap/sash which are fitted as standard to the front seats.

The seats are extremely comfortable. They can be adjusted for height and rake and the squabs are also adjustable. The steering wheel has adjustment for rake only but this, combined with the seat adjustment makes for a driving positon to suit even the most fastidious.

With the windows up noise in the coupe even over rough Belgium pave road surfaces (where we took the cars for pre-release tryout) was very low. There's very little back wash turbulence when the hood is down even at 100 mph and the noise when the windows are lowered at high speed with the hard top in position is tolerable. However, for hotter climates — even the south of France — to get the best from this car would be to use the Delaney-Galley air-conditioning system.

Ride

The ride over rough surfaces is very good, and the bumps are soaked up nicely by the all independent system. It's not the best I've met. You can feel it working on anything but a smooth road and under certain conditions (say braking in a fast corner) you upset the the balance and the tail will come out. The same applies under heavy braking when the front suspension seems to dive considerably. This has probably been brought about through compromise. Despite this, and the stupidity of four turns of lock with the good power-assisted rack and pinion steering, I found the car safe and relaxing.

If the tail does break away during a harsh manoeuvre correction is simply a matter of flicking the wheel. I've yet to try it in the wet.

I liked the overdrive car with its long loping gait: just over 4000 rpm and you cruise at the 'ton' in considerable silence. The automatic is the most responsively set Borg-Warner I've ever

come across and selection of 2 or 1 on the P.R.N.D.2.1 quadrant is rapid. There's no waiting frightening seconds before the ratio is engaged. Kickdown is the same. The torque of the engine is eminently suited to the automatic.

I liked the map pockets in the doors, the fact that you can ask a couple of people to sit in the back with the hard top on and they can be reasonably comfortable.

The boot carries the spare wheel and the fuel tank under the flat floor. This leaves a maximum height of 13 in. and a minimum of eight in. Width between the wheelarches is 35 in. maximum width is 54 in. Capacity is 9 cu. ft. which means you've room for two 28 in. suitcases and perhaps a grip or two.

Performance is not to be sneezed at. The Stag weighs about 33.5 cwt gross — that's with everything aboard, so it is not light. Basic kerb weight is 25 cwt or with optional extras including the hard top about 27 cwt. But you can push all this up to 30 mph in 3.5 sec. to 40 in 5 sec. to 50 in 7 sec. to 60 in 9.5 sec. to 70 in 12.5 sec. to 80 in 16 sec. 90 in 21.5 sec. and to 100 in 29 sec. Top gear acceleration is good as can be expected with that torque. 20-40 mph, 30-50 mph and 40-60 mph all come up in 7.5 sec. 50-70 takes 8 sec. and 60-80 takes 8.5 sec. 70-90 takes 10 sec. and 80-100 13 sec.

Fuel consumption we didn't have time to take and the factory hadn't done their homework in this direction either. Judging by the way the fuel gauge registered on the 14 gallon tank I'd estimate an average 22 mpg.

This is a good car. It has its shortcomings but they are indeed few. The thinking is right and the result augers well for the first generation of the new BLMC giant. The Triumph Division certainly knows where it is going (next month I'll have some more news from there). The other specialists, Jaguar and Rover are doing things that will keep them to the forefront. I wonder what Harry Webster can come up with from the trailing Austin-Morris Division? Only time will tell. ●

STAG V8

Continued from page 28

driver is cornering fast. The framed windows of the wide opening doors are electrically controlled from the centre console. Internally the Stag is well finished, with multi-adjustable seats and aerated PVC coverings. The dashboard with its curved instrument panel taken from the 2.5 PI is well-laid-out and the instruments most easy to read. "Eye ball" socket ventilation on either side of the dashboard and central facial vents are included. The overdrive switch is on the top of the column. The left stalk

MOTOR TEST No. 42/70 — Triumph Stag

MOTOR TESTED

Al fresco in style

Very comfortable and well appointed; excellent performance,
ride and roadholding; lavish hood and heavy hardtop difficult
to erect; very easy to handle but manners and brakes imperfect;
wind noise high, boot space modest

Under the new code of permissiveness Triumph allow themselves
to issue a discreet warning to Mercedes Benz and Alfa Romeo in
their Stag advertisements. If they can produce the cars to back
the threat, it's a warning that the opposition will not take lightly,
even though it may be only image building. Although the new
Triumph doesn't have quite the sporting spirit of the Alfa 1750
GTV, or perhaps the prestige of a Mercedes 280SL, it does have
certain qualities—above all style and versatility—that no rival
import can match at the price. It has no British counterpart, of
course, so here at least it enjoys a monopoly in a sector of the
market that has long been neglected. For this reason alone it can
hardly fail to succeed.

Costs have risen so much in the past year or so that the Stag's
£2000 price tag—more or less according to equipment—seems
to us quite a modest outlay for such a striking, thoroughly
modern V8 coupe that will exceed 120 mph, seat four
adults—two of them in exceptional comfort—and successfully
combine the roles of an *al fresco* fun car with that of a
civilized town carriage.

In some respects—seating, ride, controls, finish, appointments
and stability at speed, for instance—it exceeds expectations. In
others it merely lives up to them: the acceleration, though good,
is no better than you'd expect of a car which, by absolute

standards, has a modest power/weight ratio; and the roadholding
is as tenacious as the fat tyres and all-independent suspension
would suggest.

But there are also disappointments. Wind noise is high, even
with the hardtop, and the engine is neither as quiet nor even as
smooth as we hoped it might be—a relative observation for by no
stretch of anyone's imagination could it be called rough and
noisy. A tendency to twitch off course when changing gear and
(for some drivers) feel-less power steering marred otherwise
exemplary handling.

It could be argued that for a small sacrifice in versatility a
fixed superstructure with detachable (and stowable) roof panels
à la Porsche Targa, 914 and Corvette Sting Ray would have
saved on cost, complication and weight. Thoughts along these
lines—not shared by us all here—stemmed from the trouble we
had in erecting (and removing) the Stag's two modes of headgear.

Despite some detail faults, though, we were certainly
impressed by the Stag's concept and quality and completely
hooked by its highly individualistic charm—at its greatest on
these cars equipped (like ours) with soft and hardtop coverage, as
well as the optional overdrive, equipment that raises the price to
£2159. If that sounds a lot consider that the Mercedes 280SL
coupe/convertible—the Stag's closest European rival in
character and performance—costs over £4655, a Porsche Targa
(left-hand drive only) even more. American V8 convertibles
don't come much cheaper; nor will they do over 20 miles to the
gallon like the Stag.

**PRICE: hard and soft top model as tested, £1602 plus £491 15s. 10d.
purchase tax equals £2093 15s. 10d. Overdrive (as fitted) £65 5s. 7d.**

Performance and economy

Triumph's completely new ohc V8 engine is in effect a doubled-up version of the PE104S "four" that helps make the Saab 99 such a good car. Both engines are likely to figure prominently in British Leyland's plans for the Seventies. Because the Triumph engine in the Saab feels so refined we had hoped the full V8, with twice as many power strokes to each revolution of the crankshaft, might set new standards in smoothness. It doesn't. Certainly it *is* very smooth, but no more so than some much larger American V8s. Despite the crossflow pipe linking the two exhausts just forward of the silencers, it has a rather throbby beat which you hear rather than feel—though there's also some vibration transmitted through the gearlever.

With 145 bhp (net) from 3 litres the engine is quite modestly rated when compared with, say, BMW's 2.8 "six" which develops 170 bhp. It also has quite a lot to do for the Stag is a heavy car—almost 26 cwt with the hardtop—so perhaps the

acceleration isn't quite so vicious as you'd expect from a sporting 3-litre coupe. To get the best from the car, our performance tests were done with the soft-top up, saving about a hundredweight without increasing the drag.

The engine was always an instant starter and completely without temperament during the warm-up period. As you'd expect for a torquey V8, its usable pulling range spans the entire rev band, from idling at 800 rpm to the red-lined maximum of 6500 rpm, which we used during performance testing but seldom, if ever, on the road. The orange sector starts at 5500 rpm which the handbook warns should not be exceeded for long periods. On Continental motorways this restriction would impose a maximum speed of 109 mph in direct top (19.8 mph per 1000 rpm with the Michelin XAS tyres on our car) so the optional overdrive (£65 extra) is really essential if the car is to be used as a long-distance express—a role for which certain qualities make it particularly well suited.

In overdrive (24.1 mph/1000) 5500 rpm corresponds to over

PERFORMANCE

Performance tests carried out by *Motor's* staff at the Motor Industry Research Association proving ground, Lindley.

Test Data: World copyright reserved; no unauthorized reproduction in whole or in part.

Conditions

Weather: Warm, dry, windy
Temperature: 56-62°F
Barometer 29.6 in. Hg.
Surface: Dry asphalt
Fuel: 97 octane(RM), 4 Star rating

Maximum Speeds

	mph	kph
Mean lap banked circuit (see text)	116.5	187.5
Best one-way ¼-mile (see text)	123.2	198.5
o/d 3rd gear	112	180
3rd gear ⎫	92	148
2nd gear ⎬ at 6500 rpm	60	97
1st gear ⎭	42	67

"Maximile" speed: (Timed quarter mile after 1 mile accelerating from rest)
Mean 109.8
Best 112.5

Acceleration Times

mph	sec
0-30	3.5
0-40	5.0
0-50	7.4
0-60	9.7
0-70	13.2
0-80	17.0
0-90	22.2
0-100	29.6
Standing quarter mile	17.3
Standing kilometre	31.6

	O/d			
	Top	Top	3rd
mph	sec	sec	sec
10-30	—	—	5.8
20-40	10.2	7.8	5.4
30-50	10.1	7.6	5.1
40-60	10.2	7.5	5.1
50-70	10.6	7.7	5.7
60-80	11.6	8.5	6.6
70-90	13.2	10.0	9.1
80-100	16.3	13.4	—

Fuel Consumption

Touring (consumption midway between 30 mph and maximum less 5 per cent allowance for acceleration)
25.5 mpg
Overall 20.9 mpg
(=13.5 litres/100km)
Total test distance 1520 miles

Brakes

Pedal pressure, deceleration and equivalent stopping distance from 30 mph

lb.	g.	ft.
25	0.47	64
50	0.90	33
75	0.92	32½
Handbrake	0.38	79

Fade Test

20 stops at ½g deceleration at 1 min. intervals from a speed midway between 40 mph and maximum speed (=78 mph)

	lb.
Pedal force at beginning	25
Pedal force at 10th stop	35
Pedal force at 20th stop	40

Steering

	ft.
Turning circle between kerbs:	
Left	33
Right	31
Turns of steering wheel from lock to lock	2.75
Steering wheel deflection for 50ft. diameter circle	0.95 turns

Clutch

Free pedal movement = ⅛in.
Additional movement to disengage clutch completely = 3⅛in.
Maximum pedal load = 35lb.

Speedometer

Indicated	20	30	40	50	60	70	80	90	100
True	20	30	40	50	59½	68½	77½	87	95½

Distance recorder 0.5% fast

Weight

Kerb weight (unladen with hardtop and fuel for approximately 50 miles) 25.9cwt
Front/rear distribution 54/46
Weight laden as tested (without hardtop) approx. 28.1cwt

Parkability

Gap needed to clear 6 ft. wide obstruction in front

-5'-9"- 6'-0" -20'-3¾"-

130 mph, a speed unattainable in normal conditions but we suspect possible under really favourable ones. The MIRA lap speed of 116.5 quoted in our tables is not a true maximum because at this speed the tyres are scrubbing away several mph on the banking. In any case our test driver confesses to lifting off momentarily for the turn at the end of the long wind-assisted straight. That the car was doing 125 mph here, still accelerating and feeling astonishingly stable, underlines its excellent high-speed cruising ability. Certainly the MIRA performance suggests a mean two-way maximum of well over 120 mph.

Despite its weight, the car surges away effortlessly and quite strongly in top gear from under 15 mph: 20-40 mph takes a smooth 8 sec., 50-70 mph no longer, indicating the consistency of the pull. Through the gears the acceleration is virtually identical to that of a Capri 3000GT: both cars reach 100 mph from rest in a fraction less than 30 sec.

More than with most cars, we suspect the Stag's performance must vary considerably according to its equipment. Taking obvious extremes, the acceleration times of a hard-top automatic with Michelin tyres must be much poorer than those of a lighter soft-top manual with the alternative Goodyear covers that effectively lower the gearing by 1 mph /1000 in top.

For such a fast and heavy car, the consumption of 4-star fuel is quite reasonable—21-26 mpg according to how and where you drive. At an average 23 mpg, the 14-gallon tank gives a useful maximum range of 320 miles.

Transmission

The four-speed manual gearbox is a strengthened version of that in the 2000 /2.5PI. It feels and sounds much the same, too. The gearlever moves in a precise and positive gate, but obstructive synchromesh makes the change notchy if you snatch at it. With easy, unhurried movements, though, it engages smoothly. Apart from baulking rushed changes, the synchromesh can sometimes be beaten. Gear whine is quite audible in the intermediates.

The clutch on our car was remarkably good—not only utterly

Above right: the front seats, adjustable for height, reach and rake, are superb: the rear bench, deeply troughed for thigh support, is passable, above. Five children, centre, is a squash but three will fit comfortably smooth but also unusually progressive, so even indelicate footwork failed to jerk the car; ideal for learners. Our measurements show the pedal travel to be quite long (which we don't normally like) and the weight no better than average, but in use we were aware only of the smoothness of its action—more like a torque converter than a clutch.

The overdrive, operated by a handy switch in the gearlever knob (some drivers still prefer a column stalk), engaged with a gentle slurr, too, without help from the clutch; under light acceleration, disengagement was also smooth but on the overrun or hard power it was jerkier.

Handling and brakes

Fat radial-ply tyres on a car with respectable all independent suspension and a well balanced weight distribution is a recipe that can hardly fail to give high cornering powers and a good hold on indifferent roads. The Stag's bond with the road is certainly excellent and to break it in the dry you've got to explore g forces that are well beyond what most people would regard as

Lifting the hardtop, above, is a two-person—preferably a two-man—job. Once in place it is easy to secure. The substantial hood unfurls from a covered well, left, and is rather more difficult to latch down

By popular request, our old test boxes have been replaced by real suitcases. See page 48 for further details. These were the only two that would fit the Stag's boot—a number 1 and 3—though there was some space left for squashable bags

the limit. Unfortunately (and unusually) we had little opportunity of assessing wet road adhesion.

In some respects then handling is every bit as good as the grip. Very light and responsive steering, seats that hold you in place and minimal body roll—not to mention the good roadholding—make hard cornering very safe and easy. But the Stag has its faults. Changing gear after a burst of hard acceleration through a corner, sometimes even on the straight, can make the car twitch off course. We suspect the reason for this irritating rather than alarming behaviour is the driveshaft splines locking up under heavy torque so that they cannot adjust in length with changes in wheel camber—most pronounced under cornering. As something must 'give' the suspension and thus the wheel twists fractionally on the rubber bushes. When the torque is released in a gearchange the splines slide, the wheel straightens and the car twitches.

To be fair, we were a lot more conscious of this inherent fault (the 2.5 PI suffers from it too) at the beginning of our test than at the end, partly because experience showed it to be more of a bad habit than a vice, partly because we found ourselves automatically avoiding mid-corner changes. For different reasons, lifting the throttle in mid corner—as opposed to breaking the drive altogether—will make the car tuck in, to tighten its line. In moderation—and it is not over pronounced in the Stag—such behaviour is not a bad thing as the car helps itself round any corner, rather than plough straight on, if you misjudge your speed. In the extreme we found that lifting off when right on the limit was the most likely way to cause a tail slide, though even then breakaway is gentle and easily checked.

It is during such untoward antics, though, that you are most aware of the absence of feel on the featherweight steering. All messages come through the seat of your pants, not through your hands, as there is little informative self-aligning tug with which to gauge adhesion and understeer. Searching for it will make for untidy, even lurchy cornering. In short, the Stag's steering is over-assisted, like that of the Jaguar XJ6, for really spirited cornering. If you don't indulge in this sort of thing, though, we'd say that it's a very good set-up, especially when judged purely on the amount of effort and twiddling it demands.

The strong winds we had for some of our test were unwelcome when taking performance figures but underlined the car's exceptional stability in adverse condition at high speed. Nothing seemed to deviate it from the straight and narrow, even at maximum speed.

The brakes on our car were less satisfactory: they juddered when applied hard at speed; faded a bit under really hard usage (though they *did* just pass our 20-stop test); and, like the steering, were too heavily assisted for our liking. Feathering off a stop was also difficult because of a rather unprogressive release action. The handbrake held the car in both directions on the 1-in-3 hill.

Comfort and control

To say that the suspension feels quite firm, even a bit jolty on bad roads and a little jiggly on secondary ones, would be true but rather misleading. The overall impression is of great stability, of a very flat-controlled ride despite any underlying disturbances. There is little of the harshness often associated with a sports car, practically none of the wallowy float you get with a really soft saloon. The compromise felt to us exactly right. The stability of the ride is emphasized by the absence of exaggerated body roll on corners, by the rigidity of the structure (the overhead bracing certainly prevents scuttle shake and body tremors), and by well-muffled road noise; radial thump is particularly subdued.

In contrast wind noise is excessive. Detachable hardtops present special sealing problems and Triumph don't yet seem to have overcome those on the Stag. The top rail seal is the worst offender; that improvement is possible we demonstrated by reducing the hiss with a strip of masking tape. Even then, unpleasant wind rush dominates all other sounds above 60 mph and is getting pretty loud at 80, especially on a windy day. Almost inevitably, wind noise is even greater with the soft top: although the hood is taut, and free from draughts, the roar of the wind became almost unbearable during our maximum-speed ▶ 23

SPECIFICATION

Overall width 5' 3½"
45"   18½"
49½"   -37-
48"
52"   48"
46½"
21½"   6½"   13½"
Front track 4' 4½"
Rear track 4' 4½"

Ground clearances
Lowest point (under exhaust) 6½"
under front suspension 7½"
under engine 8"

Screen frame to floor 37"   Floor to roof 40½"
4' 4½" Unladen height
28"   14½"
37"
15½"   23"
19"   23"
23¼"   27¼"   7"   23"   27"
17"   20½"   19¼"   9½"   17½"   9¼"
21"   14½"
Bottom of door to ground 14½"
8' 4"
14' 6½"
Height of male figure 5' 10" approx.

23¼"
33"
19½"
12½"   27¼"
51"
25"
18½"

Seat measurements taken with seats compressed

Engine

Block material	Chromium iron
Head material	Aluminium alloy
Cylinders	8—90° Vee
Cooling system	water, no loss system, thermostatically controlled flow
Bore and stroke	86mm. (3.385in.) 64.5mm. (2.539in.)
Cubic capacity	2997 cc (182.9 cu. in.)
Main bearings	5—steel backed lead bronze with lead indium overlay
Valves	Overhead camshafts
Compression ratio	8.8:1
Carburetter(s)	2—Stromberg side draught—175 CDS
Fuel pump	SU electric. Diaphragm type. Inertia switch in engine bay
Oil Filter	AC. Delco Full Flow—replaceable paper elements
Max. power (net)	145 bhp at 5,500 rpm
Max torque (net)	170 lb.ft. at 3,500 rpm

Transmission

Clutch	Laycock—single dry plate diaphragm spring type—9in dia. hydraulically operated
Internal gear box ratios	
Top gear	1.00
3rd gear	1.386
2nd gear	2.10
1st gear	2.995
overdrive top	0.82
overdrive third	1.135
Reverse	3.369
Synchromesh	All forward gears
Overdrive type	Laycock—electrically operated on top 2 gears
Final drive (type and ratio)	Hypoid bevel gears, 2 pinion differential—3.7:1
Mph at 1000 rpm in:-	
O/d top gear	24.1
Top gear	19.8
O/d 3rd gear	17.4
3rd gear	14.3
2nd gear	9.45
1st gear	6.62

Chassis and body

Construction	Integral construction—steel sub-frame at rear

Brakes

Type	Disc/drum, servo-assisted. Mechanically operated handbrake to rear wheels
Friction areas:	
Front	24 sq.in. of lining operating on 220 sq.in. of disc
Rear	78 sq.in. of lining operating on 127 sq.in. of drum

Suspension and steering

Front	Independent by coil springs and wishbones: anti-roll bar
Rear	Independent by coil springs and semi-trailing arms.
Shock absorbers:	
Front and rear	Telescopic hydraulic dampers
Steering type	Rack & pinion
Tyres	Michelin 185 HR-14 radial ply tubeless
Wheels	Steel disc
Rim size	5J

Coachwork and equipment

Starting handle	No
Tool kit contents	Combination tool: plug spanner wheel nut spanner; w/trim removal tool; tool pouch
Jack	Scissor type
Jacking points	4, under sills adjacent to each wheel
Battery	12. volt negative earth 56 amp hrs capacity @ 20 hr. rate.
Number of electrical fuses	11
Headlamps	4 Quartz halogen
Indicators	Front & rear & indicator repeaters in front wing side panels
Reversing lamp	Yes
Screen wipers	2 speed.
Screen washers	Twin nozzle electrically operated
Sun visors	2—vanity mirror in passenger side
Locks:	
With ignition key	Ignition & steering column lock, side doors & petrol filler cap
With other keys	Glove compartment & luggage compartment
Interior heater	Smith's air/mix heater/demister
Upholstery	PVC leathercloth with basket weave pattern on seat facings
Floor covering	Moulded pile carpet with felt underlay
Alternative body styles	Available with soft top or hard top or both
Maximum load	943 lb (Difference between kerb & gross vehicle weight)
Maximum roof rack load	112 lb. (hard top only)
Major extras available	Hard top, air conditioning unit, Laycock overdrive, Borg-Warner automatic transmission

Maintenance

Fuel tank capacity	14 galls
Sump	8 pints SAE 10W 20W/50
Gearbox	2¼ pints SAE 90EP
Rear axle	2 pints SAE 90EP
Steering gear	1¼ pints Type A (Power steering reservoir)
Coolant	18½ pints (2 drain taps) including heater
Minimum service interval	6000 miles

Chassis lubrication	None
Ignition timing	14° btdc
Contact breaker gap	0.015in.
Sparking plug gap	0.025in.
Sparking plug type	Champion N–11Y
Tappet clearance (cold)	Inlet 0.008in. Exhaust 0.018in.
Valve timing:	
inlet opens	16° btdc
inlet closes	56° abdc
exhaust opens	56° bbdc
exhaust closes	16° atdc
Rear wheel toe-in	$0^{-\frac{1}{16}''}$
Front wheel toe-in	$\frac{1}{16}''-\frac{1}{8}''$
Camber angle	Front 1° Pos. ± 1° Rear1½° Pos. ± 1°
Castor angle	2° ± 1°
King pin inclination	10½° ± 1°
Tyre pressures:	
Front	26 p.s.i.
Rear	30 p.s.i.

Safety Check List

Steering Assembly

Steering box position	Forward and above engine bearer
Steering column collapsible	No
Steering wheel boss padded	Yes
Steering wheel dished	Slightly

Instrument Panel

Projecting switches	None seriously
Sharp cowls	No
Padding	Along top and bottom of facia

Windscreen and Visibility

Screen type	Zebra zone toughened glass
Pillars padded	Slightly
Standard driving mirrors	One inside
Interior mirror framed	Yes
Interior mirror collapsible	Yes
Sun visors	Two

Seats and Harness

Attachment to floor	By bolted slides
Do they tip forward?	Only after releasing side catch
Head rest attachment points	No
Back of front seats	Firmly padded
Safety Harness	Yes
Harness anchors at back	No

Doors

Projecting handles	No
Anti-burst latches	Yes
Child-proof locks	No

1 map reading light. 2 fan. 3 ventilation grilles. 4 radio (extra). 5 warning lights. 6 battery condition. 7 temperature. 8 speedometer. 9 brake failure warning light. 10 rev counter. 11 clock. 12 fuel gauge. 13 fresh air vent. 14 choke. 15 heater controls. 16 interior lights. 17 and 19 windows. 18 handbrake. 20 rear window heater. 21 cigar lighter. 22 panel light rheostat. 23 washer/wiper. 24 indicators/horn/dip

THE SECRET OF SURVIVAL FOR A small manufacturer in a world of giants is to find a niche in the market —to locate a gap that British Leyland, Ford and the rest have ignored, and to concentrate on filling it effectively.

Reliant, under the able guidance of Ray Wiggin, have been doing this for some time. Although their bread and butter business continues to come from three-wheelers, and from setting up package deal vehicle plants in developing countries, there is increasing emphasis on the jam of the sporting Scimitar range. We make no apologies for returning to the GTE—it is one of the most interesting cars produced in Britain and certainly one of the most thoroughly worthy. And it is unique in that it supplies genuine two-plus-two seating accommodation, plentiful luggage capacity, fine handling and the lazy, loping power of an underdeveloped three-litre engine at only just over £2000.

At least it *was* unique until a few months ago, when British Leyland's Triumph division introduced the Stag. The first few production examples are beginning to filter on to the roads now, and they are remarkably comparable with the GTE in specification as well as in price. This is not so surprising when you realise that the Triumph people themselves are dab hands at finding gaps in the market and plugging them under the very noses of their rivals. This habit started in the days before Leyland took over Triumph, when the Coventry company was indeed struggling for survival against Ford, BMC, Rootes and Vauxhall. More recently it has sheltered safely under the Leyland wing and now, as part of the British Leyland Motor Corporation's Specialist Car Division, is still charged with the same basic role.

Hence the Stag. It makes no pretence of being a sports car in the traditional sense of the phrase. Neither, although BLMC would have you think otherwise, does it quite qualify as a GT, either in the original or in the modern, devalued meaning. In fact it is a true, straightforward personal touring car—a throwback to the tourers that became a halfway house between saloons and two-seaters between the wars. As such, it has little direct competition but a lot of appeal, if BLMC have done their market research correctly, to the man who wants to move away from the staid dignity of a saloon, yet not *that* far away.

Its nearest rival, Reliant's GTE, achieves very much the same end although it does so by way of an entirely different route. It, too, is a real tourer, suited to long, laden journeys with two adults or a young family (neither car has much back seat space to offer anyone over early-teens size). But it has more of the old fashioned sports car in its makeup, and this shows immediately you get behind the wheel. It is obvious, too, in the design, for under the skin the Reliant is simplicity itself whereas the Stag is really rather complex.

Much of the Triumph's complexity, however, stems from the unusual and laudable degree of attention the designers have paid to details. By comparison much of this minutiae is missing from the GTE, which is all the more a pity when you realise that in hand-assembled, limited-output products like this there is much more opportunity to incorporate the thoughtful little touches that can really civilise a car.

STYLE AND ENGINEERING

The debt the Stag owes to the 2000 and 2.5PI Triumphs is instantly visible. The styling around the front is almost identical to the 2000's. From that point back, however, the shape differs to suggest the Stag's sporting qualities with a slight drop in the waistline at the cockpit before humping up over the rear wheels to finish once more with the saloon's smiling, sheet-metal flourish. In fact this similarity is a case of chicken and egg, for the Stag was in fact evolved first.

With the hardtop and hood both out of the way, the Stag's built-in roll cage does nothing to detract from its appearance. Overall, the styling bears the unmistakable stamp of Giovanni Michelotti, Triumph's main consultant in this field for many years.

Equally, the GTE's lines are clearly the work of Tom Karen, head of the Ogle design consultancy and responsible for the external appearance of most of Reliant's more attractive products. The GTE has a higher, narrower look than its rival, emphasised by the way in which the roofline is carried straight back, breadvan-style, to achieve the estate-car-like rear end. At the back the GTE scores an aesthetic victory with its uncompromisingly vast rear window-cum-tailgate, a sharp contrast to the Stag's con-

ventional boot and rear-end styling, w echoes of the more mundane saloons.

The Reliant like most of its kind glassfibre bodywork and the finish, althou better than it used to be, is still not up that achieved on the Stag's steel panels. the other hand the metal is more expens to repair, and corrosion-prone.

The Stag's chassis/body is the custom unitary construction affair, using a modif 2000 floorpan. The Reliant has a separ ladder-type chassis with cruciform braci welded up from stout steel tubes.

Suspension on the Reliant is by dou wishbones and coil springs at the front. the back the engineers have avoided potential pitfalls of independence and st to a live axle located by trailing arms f and aft and a Watt linkage in the late plane. The Stag has MacPherson struts front, with semi-trailing arms and c springs for the rear wheels. In fact, this a much of the rest of the running gear a other components come from the 2000/2.5

The Stag's steering, too, is borrowed fr the saloons. It has power-assistance standard, by courtesy of Adwest. The Reli also uses a rack and pinion system but some reason cannot be obtained with ser

In considering cars like these the deta of design are of as much importance as major facets. In this instance, it is high relevant that the Stag as a result of its salo background has plentiful compliance bu into its suspension and steering whereas Scimitar has relatively little. This has considerable effect in determining the respective characters and behaviour.

GIANT TEST

RELIANT SCIMITAR GTE v TRIUMPH STAG

The wheels on both cars are ordinary ...ssed steel, thinly disguised by black and ...ome trim (à la Vitesse, TR6 and others) ...the Triumph and by equally unappealing ...ssfibre moulded covers on the GTE. The ...ention in both cases is to suggest that ...wheels are rather more exotic than they ...truth are. Braking in either case is by ...r identical power-assisted disc front/drum ...r systems.

The Stag's V8 engine is a newcomer and ...e of uncertain future in view of the ...stence of the ex-GM alloy V8 which ...tish Leyland acquired with Rover, not to ...ntion the perennially expected efforts in ...s field from Jaguar. At all events the ...iumph engine is a pleasing design and one ...t deserves wider application.

As a result of choosing the lusty Ford ...gine Reliant have also saddled themselves ...h the much less desirable gearbox that ...companies it. As ever, the second ratio is ...pelessly low and the change action no ...re than fair. The Stag has a modified ...rsion of the much sweeter 2.5PI gearbox ...d can be ordered with overdrive on third ...d fourth at an extra cost of £65. Overdrive ...sts £72 extra on the GTE.

Both cars are also available with Borg ...arner automatic transmission, at £104 ...ore for the Stag and £139 for the GTE.

SE OF SPACE

There's little to choose between these ...o in major dimensions. Both cars are quite ...nerously proportioned and no attempt has ...en made to obtain compactness. Externally, ...fàct, they are of medium saloon size, with overall lengths near 14.5ft and widths nearing 5.5ft. The use made of the space so provided is another matter. Long engine compartments are necessary, partly for reasons of styling and partly because the power units themselves are set back from the front axle line in the interests of weight distribution. V-type engines, even a six like the Ford used by Reliant, never save as much space as they should. Obviously they are greedy of width, but length, too, goes by the board, especially when servo pumps, alternators and other ancillaries have to be hung on the front of the block because the already restricted side space has been hogged by the exhaust manifolds. Reliant, however, do manage to cram the spare wheel into the front of the engine compartment.

On wheelbases measuring not much over 8ft all this means that passenger space is at something of a premium. Both cars provide ample room around the front seats. Back seats are another story. The Triumph's is inviting because it is well upholstered and of reasonable width. Leg- and, particularly, knee-room are barely acceptable unless the front seats are well forward, while headroom is insufficient for anyone over 5ft 10in or so. The Reliant's back seat is divided into separate buckets by a folding armrest and although it locates the occupants better than the Triumph bench it gives them no more space for the extremities.

The Reliant's seat backs fold to extend the estate car-like luggage compartment that stretches back to the tailgate. The Stag, being basically an open car, has to make provision for the hood to fold into a compartment around the back seat, a prime reason for the restricted space in that area. Behind, there is a normal boot of none too generous capacity.

Space-saving rear suspension systems mean that room has been found in both cars for outstandingly generous fuel tanks.

COMFORT & SAFETY

In contrast to the coupé bodywork of the Reliant, the Stag is basically a convertible for which a metal hardtop is an expensive and desirable option. It adds £98 to the price, though anyone who disdains open air motoring—or doesn't mind risking being caught in the rain with the top down—can save £56 by dispensing with the hood altogether and just having the hardtop. Because it has a comparatively long passenger compartment to cover, and because it contains a lot of glass, the hardtop is no lightweight. Undoing the quick-release catches that retain it is no problem; lifting it off, and finding somewhere to stow it, are not so easy.

The hardtop incorporates a heated rear window, for which the connector plugs-in automatically as the top is fitted on to the cockpit. The rear side windows are hinged at the front to act as vents. The top fits very snugly. In British weather, at least, there is little incentive to remove it. Those who do will find that the rather floppy and ugly hood, neatly hidden away under a panel, folds up and into place fairly easily. It has a zipped-in back window for extra ventilation when one keeps it erect to ward off Mediterranean sunshine. With the hood down the wind whistles irritatingly around the roll cage but doesn't buffet the occupants as

photography: Ivor Lewis

much as in an open two-seater.

The Stag's controversial cage is so positioned as to present no obstruction to headroom. The only time when it does interfere is if one turns to reach back over the very high squabs of the front seats into the rear compartment. Its padded vinyl covering can be unzipped for cleaning.

We preferred the front seats in the Stag, mainly because they have a simpler, more effective method of rake adjustment than the Reliant's as well as being more comfortable. The Reliant seats are firmer but do give much better lateral support. A minor disadvantage with the Reliant is that in front one sits closer to the floor, which can be tiring for the legs in addition to diminishing slightly the driver's forward view. We approved strongly of the Reliant's driving position, however, in which the controls are correctly laid out and the nicely angled steering wheel has a fairly thick rim of smallish

diameter. All round visibility is good in both cars.

The Stag uses the large-diameter wheel of the 2.5PI, adjustable over a limited range for both rake (2in) and reach (4in) once a clamping lever under the dash has been released. Even with all the travel used up the angle of the wheel remains much less vertical than our drivers like. This apart, we found nothing to complain of in the Stag's controls. They are almost identical to those of the 2.5PI, which is no bad thing.

The Stag facia looks like that of the saloons and is covered with matt-finished wood veneer. It houses a generous complement of instruments, plus switches that are simple enough to locate in a hurry. The lighting control is on a rotary switch projecting from the column. In fact the entire control system, even down to the single dial containing a multiplicity of warning lights, will be entirely familiar to ▶

Instruments: 1 Speedo **2** Fuel **3** Water Temp **4** Oil Pressure **5** Tacho **7** Ammeter **Warnings: 8** Ignition **9** Main Beam **10** Oil Pressure **11** Indicators **12** Water Temp **14** Handbrake **15** Fuel Low **16** Choke Control Warning **Controls: 19** Choke **20** Ign/Start **21** Indicators **22** Lights **23** Dip **24** Flash **25** Horn **26** Panel Lights **28** Wipers **29** Washers **30** Heater **31** Fresh Air Vent **Special Items: A** Cigar Lighter **B** Clock **G** Rear Window Demister Control **H** Blower **I** Electric Window Control **P** Brake Light Fail **Q** Overdrive Control **T** Rear Window Wiper **V** Voltmeter

	GTE	**STAG**
PRICES	At £2019 a mere £23 more than the basic Stag but £75 less than the more nearly comparable hardtop version. Adding £33 for a heated rear window to match the Stag's standard one makes the differential only £42	At £1996, or £2094 when fitted with both hard and soft tops, the most expensive Triumph yet produced. Priced neatly to fit into a niche in the 2 plus 2 market occupied hitherto only by Reliant

ACCELERATION from standstill in seconds

GTE	STAG
18.0 24.2 33.3	17.9 22.9 32.3
13.5	**13.6**
10.0	10.1
7.4	7.5
5.1	5.3
2.9	3.6

FUEL

GTE	STAG
23 mpg overall	**21** mpg overall
★★★★	★★★★
28mpg driven carefully	25mpg driven carefully
375–450 miles range	280–335 miles range
17 gallons capacity	14 gallons capacity

SPEEDS IN GEARS

GTE	STAG
mph 87	mph 91
38 o/d 106	41 o/d 101
54 114	60 112
o/d 121	o/d 118
top speed	top speed

HANDLING

GTE	STAG
Greater cornering power than Triumph on smooth roads, but more easily disturbed by bumps. Mild initial understeer on Pirelli Cinturato radials, changing progressively to oversteer and an impending slide. Grip maintained well in the wet	Excellent cornering power on Michelin XAs radials. Strong understeer emphasised by power-assisted steering, turning eventually to easily controlled oversteer. Adhesion remains good in wet and/or on poor surfaces

LUGGAGE CAPACITY cubic feet

Tone indicates seats folded

BRAKES
RESPONSE in normal use. Deceleration (percent g) vs pedal load (lb)
A=Stag
B=GTE

FADE
peak deceleration achieved in 10 crash stops from 60mph at one minute intervals
A=Stag
B=GTE

DIMENSIONS	GTE	STAG
	inches	inches
wheelbase	99.5	100
front track	55	52.5
rear track	53	52.8
length	171	173.75
width	64.5	63.5
height	52	49.5
ground clearance	5.5	5
headroom, front	33	34.5
legroom, front	28	30
headroom, rear	32	32.5
kneeroom, rear	6	5
ENGINE		
material	iron/iron	iron/alloy (heads)
bearings	4	5
cooling	water	water
valve gear	pushrod ohv	single ohc
carburettors	1 Weber 40 DFAI	2 Stromberg 175-CDS
capacity cc	2994	2997
bore mm	93.67	86
stroke mm	72.42	64.5
compression to 1	8.9	8.8
net power bhp	128	145
rpm	4500	5500
net torque lb ft	192	170
rpm	3000	3500
TRANSMISSION		
control	floor lever	floor lever
synchromesh	1-2-3-4	1-2-3-4
ratios to 1 1st	3.16	2.99
2nd	2.21	2.10
3rd	1.41	1.39
o/d 3rd	1.16	1.13
4th	1.00	1.00
o/d 4th	0.82	0.82
final drive ratio	3.58	3.70
tyre size	185/14	185/14
rim size	5.5	5
SUSPENSION		
front	double wishbones, coil springs and telescopic dampers	MacPherson struts, coil springs and telescopic dampers
rear	live axle, trailing arms, Watt linkage, coil springs and telescopic dampers	semi-trailing arms, coil springs and telescopic dampers
LUBRICANT		
engine oil	10W/30	20W/50
sump, pints	9.5	9
change, miles	6000	6000
other lube points	7	1
lube intervals	3000	6000

AIR	24psi	rack and pinion	26psi	rack and pinion
BRAKES	disc 10.6in		disc 10.6in	
STEERING	35ft turning circle	3.6 turns lock to lock	34ft turning circle	4 turns lock to lock
AIR	24psi		26psi	
BRAKES	drum 9in		drum 9in	
WEIGHT	2500lb		2632lb (3024 with optional extras, as tested)	

▶anyone with experience of the related Triumph saloons.

The Reliant's dashboard layout is in the tradition of such cars—lots of gauges spread around and away from the matched speedo and rev counter. Down on the central console are the various switches. The setup takes a little puzzling out but works well enough.

Interior trim in the Reliant is entirely in black, regardless of the external colour. The Stag is available with a choice of trim colours. Both cars have vinyl upholstery; internal finish is to a high though not luxurious standard.

Borrowing again from the 2000, the Stag boasts a highly comprehensive and efficient heating/ventilating system that makes the front quarterlights (opened by turning a knob) quite superfluous. The Reliant's arrangements provide rather coarser adjustment between full heat and cold air but nonetheless work well enough. Power-operated windows are standard on the Stag.

Both cars differ from the norm in the matter of wipers. The GTE has a wiper and washer unit to clear the big back window—a job it does well. The Stag follows racing practice by fitting a pantograph arm to the windscreen wiper on the driver's side. It forms a parallelogram with the main arm and keeps the blade near-vertical.

Dual headlamps are common to the Stag and the GTE. Oddly, for these are fast, far from inexpensive cars, only on the Triumph has the opportunity been taken to fit quartz halogen bulbs.

The Stag also scores on interior illumination. A cunning light is let into the glove compartment lid so that it shines in and at the same time sends another beam downwards for map reading. Other lights illuminate the footwells and still more are built into the door armrests. When a door is opened the ground beneath is illuminated and a red light shines rearwards.

This is only one aspect of the Triumph's safety story. Like the Reliant it has a thickly padded scuttle surround and a collapsible steering column (the Reliant also has an impact-absorbing steering wheel). But there are many hidden details such as the inertia switch that cuts off the fuel supply if the petrol pipes are severed in an accident, or if the car turns over. An inversion is in any case made a safer affair than in most open cars by the provision of the stout roll cage hooped over the cockpit and linked to the top of the windscreen. Brought into the original design at a time when the US government was expected to insist on roll protection in open cars—something it has still to do—it was left in place, not least because it adds greatly to the stiffness of what would otherwise be a rather floppy body/chassis structure.

The Stag is much the quieter of the two. Its characteristically uneven V8 exhaust beat is audible but only just so, vibration negligible (as you would anticipate with eight small cylinders), the transmission is well insulated from the body structure, tyre thump and roar are equally well controlled by suspension insulation and wind noise

is at a low level that few comparable saloons can match. The Reliant suffers from an engine that is inherently much rougher running and is mechanically less refined. It makes its presence felt during acceleration but softens to a completely acceptable noise level once a steady speed has been attained. Much firmer springing than the Stag's, plus a good deal less rubber insulation and compliance, mean that road noise is a good deal more noticeable, as is wind roar over 100mph. Up to that point, oddly enough, it is almost non-existent.

Thanks to soft suspension, which allows a certain amount of body roll when cornering, the Stag has a smooth, even ride that makes a strong contrast with that of the Scimitar. The Reliant rides firmly, bumps are heard and sometimes felt and, on French roads, a well-laden Scimitar bottoms at the rear from time to time. But like most such sporting cars, the Reliant gets better as speed builds up; over 60mph it gives a smooth ride.

PERFORMANCE, HANDLING, BRAKES

It's been a long time since we last tested a pair as evenly matched as this. A mere 3mph difference in maximum speed, within a tenth of a second of each other from 0 to 80mph and still only a second apart in reaching 100mph. All of which might come as something of a surprise, for the Stag has substantially more power (but less torque, admittedly), and the GTE, handsome as it is, looks considerably bulkier.

The Stag is held back to some extent by its high first gear, not to mention extra weight, though on the other hand the engine is a willing revver. The Reliant is aided

Life inside both the Stag and the Scimitar is quite a comfortable affair if you're quick enough to get the front seats, but living in the back is a bit cramped for anyone apart from children. The Stag (top right) probably has the more expensive air about its living quarters since it has those little extras, such as electric windows, which make for real luxury motoring. Under the bonnet of the Scimitar is everything bar the kitchen sink, including the spare wheel and, of course, the Ford 3litre power unit, while under the Stag's bonnet (bottom right), there is just a great hunk of engine. The side view of the cars (below) shows up the Scimitar's box-like back end in comparison with the smoother Stag lines, while from the front you can see how two designers thought the front end of a grand tourer should look in 1970

against the watch, though hindered otherwise, by the low Ford second gear. Up to a point, on the road, one can overcome this defect by the simple expedient of ignoring the rev counter and hanging on to 6000rpm. This is a full 25 percent faster than the maximum net power speed and the engine feels rather distraught. Acceleration, as well as engine life, benefit by changing up much earlier.

Because of the improvements made in saloons in recent years, neither of these cars can truly be considered fast. A BMW 2800 will outrun them with ease and several other under-three-litre models would give them a gallop for their money. Their forte lies in providing reasonably high performance at what is nowadays little more than a medium price. Particularly when fitted with overdrive, they are both splendid machines for motorway cruising at 100mph and more. They are also gratifyingly economical. We have noted in the past the Reliant's frugal fuel consumption, especially when cruising on open roads. The Stag transpires to be nearly a rival for it in this respect. In both instances much of the economy can be traced to high gearing, reasonable mid-range torque and an ability to bowl along at a goodly pace in no more than the proverbial whiff of throttle.

The Stag is easily the more restful car to drive over long distances, being quiet and smooth by any standards, let alone the not very high ones of the Reliant. Similarly, the Stag is a much softer car in the suspension department. This gives rise to body roll during brisk cornering but pays off in facilitating much better adhesion than the Reliant's on bumpy surfaces. The Stag,

thanks to compliant springs and an independent rear end, has outstanding grip at the back, enabling one to be liberal with the throttle even when accelerating out of the tightest corners. In racing parlance, it puts the power down on the road. The Reliant, with much harder suspension and a live rear axle, rolls much less and still has very good traction but is more easily joggled off line by bumps, especially at low speeds.

Notwithstanding such shortcomings, the GTE is still the more enjoyable car to drive along winding, country roads. Primarily this is because it is altogether a more responsive, taut machine. In particular the steering is admirable—not unduly light, but precise and reasonably quick. The Stag is fitted as standard with Adwest power-assistance, a better steering servo system than any we know with the outstanding exception of the German ZF. Good as the Adwest is, it is excessively low geared and robs one of road feel, though it is not so ridiculously light and hypersensitive as some rival designs. Both cars have cumbersome turning circles.

Given a smooth surface the GTE displays better roadholding than the Stag by a small margin. Both cars offer excellent adhesion, attributable at least in part to the fact that in both cases the makers have standardised on a single make and type of tyre and can therefore develop their respective designs to get the best from them. The Stag is on Michelin XAs and the wider-rimmed GTE on Cinturato. Providing one keeps a light grip on the wheel the Scimitar feels entirely stable at maximum speed. The Stag is a little less reassuring in open form but came right up to scratch when the centre of pressure

was changed by fitting the hardtop.

Understeer is the dominant characteristic in both cars. It is more pronounced, and less easily overcome with the throttle, in the Triumph. The Reliant comes closer to neutral handling and can be brought closer still on a fast road by judicious application of torque in the bends.

Uncharacteristically, the Reliant proved more responsive to pedal pressure in our brake tests, needing less effort for a given rate of deceleration. Its braking, however, remained satisfactorily progressive, as did that of the Triumph. Under duress the Triumph's brakes faded fractionally and then, improving with heat, came back to their original, full power. Those of the Reliant showed a slight and steady fade pattern that would be too small to show up in normal, even arduous, driving.

IN CONCLUSION

Anyone with £2000-odd to spend and a yen for semi-sporting transport could until recently have made a beeline for the Reliant. Now the advent of the Triumph has complicated the issue, and the choice becomes a difficult one. Evenly matched on performance and very nearly so on fuel economy and handling, these two differ—on paper—only in comparatively minor matters.

Yet the real difference lies in their natures. The Stag is in every way more sophisticated, a softer car leaning towards the saloon end of the spectrum. The GTE is simpler, harsher, more nearly a sports car that has been adorned with practical bodywork. It is the more satisfying of the two to drive hard, but the less relaxing. Its unique bodywork makes it particularly attractive. ●

THE STAG— AT LAST

The Editor Belatedly Road-Tests British Leyland's New V8 3-litre Triumph Convertible

The Triumph Stag photographed outside the Buckley Arms Hotel at Dinas Mawddwy, not far from Bwlch-y-Groes, the once-popular 1-in-6 test hill. It was here that members of The Autocar's staff stayed 46 years ago, when reporting the RAC Small Car Trials. They naturally tried their 12/50 Alvis up the famous pass, ascending it in 1st, 2nd and 3rd gears. (The Stag went up fast in 2nd and 3rd gears.) This Welsh hotel still serves trout fresh from the Dovey river but its tennis court and private golf course have gone with the passing of the years.

LAST MONTH I felt obliged to explain in an editorial why MOTOR SPORT had not published a report on the controversial new Triumph Stag convertible. I have since driven this new Coventry car, but it was touch and go, inasmuch as on the appointed Friday when I was to drive it, the telephone rang just before 1 p.m. and Simon Pearson of the S-T Press Office enquired when would I like my Stag? "Oh, by 3 p.m., to beat the traffic congestion, would be fine", I replied, "or 4 p.m. if that would be more convenient." "I'm afraid it will be more like 5.30", said the distant voice, "because there has been a hitch and we are still working on it." "Where is this stricken Stag?" "In Coventry." Apparently a lock had failed. I said I practically never lock a car, especially other people's. But it wasn't that kind of lock which had gone wrong; apparently either you could have ignition but couldn't steer, or could steer but not run the engine. . . .

I felt they had left it rather late to discover this, the test having been agreed some three weeks beforehand; eventually I left London at 10.30 p.m., arriving home in the early hours of the Saturday morning. It's all part of this road-testing job, of course, but I wonder how often the BLMC PROs hang about of an evening waiting for motor cars which haven't arrived? If Lord Stokes thinks my September editorial was spiteful, he should now think again! As I waited I contemplated testing a Saab 99 instead, which would at least be driving behind *half* a Stag power unit, and I wondered how this Coventry Alfa/Mercedes-eater would impress one who has named the Stuttgart products as the best-engineered cars in the World and who enthuses over those from Milan, although I have yet to drive an Alfa Romeo with power steering.

The late arrival of this long-postponed Stag at least enabled me to have a good preliminary thrash in it over empty night roads. But taking over an unfamiliar car in the dark isn't the most pleasant of motoring experiences, especially when you discover that, because of changed arrangements, you haven't sufficient money to fill the tank. However, I contrived to get the petrol tank about ¾-full, sank gratefully into a reasonably comfortable but spongy driving seat, was faced with a generously-stocked facia and a multiplicity of controls, found the

wiper blades worthless, cleaned the screen with my handkerchief, and set off. Very powerful Lucas dual quartz-halogen headlamps were obviously going to make light of my darkness but the cut-off was an alarming contrast. I found substantial left and right stalks, the right one doubling up for turn-indicators, flashers, a muted, shrill horn, and the lamps-dipping, which I don't altogether approve of on expensive cars, and which on this one had a long reach when in the full-beam setting. The 16-in. dia. steering wheel had a laced-on leather-covered rim, a gale of air blew at me from universally-adjustable central fresh-air grilles, until I later discovered how to turn them off, when the dribble of air from the additional gimballed vents at the facia extremities was quite inadequate. Interior trim is in non-dazzle black and the screen sill has a tray for picnic cups.

I thrust my way out of night-life London and was skirting Oxford satisfactorily soon, without seeming to have driven very hard. The Stag's V8 2,997-c.c. five-bearing engine is very reasonably smooth, but without the exhaust "wuffle" characteristic of its type. No need to discuss why a two-plane instead of a single-plane crankshaft is used, but worth noting that it is drastically over-square, at 86 × 64½ mm., and that it develops 145 (net) b.h.p. at its peak speed of 5,500 r.p.m., which is only 8 b.h.p. more than Ford's push-rod o.h.v. V6 gives at 750 fewer r.p.m. There is a chain-driven overhead camshaft above each cylinder bank, and twin sidedraught Zenith-Stromberg 1.75CD carburetters. An 8.8-to-1 c.r. provides for 4-star fuel.

Fumbling about in the dark I found a slide on the gear-lever knob which brings in, or cuts out, overdrive in 3rd and top gears (it is an optional extra). Later I found that this slide uncovers legends "In" and "Out", which would be appropriate to some cars which have to be rowed along on the gear-lever but not to the Stag which, although it is outpaced by almost all the comparable GT cars such as the Ford Capri 3000 GT, Reliant Scimitar GTE, Alfa Romeo 1750 GTV, Porsche 911T and Mercedes-Benz 280SL, somehow feels faster than it is and decently disposes, smoothly and quickly, of the slower-moving traffic. In fact, a 0-to-60-m.p.h. time of 10.7 sec. and a s.s.

¼-mile time of just under 18 sec. is not impressive for a 1970 3-litre car; the product of 145 b.h.p. and a kerb weight of 26 cwt. puts the Stag in the fast-tourer rather than the GT category.

As the traffic thinned out I was able to go faster and it was then that I added a third dislike to two others already evident, and one which makes the Triumph Stag quite unacceptable to me in its present form. The too-notchy gear-change controlled by a tall central lever I had put down as typically Triumph, and an irritating rattle coming from my left was traced later to free movement on the part of the empty passenger's front seat. This third misfortune relates to the power steering. The action is fairly light and smooth but with no feeling whatsoever of what the front wheels are doing, to the extent that they feel all the time to be about to break away their road grip. This prompts the driver to apply correction, and as the steering then becomes lighter, to over-correct, with the result that cornering becomes a very ragged business, feeling as uncomfortable as it looks. I tried to get used to this inconsistent power-assisted steering and in sober driving it is just about acceptable and reasonably geared (2¾ turns, lock-to-lock), with a very small turning circle. But as soon as I drove fast, or anticipated having to chuck the car about, the lack of positive feel to the steering became horrid. The sensation of the front wheels tucking in as lock is applied to combat what is actually understeer, is most disconcerting. Another peculiarity is that when the throttle is backed off after accelerating hard, as when changing gear, the back-end of the car gives a slight lurch.

Power-assisted rack-and-pinion steering is standard on the Stag— there is no option. This was presumably deemed necessary to woo the American customers but it is a great pity that something better isn't used. I would put up with strong-arm parking for precise manual control. I recall how the 4-litre Rolls-Royce-engined Vanden Plas Princess was ruined by light/heavy/light power-assisted steering, and the unfortunate Stag seems to have inherited something of the same sort. There is no excuse, for ZF and others have shown how effective good power steering can be. The column is adjustable to suit different requirements.

The Triumph Stag sent for appraisal was Pre-Production Car No. 7, but I assume catalogue cars are identical. The horrid steering apart, what can one make of it ? It is a convertible after the style of a Mercedes-Benz 280SL, with very nice Michelotti styling reminiscent of a Fiat Dino, and it was conceived for release in 1968. It is nicely finished, is a reasonable 2+2 coupé for which an optional hard-top is available to cover the fully-disappearing hood which has the protection of an elaborate (detachable) roll-over frame and would have been an excellent substitute for the late-lamented Sunbeam Alpine which Chrysler UK had to put down because of its 4.2-litre Ford V8 engine. It is, alas, not an easy hood to stow or erect—see pictures.

The interior of the Stag is essentially Triumph, which I have never much liked. The simulated dull-wood facia has a rather restricted lockable cubby on the left, complete with map-cum-interior lamp, dials to the right. The latter comprise expensive-looking, closely-calibrated Smiths speedometer and tachometer, a clock, fuel gauge, water thermometer and voltmeter but, curiously, no oil-pressure gauge. As my early-morning journey progressed I had not only a blue full-beam light shining in my weary eyes but an intermittent flashing from Triumph's all-services-light-up cluster, saying "Fuel". As petrol supplies scarcely exist in darkest Radnorshire after dusk and I was skint anyway, this ruined what pleasure I was trying to obtain from flinging the Stag in untidy lines round the corners. I need not have worried, for this unwelcome warning starts when the tank has nearly seven gallons in it—and is consequently ignored, dazzle apart, until the thing runs dry with the fuel gauge indicating just above empty! The lamps are switched on by a rotary switch to the right of the steering column, as if Spencer King or one of his team had been driving a Hillman Avenger, although the Stag's rotator is smaller and provides for parking lights as well as side- and headlamps. The controls are well endowed with symbols or lettering; there was one small knob with a mysterious inscription on it, which turned out to be the rheostat panel-lighting control. Down on the console you get

"The office" of the Stag, showing leather-rimmed, padded steering wheel, layout of instruments, long central gear-lever and press-buttons on the console for the electric window-lifts and interior lights.

the tumbler switches for the window lifts, rather close set to the central hand-brake, with its man-sized grip, when this is off; a similar switch which brings in two forward-facing interior lamps, and on the upright wall of the console there is a Triumph press-button radio, some well-contrived heater controls, and a pull-out ash-tray. The facia has a brake-failure warning light directly before the driver and other lights, in the cluster, for brake on, choke in use, high temperature, etc. Big knobs on the console wall pull out to bring in the choke, effective Triplex rear-window heater (with tiny in-use light), cigar-lighter and 2-speed fan. The l.h. stalk control provides for two-speed screen wiping and washing. The electric window lifts are excellent in themselves but as they require the ignition to be on before they will function, and the ignition key is needed to open the fuel-filler flap, the uncomfortable situation arises where the driver has to wait in driving rain with his window down while the car is refuelled.

British Leyland have really tried to make this the Mercedes-Benz/Alfa Romeo slaughterer they claim it to be. The doors have convenient grabs-cum-arm-rests, locks actuated by convenient small handles below the door-opening handles, knob-operated quarter-lights, and red warning lights on the doors. Opening them brings in courtesy lights, one each side of the transmission tunnel. The external lift-up handles, however, were stiff and not pleasant to use. The rear compartment side windows have good toggles for opening them as vents. The three-spoke steering wheel has a padded boss. The front-seat passenger has an under-facia shelf and there are elastic-edged pockets on the doors and backs of the seat squabs. The front seats have conveniently-placed release knobs for tilting them to give access to the deeply-welled back seat, and they can be raised by winding a crank handle, as well as possessing squabs easily adjustable by operating the long, plated side levers. These seats are of decidedly generous size but the upholstery is, alas, p.v.c. The doors have effective "keeps". The very deep, if shallow, 9 cu. ft. boot has a clear floor and is illuminated. Reversing lamps, and the heated back window if a hard-top is ordered, are fitted as standard. There is a wobbly anti-dazzle mirror. The wheels have stainless-steel trims and are shod with 14-in. Michelin XAS tyres. There are two keys, the long one for ignition/steering lock, the fuel-filler flap and the doors, the smaller one for the boot and glove box. An instruction book covered in imitation leather has been prepared for the Stag. The shape of the back seat well suited the Motoring "Dog", who, after having had her first puppies at the age of nine is now travelling again, and far more comfortably in the Stag than on the bouncy shelf of a Triumph TR sports car in which she once rode. But for adult humans head-room is somewhat restricted.

The conservative iron-block, alloy-heads, cross-flow engine of the Stag fires up promptly if given a little choke and runs smoothly from idling speed to its peak of 5,500 r.p.m. It will pull away from 500 r.p.m., or 10 m.p.h., in the 3.1-to-1 top gear and, trying to conserve fuel on my initial nocturnal acquaintance with it, I used top and o/d top gear satisfactorily for most of the journey. At 2,500 r.p.m. in top gear the accurate (at this speed) speedometer shows 50 m.p.h., or 60 if o/d is engaged, and at the legal maximum permitted on British roads the engine is running smoothly at less than 3,000 r.p.m. It will give just over 100 m.p.h. in o/d 3rd gear, and achieve 117 m.p.h. flat-out in its highest ratio. Two tail-pipe extensions which look like something from a battlefield probably assist in muffling the exhaust note so that Stag motoring is accomplished quietly, yet with a satisfying purposeful exhaust note when you open up. A good deal of exhaust heat is exuded under the car.

The gear-lever has weak synchromesh and a long travel, the clutch is heavy and a trifle sudden, and the servo-assisted disc/drum brakes are satisfactory without being outstanding; they tended to squeal under light pressures. The ride is soft but well-damped, roll being well controlled except when cornering very fast. Rear-wheel adhesion is apt to be lost on slippery surfaces when accelerating, but the ultimate cornering ability is high.

The fuel tank holds 14 gallons and in fairly gentle motoring I obtained a m.p.g. figure of 22.5 m.p.g. Driving harder, this decreased to 20.8 m.p.g., an overall figure of 21.4 m.p.g. The petrol gauge is unhappily optimistic.

The exterior *decor* of this handsome, compact fast-tourer is confined to the name "Triumph" in the rubber-tipped bumpers and a stag badge, although zoologists will not recognise the depicted animal as a stag, with its unnatural, overweight antlers. The name "Stag" is engraved on the steering-wheel boss, and name and motif appear on the sides of the tail. A clever feature is angling of the o/s wiper blade so that it sweeps right to the edge of the screen.

Turning to details, some of the luxury aspect of the Stag rubs off when gear-lever rattle between about 3,300 and 4,300 r.p.m. in 3rd gear (I thought this was a thing of the past, but met it again recently on the smallest Opel and now on the Stag) and wind noise, even with the hard-top in use, intrude. The pedals, labelled "L" for Leyland, are large but off-set to the o/s, which brings the brake pedal rather close to the accelerator, but gives room for a clutch-foot rest. There is not a lot of elbow-room and the padded anti-dazzle vizors are rather tricky to clip back; the driver's carries the five-stage sequence for lowering and raising the soft-top. The self-propping forward-hinged bonnet is light and lifts to reveal the V8 engine with its Stanpart

68▶

THE TRIUMPH STAG CONVERTIBLE

Engine : Eight cylinders in a 90° vee, 86×64.5 mm. (2,997 c.c.). Overhead valves operated by single overhead camshafts. 8.8 to 1 compression ratio. 145 b.h.p. (net) at 5,500 r.p.m.

Gear ratios : 1st, 11.08 to 1; 2nd, 7.77 to 1; 3rd, 5.13 to 1; o/d 3rd, 4.2 to 1; top, 3.7 to 1; o/d top, 3.04 to 1.

Tyres : 815×14 Michelin XAS, on bolt-on steel wide-rim wheels.

Weight : 26 cwt. 0 qtr. 0 lb. (Empty, but ready for the road with hard-top on and approx. half-a-gallon of petrol.)

Steering ratio : 2¾ turns, lock-to-lock (power-assisted).

Fuel capacity : 14 gallons. (Range approx. 300 miles.)

Wheelbase : 8 ft. 4 in.

Track : Front, 4 ft. 4½ in.; rear, 4 ft. 4⅞ in.

Dimensions : 14 ft. 5¾ in. × 5 ft. 3½ in. × 4 ft. 1½ in. (high—hood up).

Price : £1,602, plus £491 15s. 10d. purchase tax. Total, as tested, £2,173 1s. 5d.

Makers : Standard-Triumph International Ltd., Canley, Coventry, England.

Performance Data

Acceleration :

0-30 m.p.h.	..	3.8 sec.	0- 70 m.p.h.	..	14.2 sec.
0-40 ,,	..	5.5 ,,	0- 80 ,,	..	18.2 ,,
0-50 ,,	..	7.5 ,,	0- 90 ,,	..	23.4 ,,
0-60 ,,	..	10.7 ,,	0-100 ,,	..	33.9 ,,

Speeds in the gears :

1st ..	.. 41 m.p.h.	O/d 3rd	.. 101 m.p.h.
2nd	.. 60 ,,	Top ..	.. 114 ,,
3rd ..	.. 92 ,,	O/d top	.. 117 ,,

Overall fuel consumption : 21.4 m.p.g.

Views of the Stag's V8 power unit and, right, *its luggage boot.*

ROAD TEST / John Bolster   Triumph Stag

Attractive 2 plus 2 with V8 engine

Before writing a road test report of the Stag, it is necessary to analyse exactly what sort of a car it is. It is certainly a GT, whatever that may mean, but probably not a sports car in the traditional sense of the term. It is far from being a sort of junior E-type Jaguar, for no attempt has been made to place an undue emphasis on performance, and it is altogether more luxurious than a TR6 or an MGB.

The Stag is propelled by a very over-square engine of extremely modern design which bears no relationship to any previous Triumph power unit. Of moderate overall length, this V8 packs 3-litres under the bonnet that is fashionably short and . permits a body with really useful rear seats to be carried on a wheelbase of only 8 ft 4 ins. The result is a car that is just the size everybody wants and in appearance it is an absolute winner— I parked it and watched the reaction of passers-by. It is only sold with. an open body, with hood or very attractive hard-top, and the problem of rigidity has been ingeniously solved with an upholstered roll-over bar that also extends forward to the centre of the windscreen. The independent rear suspension permits the rear seats to be carried low, which allows the roof line to sweep down attractively in a way which is usually denied to four-seaters.

The Stag, then, is a compact car of delightful appearance which is rather more than a 2 plus 2. It has a big enough engine to have an effortless performance but, although this is of advanced overhead-camshaft design, it is in relatively "soft" tune. Very great trouble has been taken to insulate the suspension from the body, with the object of

reducing road noise to a minimum, and a bridge-pipe between the two exhausts systems avoids "V8 beat," while a viscous fan drive cuts down noise from this source.

The car is of solid construction and not particularly light, which one can sense from the way the doors close. The steering can be instantly adjusted both for rake and length of column, without stopping the car if desired. The seats are very comfortable and there is ample leg room for tall drivers, the minor controls all being sensibly positioned, as in the other Triumph models. The engine starts instantly from cold, but the test car sometimes had to be spun for a few moments when hot.

Very quiet and smooth, the V8 engine seems equally happy at any speed in its considerable range up to the red line on the rev-counter dial at 6500 rpm. Though an overdrive is available, it is impossible to over-rev on the direct top gear of the manual transmission or of the Borg-Warner automatic. The latter option was fitted to the test car and suited the characteristics of the engine very well. In manual form the Stag is capable of about 118 mph, but in automatic form I timed it at 115.4 mph, while one loses about half a second from a standstill to 60 mph. The speedometer registered 124 mph at maximum speed. Obviously the choice of transmission is a personal matter, the automatic appealing more particularly when there is a lot of town and traffic work.

The Stag has power-assisted steering as standard, and this is in keeping with its luxurious rather than sporting character. The lightness of the steering may be a little disconcerting at first but one soon takes it

for granted, and I often forgot about it. Th car is very stable at high speeds, requirin absolutely no " holding," even in gusty wind This exceptional stability is bought at th expense of a fairly marked understeerin characteristic which can be reduced by th application of power but not entirely cance led out. The tyres stick to the road very we never bouncing over bumps, and in gener

The upholstered roll bar solves the rigidi problems.

one does not feel that the car has a relatively short wheelbase.

A very comfortable ride is achieved without any wallowing, and there is also less roll on corners than would be expected. Perhaps the most impressive feature is the insulation of road noise; in spite of using Michelin XAS steel-braced tyres, there is literally not a sound when one deliberately drives down a line of catseyes. Like all the other controls, the brakes are light to use and stand up to hard driving.

With the hood down and stowed beneath its decking and the windows raised—at the touch of a switch—the car is remarkably silent and most of the draughts are subdued. This is ideal motoring when the weather permits it. With the hood raised it is a different story for the wind roar at speed makes conversation impossible, though the fabric does not actually flap. The hood is very neat but by no means easy to raise or lower—it would be best to fit the hard-top when winter comes. The hard-top looks very much a part of the car and at a casual inspection the Stag could be mistaken for a fixed-head coupé.

Much of the charm of this Triumph resides in the effortless performance of its engine. It has no preferred cruising speed, and there is a reserve of power that makes this an easy car to drive under all conditions and a splendid companion for long journeys. The four quartz-halogen headlamps let the miles or kilometres pass easily at night, and there is copious adjustable fresh air ventilation to stop the interior from becoming stuffy. The detail refinements are too numerous to mention, but this is a very well-equipped car.

At the start of this report, I said that it was necessary to analyse exactly what sort of a car the Stag is. Perhaps it is a revival of the "open touring car" of ancient times, or maybe it is something entirely new. It is certainly a very pleasant vehicle to use for getting around, and nobody minds being seen in really good looking cars. Above all, it is more than reasonably priced as such things are reckoned today, and the demand is bound to be enormous.

The Stag has clean lines and is attractive as either an open car or with the hard top.

The 3-litre V8 engine is very over square, being of extremely modern design (above). The interior is very comfortable and the controls sensibly positioned (below).

SPECIFICATION AND PERFORMANCE DATA

Car tested : Triumph Stag open 2 plus 2, price £1996 including tax. Extra : Automatic transmission, £105.

Engine : Eight cylinders, 86 mm x 64.5 mm, 2997 cc. Single chain-driven overhead camshaft per bank Compression ratio 8.8 to 1, 145 bhp (net) at 5500 rpm. Twin horizontal Stromberg carburetters.

Transmission : Borg-Warner Type 35 automatic transmission, ratio 1.0, 1.45 and 2.39 to 1, multiplied by torque converter reduction of 1.0-2.3 to 1 Hypoid final drive, ratio 3.7 to 1.

Chassis : Combined steel body and chassis. Independent front suspension by MacPherson struts with lower wishbones and anti-roll bar power assisted rack and pinion steering. Independent rear suspension by semi-trailing arms and coil springs with telescopic dampers. Servo-assisted disc front and drum rear brakes. Bolt-on steel disc wheels fitted 185-14 radial ply tyres.

Equipment : 12-volt lighting and starting with alternator. Speedometer. Rev counter. Voltmeter. Water temperature and fuel gauges. Clock. Heating, demisting and ventilation system. 2-speed windscreen wipers and washers. Flashing direction indicators. Cigar lighter. Reversing lights. Electric window actuation. Radio (extra).

Dimensions : Wheelbase 8 ft 4 in. Track (front) 4 ft 4½ in; (rear) 4 ft 4¾ in. Overall length 14 ft 5¾ in. Width 5 ft 3½ in. Weight 1 ton 5 cwt.

Performance : Maximum speed 115 mph. Standing quarter-mile 16.9 s. Acceleration : 0.30 mph, 4.0 s. 0-50 mph, 7.2 s. 0-60 mph, 10.0 s. 0-80 mph, 18.8 s. 0-100 mph, 29.8 s.

Fuel consumption : 18 to 24 mpg.

TRIUMPH STAG (AUTOMATIC)

¼ mile

Max. speed 115 mph

MPH

SECONDS

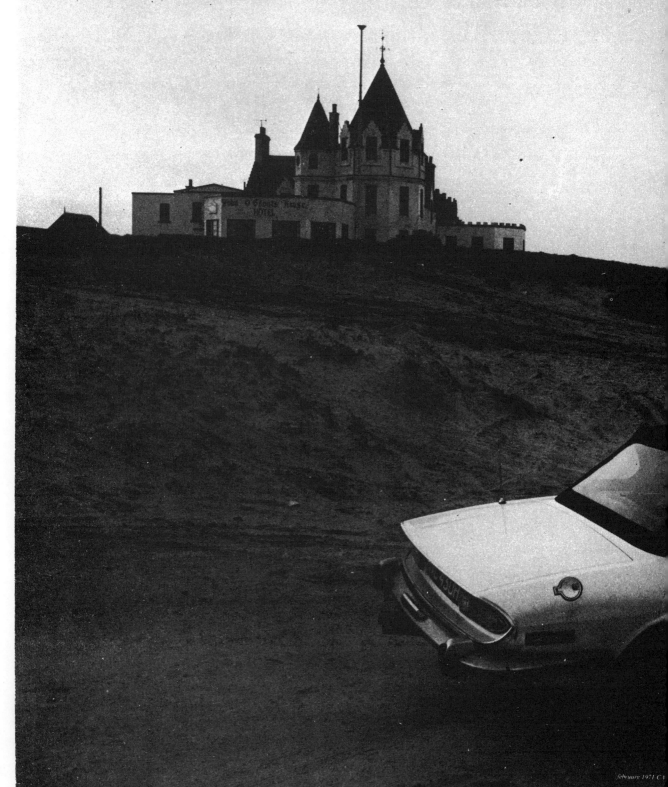

Ian Fraser takes the *Stag express to Scotland*

OU MAY SAY THAT WE WERE QUITE MAD. AND
rtainly that we cheated as well. After all, who
ut the deranged bent on deception would take
drophead to John o' Groats for a winter weekend
d break the rules by not starting from Land's End?
rainstorms notwithstanding, we decided that we owed the
riumph Stag a healthy run within its homeland and to
this utilised a spare weekend by converting it into a leisurely
00mile journey between 9.30pm on a Friday and 1.30am on
e Monday.

Although we did not start from Land's End, since we were
t indulging in anything as vulgar as a record attempt, our
urney began and finished at Portsmouth; in a sense the south-
rth-south aspect was achieved but possibly not to the entire
tisfaction of those people who have in the past set out with
eat determination to go from one end of the country to the
her and back again in the shortest possible time. Our journey
as somewhat different since it did not matter two hoots if we
t to John o' Groats or not—which is probably the reason
e made it without any difficulty at all.

Primarily we proved some things about the Stag which shorter
unts would have failed to reveal. The car itself turned out to
a soft-top with a manual transmission and overdrive, although
e had vaguely hoped that it might have been equipped with
e optional hardtop. In retrospect it was to our benefit that
r friends at Triumph provided a drophead, despite its short-
mings. The Stag is not a sports car and does not claim to be,

although its lack of clear definition is one of its sales advantages.
For the sort of journey we did it would have been hard to find
a better car and certainly difficult to locate one as suitable
among the ranks of sports cars of comparable price. But please
do not think that we are defending the Stag. Far from it; in fact
we were able to turn up some basic weaknesses which would
have made sports cars puff out their power bulges with pride.

As L J K Setright said recently, the only true sports car
feature of the Stag is the size of the luggage compartment, which
was brought home to us as we started to pack the vehicle. We
were able to fit a couple of reasonable bags and odds and ends
into the boot but the leftovers ended up on the back seat (we
had hoped that the Stag would prove to be a family two-plus-
two—and it would be for gentle journeys requiring not much
more than a picnic lunch to be carried in the stern—but it
would be out of the question as a holiday transport for two
adults and, say, two children). Perhaps the best thing about the
Stag's luggage compartment is its clear and unobstructed shape,
and, being fully lined, it would be possible at a pinch to dispense
with bags altogether and turn the boot into a wardrobe. Some
of the weather we encountered on the way north was so bad
that had our bags come floating out of the boot like barrels
over Niagara Falls we would not have been all that surprised, but
the compartment proved to be completely waterproof. The
disadvantage of carrying tempting things like camera bags on the
back seat is that the light-fingered fraternity would have very
little trouble helping themselves.

Our voyage started in teeming rain at 9.30pm when we set ▶

photography Ian Fraser

▶ sail for London, our first refuelling stop. Mistakenly, we decided to press on for a couple of hours instead of having dinner right there and then in London. When we did stop an hour or so later we must have selected the worst motorway eatery known to man. For that reason we will not alarm you with the sordid details of what must be the epitomy of poor eating. By 3am we were well clear of the M1 and making reasonable progress on the M6 despite violent crosswinds, heavy rain showers and gallons of dirty water being thrown up by lorries. Rather than continue the unequal struggle in a tired condition we found ourselves a quiet corner in a motorway-services car park, reclined the Stag's seats and slept for two hours before continuing northwards. At the moderate speeds dictated by the conditions and not having any desire to see if we could outrun the law in their XJ6s, the Stag proved to be remarkably economical, allowing us to reach Carlisle before refuelling—some 305 miles on 12.5 gallons, or 24.4mpg. The fuel-tank capacity of 15 gallons therefore provides a moderate-cruising range of well over 300 miles with reserves, thus making reasonably high point-to-point averages possible without really trying.

Our aim was to make our headquarters in Perth before setting course to John o' Groats. We arrived in the tidy, prosperous town just on 9.30am as the sun was making its attempt to break through. Our AA guide indicated a good hostelry called the Station Hotel, so we checked into that large and extremely clean establishment, obviously built during the great Victorian train era but having declined little in subsequent years, especially the service. The staff cheerfully prepared a late breakfast while we bathed and changed clothes prior to continuing north. We figured that if we were to get to John o' Groats before sunset we would need to be there by 3.30 or 4pm at the latest, so the Stag would have to work quite hard on the narrow but virtually traffic-free roads.

The overnight run to Perth had revealed several important things about the Stag, not the least of which was its comfort. Neither of us had suffered any discomfort from the seats which, admittedly, were pushed back far enough to make it impossible for even children to be carried in the rear, thus leaving ample legroom in the front. While the Stag's seats really are good, we were less impressed by the hood, which flapped very badly at speeds around 85 to 90mph whereas the racket at 100mph must surely be akin to going through the sound barrier in a Vickers Vimy—unbearable enough to make 85mph just about the maximum sustained cruising speed. We were also driven to distraction by the totally inadequate illumination for map reading. There are a number of lights in the cockpit but none of them are bright enough or sufficiently well placed to make navigation anything less than a hideous task of torment.

Despite the rush from Perth to the Inverness fuel stop, the Stag managed a highly creditable 25.6 mpg overall from Carlisle at an average speed for the 269 miles in the mid-60s. The remaining 139 miles to the top of Scotland were a matter of some desperation to try to get there while there was still daylight. This was helped by the discovery that turning off the A9 at Bonar Bridge and rejoining it near Mound Station represented a 12 mile saving as well as providing some truly spectacular scenery, again with very little traffic apart from the occasional transient fisherman or hunter, lurching dog-laden Renault 4Ls along at a healthy rate.

Inevitably, John o' Groats was mildly grotty and bleak, although the air was clear enough for the houses on Stroma to be visible, with South Ronaldsay merely a shape in the distance. Our calculations revealed that we had averaged 62mph from Inverness and had, indeed, arrived pretty much as planned. Again the Stag proved itself as a comfortable tourer with very safe and predictable roadholding, although we became disenchanted with the standard-equipment power steering and its inherent lack of feel as we rushed up the coast. Maybe the steering would have been better had the excessively large wheel been of smaller dimensions. It felt too big and awkward and there was just not enough feel to get the understeer set-up nicely in corners. On a similar tack, the brakes—disc front, drum rear you will recall—were not totally to our liking, the main problem being lack of feel once more, due perhaps to the use of split hydraulics. Anyway, that does not alter the fact that they worked well. Only after some really violent use did they show any sign of fade and even then recovery was fast enough and complete. The balance was good, too. Once or twice we got onto the brakes very hard indeed, but the Stag pulled up straight without the rear drums locking-up prematurely, as we half expected they might, and there was little enough dive to keep the headlamps effective.

Although not as sophisticated as it could be, the rear suspension worked well enough for us. As with the TR6 there is quite a lot of squat under hard acceleration, the disadvantages of which are largely cancelled out by the well-controlled and comfortable ride. On the sometimes choppy and difficult roads in the Highlands the Stag's suspension smoothed out the worst of it quite fusslessly and also gave the impression of being much more rigidly constructed than is the case with the majority of open vehicles. Of course, what success the Stag has in this direction is helped enormously by that controversial roll-cage arrangement which, we suspect, is intended more to tie the body together than to overcome problems of gravel-rash on the scalp. Some of the hood noise that assailed our ears at high speeds was due to the fabric belting out a tattoo on the cage.

The three-litre V8 engine with its single overhead camshafts, behaved faultlessly, providing good power and torque up to and beyond the red line on the tachometer. However, its standing start acceleration was somewhat handicapped by the very high first gear which gives better than 40mph, but leaves second too low with its maximum of just on 60, while third runs to 91. On a number of occasions we found ourselves floundering about between second and third and then having to make do with third. It would have been rather nice if the overdrive also worked on second to bridge the gap. As it stands an indicated 80mph in direct third equals 5500rpm or 4600 in o/d third, while it represents 4100 in top and 3250 in o/d. We thought the change lever was a bit notchy but having the overdrive engagement switch on the knob simplified things quite a lot. We also thought the instrument display should have included an oil pressure gauge while the legibility could have been better, especially at night. On a similar tack, the dipper arm on the steering column went too far away on the high-beam position to be readily retrieved in a hurry without taking one's right hand off the wheel.

Our return from John o' Groats (so named after Dutchman John de Groot who is reputed to have run the Orkney ferry in the late fifteenth century; eight of his descendants became joint owners of the estate and to obviate problems of precedence they built an octa-

gonal house with eight doors leading to an octagonal table; the house has long since vanished, although the local hotel, built in 1875, recalls it with an octagonal tower) to Perth was more leisurely and the refuelling stop at Iverness revealed that the 278 miles from there to the top and back again had consumed 12.2gallons which was rather better than we had anticipated. In sudden fear of missing our only real meal of the day, we pressed on back to Perth on mostly wet roads, the slop thrown up from them seriously damaging our capacity to illuminate the way ahead. And slipping along the floor of the valley between the Monadhliath Mountains and the Cairngorms we were attacked by an enormously strong wind and rainstorm which tried very hard to push the Stag off the road or, at the very least, carry off the hood. Such an acid test proved convincingly enough that the car is very stable directionally and that the weather equipment is made of stouter stuff than anything the Scots can blow at it. We were less fortunate in resisting the onslaught of a particularly

well-driven and extremely fast Lotus-Cortina in the hands of a local who was obviously practising for something important.

The obliging people at the Station Hotel, back in Perth, were quick to organise us a pleasant meal even though we had arrived back right on the death knock at 9.30pm. We were gone again by 10am Sunday, the Stag making its first cold start since some time in the forenoon on Friday. In a rare moment of bravado we decided to take advantage of crisp sunshine by lowering the top, the instructions for which are placarded on the driver's sun visor. Best as a two-man task, the hood nevertheless folds quickly and disappears from sight under the rear-hinged metal tonneau. Having released the tonneau it then refused to lock down again on the driver's side so we had to tolerate a few rattles and booms on our gentle journey over the black ice en route to Crieff via Dunkeld—a notably attractive little town on the banks of the Tay, with a recorded history of more than 1000 years and a medieval cathedral, to say nothing of the fact that this is exactly

where the Jacobite Highlanders routed William III's army in 1689. Besides providing us with a warming lunch, Crieff is also the tourist gateway to the Highlands, a role it fulfills more in the warmer months than during our visit. The insanity of open-air motoring having lapsed after our aimless wanderings through the highly diverse and staggeringly beautiful scenery, we turned the Stag's nose south again, towards the Forth Bridge, Edinburgh, the A1 and then the M1 to London. Cruising gently in the 70 to 80mph region in overdrive top (traffic density, accident rate and police activity making anything higher a risky procedure) the Stag returned 29.5mpg. We were back in Portsmouth, opening the front door, by 1.30am Monday, regretting only the limited time we had been able to spend in the Highlands. The Stag performed faultlessly, having found few rattles and lost none of its tune, but just as we left the petrol station in London, the Stag's speedometer groaned as the needle whipped around the dial before dropping back to the zero stop. Stone dead. ●

The Stag's hood (far left) proved to be weatherproof but too noisy at speed, although it was quick to raise and lower, while U-shaped panel is metal tonneau to cover hood well. Controversial roll cage helped keep the body nice and tight (centre) over the uneven roads we encountered in the Highlands. We braved the freezing temperatures (top) to lower the top and take advantage of the few moments of feeble winter sunshine that did nothing to disperse some evil patches of black ice

AUTOTEST

Triumph Stag Automatic (2,997 c.c.)

AT-A-GLANCE: British Leyland's sporting 2+2 with automatic transmission. Performance still very brisk, but some worsening in fuel consumption. Noise level not much affected. Very comfortable and well equipped, with good handling but power steering lacking in feel for fast drivers.

MANUFACTURER

Standard-Triumph International Ltd., Canley, Coventry.

PRICES

Basic	£1,825.00
Purchase Tax	£559.93
Seat belts (approx.)	£14.50
Total (in G.B.)	£2,399.43

EXTRAS (inc. P.T.)

Automatic Transmission*	£104.45

*Fitted to test car

PRICE AS TESTED £2,503.88

PERFORMANCE SUMMARY

Mean maximum speed	112 mph
Standing start ¼-mile	17.9 sec
0-60 mph	10.4 sec
30-70 mph through gears	10.1 sec
Typical fuel consumption	20 mpg
Miles per tankful	300

IT is now just a year since the Triumph Stag was first announced. For some people, it has been a frustrating year of waiting for their Stag to materialize, because the moment the car arrived, demand shot well ahead of supply and stayed there. As we said in our Stag road test (30 July 1970), we were hoping to add an example to our long-term test fleet. Even though we were high in the queue, we had to wait some considerable time before we were able to take delivery of the Stag (with automatic transmission) which forms the subject of this test and will of course also be reported on in the usual way when it has done 10,000 miles.

It may be remembered that our original, manual transmission test car (one of the pre-production batch) returned rather disappointing performance figures. We therefore took the opportunity of trying another manual car while we were completing the test on the automatic, with the double object of updating our performance figures and comparing the two versions.

The automatic car is the result of a simple substitution of the Borg-Warner 35 transmission for the original four-speed manual gearbox and overdrive; nothing else is changed. Since the tyre size and the final drive ratio are unchanged, the overall gearing (giving 19.8 mph per 1,000 rpm, assuming no torque converter slip) remains the same. The transmission is controlled by a lever on the central console, moving in a conventional gate marked with Park-R-N-D-2-1 positions.

Performance and consumption

The Borg-Warner transmission on our test car was set to give fairly relaxed performance, with automatic up-changes coming at 37 and 63 mph, even on full throttle. These change points did not take the engine to the 5,500 rpm power peak, and contrasted with the 54 and 89 mph which represented the 6,500 rpm limit in the lower ratios. The kick-down points were similarly low; 34 mph for the change down from intermediate to low, and 53 mph from high to intermediate.

Clearly, it should be possible to improve on the times for a fully automatic acceleration run by holding on to the lower ratios. It is a tribute to the stepless nature of the Stag engine's torque curve that, while this proved to be the case, the improvements were far from spectacular. In particular, there appeared to be little point in going beyond the power peak, and it must be said that the present settings are a good deal more intelligent than a keen driver might think at first. In absolute terms, the automatic Stag is respectably fast. By taking the engine up to the 2,100 rpm torque converter stall point against the brakes, a standing start can be made with a little cheep of protest from the tyres. The time to 30 mph was 4.1 sec; this was the only time which did not represent an improvement on the original manual-gearbox test car. For example, 60 mph took only marginally more than the magic 10 sec, and the quarter-mile was covered in under 18 sec.

The manual gearbox car tried this time, however, proved a good deal faster. In spite of having to carry two of our heavier testers, it matched the manufacturer's claims very closely, and actually improved on the claimed 0-60 mph time. Our table compares the performance of this car with that of the first test car; it can be seen that while there is little change in the bottom-end figures, those in the mid-range and at the top end are much improved. Perhaps strangely in view of this, we were unable to obtain much improvement on the original maximum speed, the car stabilizing at 116 mph (123 mph indicated) on a very long, level run. This is well below the power peak in overdrive top gear, whereas the maximum in direct top takes the engine to the far side of the peak. The automatic car achieved a mean of 112 mph, coming very close to the maximum of a non-overdrive manual car.

Despite the improvement in the mid-range performance of the manual car, it returned a marginally better fuel consumption than before. The automatic, driven in much the same way during the test period, managed only 17.2 mpg, a deficiency of almost exactly 20 per cent, and rather more than one would normally expect. It could well be that the looseness of the manual car (which had covered almost three times the mileage) accounts for a good deal of this difference. The steady-speed figures for the automatic show that it is using no more fuel at 40 mph than at 30, and scarcely any more at 50 mph; so it looks as though low-speed commuting is hardly the most economical way of using the automatic.

Good cruising

Both cars proved very relaxed when cruising at 70 mph, with very little difference in noise level, even though the automatic's engine was turning over a good deal faster. As speed was increased, it was wind rather than mechanical noise which became intrusive, so that there was still little to choose between the two. Only at really high cruising speeds — 100 mph or more— did the automatic start to suffer from an

The Stag's air of interior quality has hardly suffered in this test car, despite the fact that it has covered over 15,000 miles. The seats are very comfortable, the controls good, and the instruments clear — although some drivers missed an oil pressure gauge

Above: the Stag's boot is large in area but rather shallow, because of the spare wheel and large fuel tank lodged beneath the floor. It is carpeted throughout, but the wooden base panels are not easy to remove and replace

Above left: because of the room taken up by the hood stowage, the back seat is rather small. If its occupants are not too large it is quite comfortable, but the lack of legroom is a problem

Left: under-bonnet accessibility in the Stag is quite good (by British standards), and the engine looks relatively small. The dipstick, however, is difficult to get at, and very awkward to replace in the dark

PERFORMANCE CHECK

Maximum speeds

Gear	mph		kph		rpm	
	R/T1	R/T2	R/T1	R/T2	R/T1	R/T2
O.D. Top (mean)	115	116	185	187	4,770	4,810
(best)	117	116	188	187	4,850	4,810
Top (mean)	113	113	182	182	5,710	5,710
(best)	—	113	—	182	—	5,710
O.D. 3rd	100	105	161	169	5,790	6,080
3rd	92	92	148	148	6,500	6,500
2nd	61	61	98	61	6,500	6,500
1st	42	42	68	42	6,500	6,500

Standing ¼-mile, R/T1: 18.2 sec 75 mph **Standing kilometre, R/T1:** 33.4 sec 98 mph
R/T2: 17.1 sec 82 mph **R/T2:** 31.3 sec 102 mph

Acceleration, R/T1:		3.9	5.8	8.1	11.6	15.1	19.6	25.7	36.9
R/T2:		3.5	5.1	7.1	9.3	12.7	16.5	21.8	29.2
Time in seconds	0								
True speed mph		30	40	50	60	70	80	90	100
Indicated speed MPH, **R/T1:**		30	40	50	61	73	85	97	108
Indicated speed MPH, **R/T2:**		31	41	52	63	73	83	94	105

Speed range, Gear Ratios and Time in seconds

Mph	O.D. Top (3.04)		Top (3.70)		O.D. 3rd (4.20)		3rd (5.13)		2nd (7.77)		1st (11.08)	
	R/T1	R/T2	R/T1	R/T2	R/T1	R/T2	R/T1	R/T2	R/T1	R/T2	R/T1	R/T2
10–30	—	—	9.1	9.0	8.2	8.0	6.4	6.3	4.1	3.9	3.0	3.0
20–40	10.8	11.0	8.2	8.2	7.1	7.1	5.5	5.6	3.5	3.4	3.1	2.8
30–50	11.1	10.4	8.4	7.8	7.0	6.6	5.4	5.3	3.8	3.7	—	—
40–60	11.3	10.5	8.4	7.8	7.1	6.8	5.6	5.4	4.9	4.3	—	—
50–70	11.6	11.6	8.8	8.3	7.8	7.6	6.7	6.0	—	—	—	—
60–80	13.2	13.1	9.9	9.2	9.1	8.7	8.5	7.4	—	—	—	—
70–90	16.1	14.4	12.6	11.2	11.9	10.2	13.7	9.8	—	—	—	—
80–100	21.9	17.1	18.0	13.7	17.9	13.3	—	—	—	—	—	—

Fuel Consumption
Overall mpg, **R/T1:** 20.6 mpg (13.7 litres/100 km)
R/T2: 20.7 mpg (13.6 litres/100 km)

NOTE: "R/T1" denotes performance figures for Triumph Stag tested in *AUTOCAR* of 30 July 1970.

.TRIUMPH STAG AUTOMATIC (2,997 c.c.)

ACCELERATION

SECONDS

SPEED MPH TRUE INDICATED	TIME IN SECS
30	4.1
29	
40	5.8
39	
50	7.9
50	
60	10.4
61	
70	14.2
72	
80	18.6
84	
90	24.9
95	
100	34.5
107	

SPEED RANGE, GEAR RATIOS AND TIME IN SECONDS

mph	Top (3.70-8.50)	Inter (5.37-12.37)	Low (8.85-20.40)
10-30	—	—	3.0
20-40	—	—	3.0
30-50	—	—	3.7
40-60	—	5.3	—
50-70	—	5.9	—
60-80	8.6	7.4	—
70-90	9.9	—	—
80-100	14.8	—	—

Standing ¼-mile
17.9 sec 78 mph

Standing kilometre
32.6 sec 98 mph
Test distance
1,050 miles
Mileage recorder
0.7 per cent over-
reading

PERFORMANCE

MAXIMUM SPEEDS

Gear	mph	kph	rpm
Top (mean)	112	180	5,660
(best)	113	182	5,710
Inter	89	143	6,500
Low	54	87	6,500

BRAKES

(from 70 mph in neutral)
Pedal load for 0.5g stops in lb

1	32	6	35
2	28	7	35
3	30	8	40
4	30	9	50
5	35	10	45

RESPONSE (from 30 mph in neutral)

Load	g	Distance
20lb	0.36	84ft
40lb	0.69	44ft
50lb	0.82	37ft
60lb	0.95	32ft
70lb	1.0	30.1ft
Handbrake	0.25	120ft
Max. Gradient 1 in 4		

MOTORWAY CRUISING

Indicated speed at 70 mph . . . . 72 mph
Engine (rpm at 70 mph) 3,540 . . . 1,495 rpm
(mean piston speed) . . . . . 1,495 ft/min.
Fuel (mpg at 70 mph) . . . . 23.0 mpg
Passing (50-70 mph) . . . . 5.9 sec

COMPARISONS

MAXIMUM SPEED MPH

Lotus Elan Plus 2S 130 (manual)	121	(£2,616)
Mercedes 280SL (automatic) . .	121	(£4,791)
BMW 2800 (automatic)	120	(£3,719)
Alfa Romeo 1750GTV (manual)	116	(£2,450)
Triumph Stag (automatic)	**112**	**(£2,489)**

0-60 MPH, SEC

Lotus Elan Plus 2S 130	7.4
Mercedes 280SL	9.3
BMW 2800	10.1
Triumph Stag	**10.4**
Alfa Romeo 1750GTV	11.2

STANDING ¼-MILE, SEC

Lotus Elan Plus 2S 130	15.4
Mercedes 280SL	17.0
BMW 2800	17.2
Triumph Stag	**17.9**
Alfa Romeo 1750GTV	18.0

OVERALL MPG

Alfa Romeo 1750GTV	23.9
Lotus Plus 2S 130	23.3
BMW 2800	19.9
Mercedes 280SL	19.0
Triumph Stag	**17.2**

GEARING (with 185-14in. tyres)

Top	19.8 mph per 1,000 rpm
Inter	13.7 mph per 1,000 rpm
Low	8.3 mph per 1,000 rpm

TEST CONDITIONS:

Weather: Cloudy but dry. Wind: 5-15 mph. Temperature: 18 deg. C. (64 deg. F.)
Barometer 29.55 in. hg. Humidity: 50 per cent. Surfaces: dry concrete and asphalt.

WEIGHT:

Kerb weight 25.3 cwt (2,835lb—1,285kg) (with oil, water and half full fuel tank.)
Distribution, per cent F, 55.7; R. 44.3. Laden as tested: 29.4 cwt (3,295lb—1,494kg).

TURNING CIRCLES:

Between kerbs L, 33ft 10in.; R, 34ft 3in. Between Walls L, 36ft 1in.; R, 36ft 6in.
steering wheel turns, lock to lock 2.8.

Figures taken at 5,500 miles by our own staff at the Motor Industry Research
Association proving ground at Nuneaton and on the Continent.

TRIUMPH STAG AUTOMATIC (2,997 c.c.)

AUTOCAR 10 June 1971

CONSUMPTION

FUEL
(At constant speeds—mpg)

30 mph	31.5
40 mph	31.5
50 mph	29.8
60 mph	26.3
70 mph	23.0
80 mph	20.6
90 mph	17.1
100 mph	12.3

Typical mpg . . . 20 (14.1 litres/100km)
Calculated (DIN) mpg 20.9 (13.5 litres/100km)
Overall mpg . . 17.2 (16.4 litres/100km)
Grade of fuel Super, 5-star (min. 100 RM)

OIL
Miles per pint (SAE 10W/40) . . 1,000

SPECIFICATION FRONT ENGINE, REAR-WHEEL DRIVE

ENGINE
Cylinders . . . 8, in 90 deg. vee
Main bearings . 5
Cooling system . Water, pump, fan and thermostat
Bore 86.0mm (3.39in.)
Stroke 64.5mm (2.54in.)
Displacement . 2,997 c.c. (182.9 cu. in.)
Valve gear . . . Single overhead camshaft per bank
Compression ratio 8.8-to-1 Min. octane rating: 97 RM
Carburettors . . 2 Zenith-Stromberg 1.75 CD
Fuel pump . . SU electric
Oil filter . . . Full flow, replaceable element
Max. power . . 145 bhp (net) at 5,500 rpm
Max. torque . . 170 lb. ft. (net) at 3,500 rpm

TRANSMISSION
Gearbox . . . Borg-Warner 35, 3-speed automatic
Gear ratios . . Top 1.0-2.30
Inter 1.45-3.34
Low 2.39-5.50
Reverse 2.09-4.81
Final drive . . . Hypoid bevel, ratio 3.70-to-1

CHASSIS and BODY
Construction . Integral with steel body

SUSPENSION
Front . . . . Independent, MacPherson struts, lower links, coil springs, telescopic dampers, anti-roll bar
Rear . . . . . Independent, semi-trailing arms, coil springs, telescopic dampers

STEERING
Type . . . . Power-assisted rack and pinion
Wheel dia. . . 15¾in.

BRAKES
Make and type . Lockheed disc front, drum rear
Servo . . . . Lockheed vacuum
Dimensions . . F 10.6in. dia. R 9.0in. dia. 2.25in. wide shoes
Swept area . . F 220 sq. in., R 127 sq. in. Total 347 sq. in. (182 sq. in./ton laden)

WHEELS
Type . . . . Pressed steel disc, 4-stud fixing, 5.5in. wide rim.
Tyres—make . Michelin
—type . XAS radial ply, tubeless
—size . 185-14in.

EQUIPMENT
Battery . . . . 12 Volt 56 Ah
Alternator . Lucas 11AC, 45 amp a.c.
Headlamps . Lucas 4-lamp tungsten-halogen, 110/220 Watt (total)
Reversing lamp . Standard
Electric fuses . 8
Screen wipers . Two-speed
Screen washer . Standard, electric
Interior heater . Standard, air-blending type
Heated backlight Standard with hard-top
Safety belts . Extra, mounting points standard
Interior trim . . PVC seats and headlining
Floor covering . Carpet
Jack . . . . Screw scissor type
Jacking points . 2 each side under body
Windscreen . Toughened
Underbody protection . Phosphate treatment prior to painting

MAINTENANCE
Fuel tank . . . 14 Imp. gallons (64 litres)
Cooling system . 18.5 pints (including heater)
Engine sump . 8 pints (4.5 litres) SAE 10W/40. Change oil every 6,000 miles. Change filter element every 12,000 miles.
Transmission . 11.5 pints ATF. Check fluid every 6,000 miles.
Final drive . . 2 pints SAE 90EP. Change oil every 6,000 miles.
Grease . . . No points
Tyre pressure . F 26; R 26 psi (normal driving) F 26; R 30 psi (full load)
Max. payload . 728lb (330kg)

PERFORMANCE DATA
Top gear mph per 1,000 rpm 19.8
Mean piston speed at max. power . . 2,300 ft/min
Bhp per ton laden 99

STANDARD GARAGE 16ft x 8ft 6in.

OVERALL LENGTH 14'5·75"
OVERALL WIDTH 5'3·5"
OVERALL HEIGHT 4'3·5"
GROUND CLEARANCE 6"
FRONT TRACK 4'4·5"
WHEELBASE 8'4"
REAR TRACK 4'4·87"

SCALE 0.3in. to 1ft
Cushions uncompressed

AUTOTEST
Triumph Stag
Automatic . . .

Stags at rest, rather than at bay. Both test cars were equipped with soft and hard tops; the hard top (which contains a considerable weight of glass) looks small enough here, but is a job for one man to lift and needs two to remove it from or replace it on the car. Nothing is changed in the cockpit of the automatic transmission car except for the transmission lever itself. The massive fuel tank, greatly appreciated during long journeys, is shaped to accept the spare wheel beside it; but beyond the usual wheel-changing equipment, there is little in the way of a tool kit

annoying low-frequency throb from the transmission. This noise, once started, could persist until the car was slowed below 70 mph.

Gear changing in the automatic car was usually smooth and quiet, even if the driver held the intermediate ratios to high speeds. The only thing to mar the performance of the transmission was the sometimes-violent 'clunk' as it changed down to first gear, or when engaging 'D' from neutral. At times, the kickdown was rather slow to operate.

In our original road test, we criticized the clutch action and gearchange of the manual car, while expressing the hope that it was non-typical in this respect. We can now establish that this was so; on this manual car the clutch was smooth in operation and required a medium operating effort, while the gearchange, though still having rather long movements, was light and precise. It was notable that the rushed change across the gate from second to third (which causes us difficulty during acceleration runs with some cars) could be made cleanly and consistently.

Comparing the brakes of the automatic with those of last year's car, their characteristics appear to have changed somewhat. A best stop, still of 1g, can now be made with only 70lb pedal effort instead of 120lb. There is a marked tendency for the rear wheels to lock first. On the other hand, the brakes no longer stand up quite so well to our fade test, showing a consistent rise in the pedal effort required and starting to smell after a few stops; it would seem that our automatic must have softer linings. The handbrake did not prove very effective on either car, whether on the test hill or in an emergency stop on the level.

Handling and comfort

The Stag's power steering (which is standard equipment, of course) has a sort of Jekyll and Hyde character which takes quite a lot of getting used to. There is a certain amount of load built into the system which, for small wheel movements or at low speeds, almost disguises the fact that there is any power assistance at all. When one really comes to throw the car around, however, one finds that the load does not increase beyond a certain point, so that the motorway impression of a system with lots of 'feel' disappears and the driver tends to over-control and has to adjust his line in mid-corner.

Once the driver is used to this, the Stag handles remarkably well for a fairly nose-heavy car. Most of the time it understeers, tending to almost neutral behaviour before the track and camber changes caused by the semi-trailing rear suspension take charge and bring the tail round. Opening the throttles wide in mid-corner on a dry road can delay the onset of the final oversteer; there is a comforting feeling of added stability as the tail tucks itself down and the car spurts on along the chosen line. In the wet, however, such a technique results only in an abrupt loss of adhesion at the back end.

Straight line stability is normally good, but is rather upset by gusty sidewinds. The Stag particularly objects to being taken through the wind shadow of large lorries in these conditions.

For long distance driving, the Stag really scores with its good ride and excellent seating. If anything, the ride feels a little firm at first, but

there is plenty of spring travel to soak up mediocre surfaces and the damping is very good indeed. The seats are well shaped and adjustable (along with the steering column) to suit almost any size and shape of driver.

In the rapidly changing weather conditions of our test period, we really appreciated the excellent heating and ventilation system in the Stag, with its easily adjusted air-blending heater. Our only criticism was that the output of fresh air from the butterfly-type vents at the ends of the facia was not very great (in either car). The heater controls are not quite as easy to reach as most of the other controls, which are mostly in the form of column-mounted stalks or knobs.

Needed in numbers

There is no doubt that the Stag is a very attractive car on many counts. We are now happy that the manual car goes better than our original figures suggested, while the automatic transmission suits the Stag very well, taking away the strain of city driving while leaving a very respectable performance. The car's handling is good, and its comfort and equipment excellent. Since we first tested it, it has risen in price, but this seems to be almost inevitable these days. More expensive or not, the queue for it is still long, and we hope that as much effort as possible will be put into satisfying the market.

RT/TEST
REPORT

TRIUMPH STAG

. . . V-8 Grand Tourer targeted to sell for just under $5,000 in the U.S.

Offering an unusual mixture of characteristics from luxury cars and from open sports jobs, the Triumph Stag is difficult to assess. As a luxury car it is small, a 2 + 2 (with moderate space in the trunk) which is 175 inches long and 63.5 inches wide. As a 3-liter sports job it takes almost 10 seconds from zero to 60 mph but goes on to 120 mph or more, handling easily but not inviting you to throw it around. As something between sports and luxury, it is an open job with excellent roll-over protection which can be converted quickly into a hardtop. It is tremendously comfortable for two people and practical for four, running very quietly indeed when hard-topped. It is very effortless to drive at normal-to-brisk speeds on any sort of road. I enjoyed my week with a Stag

tremendously, and thought it excellent value for money at a factory price about 20% below a Jaguar XJ6.

Triumph developed this Stag out of their 2000-2500 series of six-cylinder sedans. There is pretty much the same underframe, shortened by six inches to give a 100-inch wheelbase. Four-wheel independent springing is much the same, with revised settings and with larger-diameter wheels to accommodate bigger brakes. Instead of an old and highly-developed in-line six, however, there is a new V-8 based on the SOHC slant-four engine which Triumph have been building for the SAAB 99.

Fewer linear inches and more cubic inches make the Stag quite fast. In overdrive 4th, 120 mph is well within the "per-

With a target price in the U.S. of about $5,000 for a bare bones car, the Stag is in a sense a replacement for the 2000-2500 sedans, not the TR6, which will be continued.

mitted continuous" sector of the tachometer, and may be an underestimate of true maximum speed across flat desert. At about 2,900 pounds curb weight with the optional hardtop, however, the Stag's luxury comes rather heavy, and the docile motor does not give spectacular acceleration. Reaching 80 mph in a 17.4 second quarter-mile, the Stag is clearly towards the "roomy and luxurious" rather than the "sporting" side of Porsche's 911 range. It is also likely to sell in the U.S. for about $5,000, less than the least exciting Porsche 911T and with equipment of a very high standard.

I tested the Stag in all the three different

The standard soft top looks as ungainly when erected as those of any previous Triumph design. It also is noisy at speed. However, one man can fold it neatly under a steel lid.

Full instrumentation in a solid walnut panel is augmented by back-up warning lights at far left. Tach reads to 7,000 rpm and the outlet at the far right is for ventilation.

roles which one example can play. As an open car with the top folded completely out of sight, as an open car with the top raised, and as a closed car made by fixing a hardtop above the folded-away soft top. Two men can lift the optional hardtop on or off with reasonable ease, and the car may be purchased with hardtop only, with soft top only or with both, as on the test job. Emphatically, the Stag is more pleasing open or with the hardtop in use than with the soft top raised.

Open, the Stag does not expose the driver and front seat passenger to as much buffeting and back-draft as do many sports two-seaters, in spite of having an open rear passenger compartment. During some of the less-cold weather of England's winter, I was able to enjoy driving the Stag as an open car without needing more than an ordinary topcoat, the heater keeping my feet comfortably warm.

There is a reassuring impression of strength when this car is open, derived from the broad roll-over hoop and its sturdy link to the windshield frame.

Whereas many convertibles shake and rattle on bad roads, this one feels stronger than many steel-topped sedans.

Some open Triumphs of the past were notable for soft tops which could be raised or lowered very quickly and easily. Times change, though, and while the Stag s soft top can be furled completely 'out of sight below a hinged metal cover (and I did manage to raise it and stow it again without anyone to help me), neither process was quick. With the soft top up the car was truly weatherproof, and rear quarter panels as well as the zip-out rear window gave plenty of all-around vision. Unhappily, by the time you were doing 60 mph under the soft top there was too much wind noise inside the car. This became louder as the speed increased, so long

Optional overdrive, with which our test car was equipped, has a handy selector on the shift knob which eliminates the time-consuming lift-off on the accelerator of past designs.

ROAD TEST

The hardtop adds nearly 100 pounds but transforms the Stag into a luxury tourer for four adults. Car is described as being utterly noiseless and draft-free when it is in place.

Roll bar offers valuable reassurance to the driver and his passengers. When the hardtop is placed in position, connection is automatically made to the defrost wires in the rear windows.

red-marked 6,500 rpm limit.

Probably if the Stag had a less tractable engine, one would be in the acceleration-providing ratios more often. The way it is, you can crawl smoothly along at 10 mph in 4th with 500 rpm on the tachometer, and whether you press gently on the gas pedal or kick it down to the floor, the Stag will accelerate away unhesitatingly. In the snarled traffic of central London, the V-8 idled and moved me a few yards and idled and moved me a few yards in the smoothest possible manner, never vibrating or stalling. Up towards the top of the speed range, there was more of a tremor on the shift lever than I had expected, but except when you touch the shift lever this is a silkily smooth V-8, and a pretty quiet one also.

Three kinds of transmission can be ordered in a Stag. I've spent a couple of hours with an automatic transmission example, and really it was altogether too smooth and lacking in sparkle. There simply wasn't quick enough response to match the car's rather sporting appearance. Four-on-the-floor is much to be preferred if your wife knows how to use it. The full maximum speed of 120 mph is available without over-revving, and you can do 110 mph within the rpm range

journeys under the soft top were unexpectedly tiring.

Drop the hardtop over the folded soft top with a friend's help, move four accessible levers to lock it in position, and the Stag is an extremely refined car once again. Automatically, as you lowered the hardtop into place, you coupled up the electric circuit to a heated anti-mist and anti-ice rear window. Except that covered-over space behind and at each side of the rear seat, in which the soft top is stowed, reduces rear seat roominess, nothing hints that this is not an ordinary two-door hardtop. Nothing except acceleration-reducing weight which has been added to make a really strong open car, with its soft top, and with a hundred

pounds of hardtop incorporating three more glass windows.

I'm afraid that perhaps I'm being *too* rude about the Stag's performance. It certainly isn't a car which has problems keeping up with its own shadow, but it could so easily handle more horsepower. Acceleration in overdrive is moderate, and feels downright slow because it is so quiet. In 4th you pick up more quickly and in 3rd better than your ears suggest, but you must downshift to 2nd for real lift-off sensations. Once down there you are in a really useful ratio which jumps you to 50 mph at 5,500 rpm where a yellow sector on the tachometer ("not recommended for continuous use") starts, and on to about 60 mph before you reach a approved for continuous driving.

A good way to spend more money is, however, to add the overdrive option to the four-speed box. Typically British, the overdrive gives a "hot shift" up or down when you move a switch, which, on the Stag, is recessed into the top of the shift lever. In 4th overdrive you could exceed 130 mph downhill without infringing the "continuous" rpm limit, or if you knew a sufficiently steep and straight hill, you could do 155 mph without actually over-speeding the engine! More to the point, 100 mph is a quiet and easy cruising gait when the law permits it, at which you have barely more than 4,000 rpm on the tachometer and are burning fuel at a rate no faster than 16 mpg. Overdrive also gives you an extra-versatile 3rd, the easy 5,500 rpm accelerates you to nearly 80 mph and then a flick of the switch without lifting off the gas produces a half-ratio shift, taking the speed on up to 95 mph at the same 5,500 rpm.

Gas mileage does not sell this kind of car, but the 16.5 gallon tank will usually take an overdrive-equipped Stag more than 300 miles. You are a hard driver if you don't get nearly 20 mpg, and it is quite easy to do better than that figure. Without the overdrive you would probably be about 2 mpg worse off on the open road, but no worse off in city traffic. An automatic transmission (overdrive cannot be added to this) might make 16 mpg look pretty normal.

Seats provided for British buyers do not have the headrests demanded in the U.S., So I can only hope that the jobs sent over the Atlantic are as fabulously comfortable. as those kept at home. You can waste a lot of time fooling with non-powered adjustments for seat height, reach and backrest angle plus moving the steering wheel up-and-down and to-and-fro, but wherever the five adjustments are when

Visibility is marred only by the excessively thick "B" posts, but these, of course, are necessitated by the integral roll bar. Rear quarter windows are fixed.

Someday stylists will realize that a functional wheel with, perhaps, a little more polish and chromed lugs is more attractive than any cover, particularly when the phoney lugs don't add up.

you get bored, you'll probably find that you are very comfortable and that you stay that way for hours and hours. Side windows on the two big doors do have power lifts, one of which was finding its job a struggle on the pre-production car which had already suffered a lot of mileage in the hands of factory testers. Air conditioning will be available in cars delivered to the U.S., whereas in more temperate Britain we are content with plenty of fresh air vents plus a heater.

Quite a lot has been spent on furnishing and equipping the Stag well, for function as well as for appearance. Minor controls and switches are all easy to find when you are wearing the safety harness. A sports car's set of clear circular-dial instruments is supplemented by a group of eight warning lamps on the polished wood panel.

Without its four-wheel independent suspension feeling exaggeratedly flexible, the rigidly-built Stag rides very, very well indeed over most any kind of surface. Bulkier sedans from which the chassis derives, after all did take 2nd place in both the London-to-Australia Marathon and the London-South America-Mexico World Cup Rallye. You never wallow, yet you never seem to hear or feel the bumps

very much. Spencer King, who moved from Rover to complete the Stag's development, shares with Colin Chapman of Lotus a belief in soft springs controlled very firmly by powerful shock absorbers. This does allow some body roll when you corner fast, but attitude changes are slow enough not to be much noticed.

Powered rack-and-pinion steering is standardized on this car, plus high-speed radial tires, which, on the test example, were Michelins. Results are good, but with no need for compromises such as limited self-centering to suit cars without power steering, I would have hoped for something even better. Ordinary driving is extremely pleasant, the steering (geared

ROAD TEST

A roll bar reminiscent of that in the last of the Shelby Cobras is standard equipment and fits under both the standard soft and optional hard tops.

Trunk holds 9 cubic feet of luggage but the prominent hinges mean that not all of this is usable unless soft duffle is wrapped around them. Note the full carpeting.

2.75 turns from lock to lock) is quick in response and you soon forget that its lightness results from hydraulic power. Ordinary driving includes staying in your lane effortlessly through curves when cruising at 100 mph. Sadly, however, there is no real "feel" to warn you when you approach the limit of tire grip, so this isn't a sports job to be thrown around for the fun of controlling slides.

Yes, it will power slide. Traction in a straight line is quite good, but when accelerating hard out of a side street you lift a lot of weight off the inner rear wheel. No spin-limiting differential is offered. Other than when using 1st or 2nd out of a tight turn, road grip seems to be good in either wet or dry weather.

At the risk of re-starting the Anglo-American War of 1812, I'll describe the Stag brakes as somewhat American in

their behavior. Discs up front and drums down aft have eager power operation, so a gentle push on the pedal produces quite sharp retardation. Measuring the best stopping distance from 60 mph, 125 feet on a good dry road which represents almost 1g deceleration throughout, was a matter of judging pedal pressure rather nicely to prevent the four wheels locking. A bit too much push, or a length of blacktop with less broken stone rolled into it, would see the Stag sliding along without any wheels rotating—and a locked radial does not give anywhere near its best grip. Also, too frequent stops without any cooling time would lead, very temporarily, to uneven braking with one or two wheels locking up earlier than the others. I can be unreservedly polite, though, about the handbrake, a sturdy pull-up lever between the seats which feels good and works as

powerfully as a handbrake on the wrong (i.e., rear) end of a front-engined car possibly can.

Although this is essentially a 2+2 rather than a full sedan, it is entirely possible to carry two men in the rear seat, and children are really comfortable behind even the tallest driver. Luggage capacity in a fully carpeted trunk is not intended for four people, especially with concealed hinges intruding upon space for rigid cases. As a two-seater there is, of course, plenty of capacity split between the trunk and the +2 rear seat. Against what standard should one judge the Stag when tabulating a rating?

It's utterly unreasonable to complain about a car being different, yet it does make the Stag difficult to assess. Emphatically, it is not a ball-of-fire sporting job as some TR owners may have hoped, but rather, it's a luxury 2+2 which runs quite fast over really long distances and has a gently sporting flavor. Very few teen-age males are likely to want Stags, whereas quite a lot of girls and mature men would seem likely to think it an extremely pleasing car at an entirely sensible price.

Joe Lowrey

V-8 adapted from two SAAB 99 blocks
Twin Solex carburetion

Eight-blade fan
MacPherson strut tower
Brake servo
Distributor

Unlike Rover, which borrowed its V-8 from ex-Buick tooling, the SOHC Triumph consists essentially of a pair of fours as sold by them to SAAB on a common crank.

TRIUMPH STAG 2 + 2 OPEN/CLOSED COUPE

PERFORMANCE AND MAINTENANCE

Acceleration: Gears:

0-30 mph	3.6 secs.—	I
0-45 mph	6.6 secs.—	I, II
0-60 mph	10.0 secs.—	I, II
0-75 mph	15.5 secs.—	I, II, III
0-1/4 mile	17.4 secs. @ 80 mph	

Ideal cruise ....100 mph
Top speed(est) ....120 mph
Stop from 60 mph ....125 ft.
Average economy (city) ....16 mpg
Average economy (country) ....21 mpg
Fuel required ....Premium
Oil change (mos./miles) ....—/6000
Lubrication (mos./miles) ....—/6000
Warranty (mos./miles) 12/12,000
Type tools required ....SAE
U.S. dealers ....500 total

SPECIFICATIONS AS TESTED

Engine ....182.9 cu. in., SOHC 2V V-8
Bore & stroke ....3.39 x 2.33 ins.
Compression ratio ....8.8 to one
Horsepower ......145 (SAE net) @ 5500 rpms
Torque ....170 lbs.-ft. @ 3500 rpms
Transmission .....4-speed, manual w/overdrive
Steering* ....2.75 turns, lock to lock
                        32.0 ft., curb to curb
Brakes* ....disc front, drum rear
Suspension ....coil front, coil rear
Tires ....185 HR 14, Michelin XAS radial

Dimensions (ins.):

Wheelbase	100.0	Front track	52.5
Length	173.8	Rear track	52.9
Width	63.5	Ground clearance	4.5
Height	49.5	Weight	2900 lbs.

Capacities: Fuel ...16.5 gals.   Oil ...4.8 qts.
           Coolant ....11.0 qts.   Trunk ....9.0 cu. ft.
*Power assisted as tested

RATING

	Excellent (91-100)	Good (81-90)	Fair (71-80)	Poor (60-70)
Brakes		88		
Comfort	96			
Cornering		85		
Details	92			
Finish	92**			
Instruments	94			
Luggage		88		
Performance		84		
Quietness	92			
Ride	96			
Room		88		
Steering		84		
Visibility	92			
Overall		90		

**Assessed on pre-production example

BASE PRICE OF CAR

(Excludes state and local taxes, license, dealer preparation and domestic transportation): $5,000 at P.O.E. East Coast (estimated).

Plus desirable options:

$ n/a Hardtop
$ n/a 3-speed automatic
$ n/a Air-conditioning
$ n/a AM/FM radio
$ n/a Chrome wire wheels
$ n/a Luggage rack
$ n/a TOTAL
$ n/a Per lb. (base price).

ANTICIPATED DEPRECIATION

(Based on current Kelley Blue Book, previous equivalent model): $ n/a 1st yr. + $ n/a 2nd yr.

n/a—not available

13,000-

Mile appraisal: Long-term Triumph

STAG

A likeable and lively car, unusually well equipped.

We have been putting in about 1,000 miles a month with our Stag and have now topped the 13,000 mark, so it is time to make a first "owner's" report. To the most pointed question "would you have bought a Stag in December, 1970 if you had known what you know now?", the answer, without hesitation, is "yes". To a further question, "has it turned out as expected?", the reply is, "not entirely".

By Maurice A. Smith DFC

THE Stag was bought more or less as a replacement for our Sunbeam Tiger II (two-and-a-bit seater), which itself followed a Tiger I and an E-type Jaguar (two-seater). It is at least a 10-year later design and had the Tiger been developed on, it would probably by now have cost much the same as the Stag, around £2,200 delivered. With hard top, hood and automatic transmission like ours, the cost is £2,350. One of the differences you really notice apart from the Stag being bigger, concerns the vee-8 engines in the two cars; the Tiger with 1.7 more litres and less weight, was always eager to go off like a rocket and it encouraged the driver to do so. The Stag is not particularly eager or rocket-like, but can readily be wound up to give a lively burst of acceleration. It will cruise continuously nearly as fast as a Tiger—say, 100 mph and is quieter, more comfortable, softer sprung and more spacious.

To live with then, the Stag is much more relaxed and relaxing in nature. Its 3-litre vee-8 engine gives a very smooth and gentle burble of power in traffic but gets surprisingly wound up and whirring if you kick down and use all it has got. From outside you can hear the vee-8 beat as a Stag accelerates away. Now the car is smooth, but originally there was considerable tremor from the front wheels and also vibration at high speed, owed to the Borg-Warner transmission according to Triumph and to the prop shaft according to B.W. This was finally corrected in April. How, we wonder, can you detect such transmission unbalance before delivery if it only starts to show up at 85 mph on its first trip abroad after running in?

That first foreign journey to Switzerland was great fun. Three of us went with plenty of luggage and the Stag was a pleasure to drive in the mountains. Light, power-assisted steering with quick response and good lock are just what

PERFORMANCE CHECK

Maximum speeds

Gear	mph R/T	mph Staff	kph R/T	kph Staff	rpm R/T	rpm Staff
Top (mean)	116*	112	187	180	4,810	5,660
(best)	116*	113	187	182	4,810	5,710
3rd/Inter	92	89	148	143	6,500	6,500
2nd/Low	61	54	98	87	6,500	6,500
1st/—	42	—	68	—	6,500	—

Standing ¼-mile	R/T:	17.1 sec		82 mph		
	Staff:	17.9 sec		78 mph		
Standing kilometre	R/T:	31.3 sec		102 mph		
	Staff:	32.6 sec		98 mph		

Acceleration									
R/T:	3.5	5.1	7.1	9.3	12.7	16.5	21.8	29.2
Staff:	4.1	5.8	7.9	10.4	14.2	18.6	24.9	34.5

Time in seconds								
True speed mph	30	40	50	60	70	80	90	100
Indicated speed mph R/T	31	41	52	63	73	83	94	105
Indicated speed mph Staff	29	39	50	61	72	84	95	107

Speed range, Gear Ratios and Time in seconds

Mph	Top R/T	Top Staff	3rd Inter R/T	3rd Inter Staff	2nd Low R/T	2nd Low Staff
0-20						
10-30	9.0	—	6.3	—	3.9	3.0
20-40	8.2	—	5.6	—	3.4	3.0
30-50	7.8	—	5.3	—	3.7	3.7
40-60	7.8	—	5.4	5.3	4.3	—
50-70	8.3	—	6.0	5.9	—	—
60-80	9.2	8.6	7.4	7.4	—	—
70-90	11.2	9.9	9.8	—	—	—
80-100	13.7	14.8	—	—	—	—

Fuel Consumption

| Overall mpg | R/T: | 20.7 mpg (13.7 litres/100km) |
| | Staff: | 19.2 mph (14.6 litres/100km) |

NOTE: "R/T" denotes performance figures for Stag manual tested in *Autocar* of 10 June 1971
*Road Test maxima in overdrive top gear

A good layout. Ample and easily managed ventilation and heating, well positioned secondary controls, multiple steering wheel and seat adjustments. The warning lamp sectored dial (left) is obscured as usual; the speedometer has kph markings as well as mph. Unfamiliar box is Readycall radio telephone, and microphone. Tape recorder selector switch replaces ashtray in centre

is needed. The engine has more torque for climbing than the normal acceleration would suggest, and it hangs on well at quite low rpm. The seats are sufficiently well shaped to give location and proper support. The vibration mentioned earlier spoiled the high-speed *autoroute* cruising but we were pleased with the mechanical quietness and relatively low wind noise.

If you get a really gusty day on a motorway, directional stability is not 100 per cent, as you might expect with that short rounded tail—those horrid fins of the 1960s had some uses—but the precise rack and pinion steering keeps you on course. It's not the smartest steering wheel we have seen and it might be smaller.

Some early talk of Stags "jacking up" and twitching on corners, owing to the half-shaft splines sticking under heavy torque and then slipping suddenly, has not been supported by this automatic car, although another manual Stag we had on test once showed signs of this in pretty extreme conditions. We followed a Stag fairly fast round Stowe corner at Silverstone during a recent test day (in a Reliant GTE) and were interested to see the busy behaviour of the back wheels and the early lift-off of the inside front one. It goes to show that the ordinary

owner, even a fast driving one, gets nowhere near the limits to which cars are tested when their ultimate behaviour is being investigated.

We are reasonably satisfied with our Stag's road-holding, cornering and ride for all ordinary purposes. If we were asked what improvements might be made, the harshness felt on rippled surfaces and occasional thump back through the steering would be one of our first suggestions for attention. There are times on wet roads when back wheel adhesion is suspect. It is also very easy to spin the inside rear wheel when moving off on a curve.

This is the first time we have opted for automatic transmission on a sporting car. It is a sign of the changing times—British automatics changing for the better and traffic congestion for the worse. We do not regret the choice, but think it high time that a cruising over-drive were available with automatic. The automatic Jaguar XJ6 is another car that needs one. Motorways are here to stay.

In appearance the Stag is obviously of the Triumph family. One rival manufacturer remarked that it was so ugly you couldn't sell one on the Continent. We do not agree, nor would we hold it up as an example to all. With luck it will take the new mandatory front bumper heights in the USA without difficulty. Perhaps its looks are an acquired taste and after 13 months we have.

It is no good buying a Stag if you need limousine accommodation. This is a compact, convertible coupé, of the true plus two kind. Average grown-ups can sit comfortably in the back without much to spare. Tall people will find their heads touch the hard-top roof. Getting in and out of the back seats (front seat catches controlled by levers high in the seat backs) is easy enough. With the hood up, back passengers have as much space, but of course, feel a bit blinkered. Wind noise becomes considerable over 60 mph, though less than in most other open cars with hoods up.

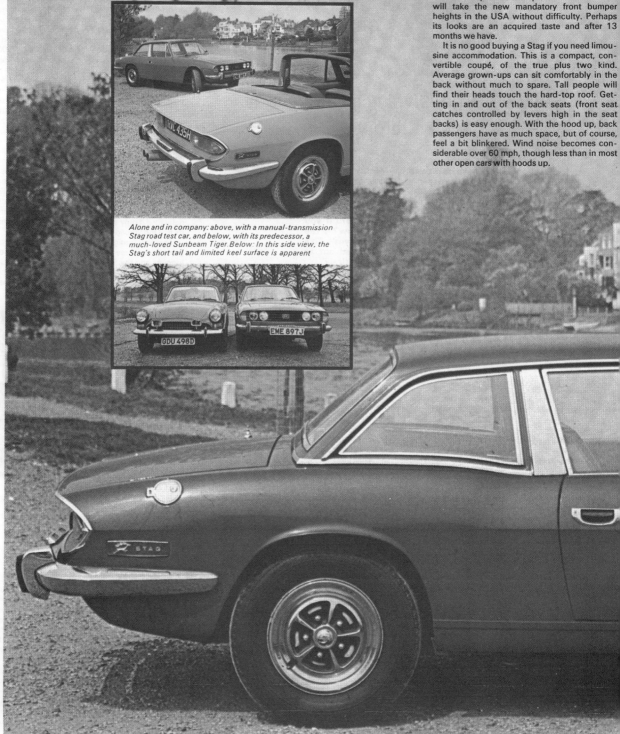

Alone and in company: above, with a manual-transmission Stag road test car, and below, with its predecessor, a much-loved Sunbeam Tiger. Below: In this side view, the Stag's short tail and limited keel surface is apparent

Many owners will buy their Stags intending to keep the hard tops on all the year round. The folding hood, surprisingly, is an optional extra. Not so, us. Either you like an open car or you don't. There is something about that rush of air, even if Nader says it is polluted! Agreed, most people will not bother to wrap up like Eskimos to go motoring, so the days of the classic open tourer have passed. Despite this, a few of us still actually enjoy putting on our Jack Brabham rally jackets and going for a topless drive—so to speak. Of course, the weather has become much worse as a result of the Americans and Russians piercing the earth's atmospheric crust with their rockets, so we also feel the need of the hard top.

Lack of rigidity has been a criticism of many open-bodies, although we are now over the days of coach-built convertibles that shook like a railway carriage. It usually needs big boxy sills like those on the E-type Jaguar to keep an open car rigid. In the case of the Stag, which has wide doors, body stiffness is assisted by having a roll-over 'cage'. This is made up of a roll-over bar extending from the rear door pillars and joined to the top of the screen frame by a central ridge member. Padded and trimmed, this cage doesn't look untidy nor detract from the open car effect.

Included in the fairly high price of the Stag are the exceptional number of desirable features which make up the value. Power-assisted steering is one of them. This gives unusually

quick, light response from straight ahead, which would be particularly valuable for emergency evasive action. It also makes the car very handy in traffic and for parking. Next, there is the two-axis adjustment on the steering column. It moves in and out and swings up or down when you release the clamping lever. This, together with the seat adjustments — back and forth, cushion tilt-up and back-rest angle, should allow anyone to get set. The low instrument panel and screen base with short, slope-away nose help to give a first class forward view. This is very much a girl's car as well as a man's.

Going on with the equipment, you get bright red lamps on the doors in the back ends of the arm rests. These are an obvious safety-feature and good courtesy lamps to help you step in and out at night—puddle lamps, Triumph call them. The hard top comes with built-in electrically heated rear window, arrangements reminiscent of those on the Mercedes 250-280 SL.

Electric operation of the windows is something we really appreciate and specially when driving solo. Opening quarter lights may not be necessary, but if you have them they should pivot open by twisting their knobs, as they do on the Stag. The hard top has extractor-type hinged side windows.

The driver's wiper arm has an articulated linkage which lines the blade up with the screen pillar, so eliminating a blind sector. Then there are the quartz halogen lamps, proper fuse panel, looking fuel filler (which like the cigarette lighter some of us would happily do without),

rheostat for instrument lighting, electric windscreen washer, boot interior lamp, map-reading lamp, twin reversing lamps, parking lamp switch, dual-intensity signal and brake lamps with signal repeaters on the sides of the wings, day-night dipping mirror, and viscous fan coupling to prevent whirr.

Some designers cut down on their bumpers. Those on the Stag are sturdy and wrap around—right round at the back—and the overriders have rubber inserts.

All the above should be standard equipment on good class cars, as they are on the Stag, yet it is surprising how few other cars have them all. We would certainly like to add the export options of fitted head-rests and hazard warning lamps. We do not like a toughened glass windscreen, Zebrazone or not. Air-conditioning can be specified but cannot be added after the car has been assembled.

Next, we turn to some troubles and short-comings. The Stag has never left us stranded or in fact, let us down at all, so that is a main point in its favour. The nearest it came to it was a rubbed through fuel pipe, attributable to stupid detail design or assembly (see picture and check your Stag). This also accounted for several days of untraced petrol smell and re-

69 ☞

stag...
TRIUMPH'S LONG-DISTANCE RUNNER

A wild, high performance sports car the Stag is not, but neither is it a 2-plus-2 limousine. Waiting halfway between the two extremes, Triumph's V8 is very desirable motoring.

IN THE DAYS BEFORE they were welded together as British Leyland, there was an outbreak of V8 engine designing at both Leyland and BMC. The first fruits appeared in the Daimler 2.5, then the Rover 3500, then half an engine appeared in the Saab 99 of all places and everyone said what a splendid unit it would be when Triumph glued both parts together and made it into an ohc V-8.

After the coming together V-8s started to be shed. The projected Jaguar one was strangled at birth, the Daimler dropped into the background and that left Rover and Triumph, Rover getting a clear lead by having its complete engine in production instead of a half for export to Sweden.

The pundits all forecast that a V-8 version of the Triumph 2000 would appear but they didn't stop to think that it would compete with the Rover 3500, made by the same firm and, in any case, they weren't aware that the petrol injection Triumph 2.5 was on the way.

Another piece of the jigsaw came to light when the design teams of Rover and Triumph were brought together and this caused everyone to forecast a Triumph 2.5 engine in the Rover 2000 body, but wrong again. Or that the Rover V-8 would be dropped. Still wrong.

Stag interior is pleasant mixture of luxury and sportiness. General layout follows 2.5 PI sedan. Steering wheel is adjustable and combines with excellent front seats for a superb driving position.

All right then, the Rover experimental mid-engined car would be refined and produced as a Triumph? Uh uh, but getting warmer. That Triumph would produce a 2-plus-2 V-8 based on the 2000 running gear with a removable top? Nobody guessed that one and it's not to be wondered at because the result is a car which doesn't fit into any preconceived slot and although you might just be tempted to say: "What about the Mercedes 350SL?" in truth, the only real resemblance is in the number of seats and the fact that the lid comes off.

The Merc is unashamed luxury almost regardless of cost while the Stag is the best that can be produced within a given price limit. Both give value for money but it's a matter of whether you wish to buy your wife beaver, lamb or mink.

It's usually a good idea to study car brochures to discover how the maker sees his own vehicle, Triumph pitch in with: "Some people think that the Continentals have the reputation for really stylish grand tourers all to themselves. Well, that reputation had to run out some time. The time is now. And the car that's overtaken them in style is the Triumph Stag. The Stag's styling is sporty, but suave. Its simple low-lying lines are impeccably cool, and give it stand-out sophistication among the lumbering herd."

That's enough of that to be going on with but it is interesting that the rest of the brochure makes great play of travelling long distances on those never-ending Continental roads and, if this is what they set out to do, then they have succeeded very well.

First thoughts on driving the Stag were: "This is a car I could go a helluva distance in" and when the test was over I still felt the same about it.

Continued on page **66**

wheels road test

STAG...TRIUMPH'S LONG-DISTANCE RUNNER
Continued from page 64

It has undoubtedly been designed with long-range straight-road motoring as the chief consideration. The seats are very good, giving support right up to shoulder level and a fair bit of wrap around as well. The padding is relatively firm, as it should be.

The engine has a moderate output at 145 bhp (5500 rpm) for a modern three-litre ohc V-8. The compression ratio is a mere 8.8:1 but I suppose we'll have to get used to these lower values now that emissions have to be controlled — and rightly so because, let's face it, we're all pedestrians when we leave our cars and any bronchitis sufferer who has had a lungful of exhaust fumes will require no convincing on the subject. The torque is good at 170 lb/ft (oddly, Triumph give it in lb/inches) at only 3500 rpm and the result is a rather friendly, almost fluffy motor which doesn't show any anger until you get the revs really high. The dumble-dum V-8 exhaust note seems completely out of keeping but it is nice to listen to for all that. Like deep-throated, man.

For test we had an automatic model with our old friends Mr Borg and Mr Warner doing the changing. Borg, who makes the upward changes, is an old smoothy most of the time unless you provoke him with a downward kick in the ribs (or in the bottom, going by his reaction), while Warner changes down sweetly at all times. You can stir them both up with the manual selector, which is very nicely placed but not so easy to use by fumble until you are used to it, and to find D or R it is best to read it to be quite sure. There is very little jerk on initial engagement.

A slightly odd feature of the brochure is that the automatic box merely gets a casual mention. All the performance glamor (and details of ratios) goes to the standard manual with its overdrive on third and top, yet all the interior pictures show the auto.

This written emphasis on the manual box suggests a point where Triumph and your tester do not agree. It would seem that it regards the Stag as a sporting device that should have a stick change but I don't — as we shall have explained when we get to the suspension.

I think of it as a nice lazy-man's car for covering a long distance at high speed with the minimum amount of effort. If it were meant to be a device for revving up and throwing into bends then it would have had a rortier motor for a start.

In passing, the basic price is $7657 but you have to have the laminated screen, another $49, and the automatic adds $342 to make the total $8048 and, provided that you're not under the impression that you are buying a sports car, it is good enough value by Australian standards.

The test car had the optional hardtop and I really can't see

Rear seat is much more comfortable than usual 2-plus-2 set-ups. It's fine for children, lacks more in width than legroom.

a lot of point in the soft top version because there is nothing more irritating at speed that hood flap and though there may be some who like motoring with the top down, they are a dying race (not yet, Cook—Ed). Bear in mind that the Stag has very good face-level cooling and that the rearward side windows can be opened on their forward hinges to act as very efficient extractors — surprisingly quiet ones, too.

There was quite a bit of wind hiss round the roof of the test car but this doesn't seem to be typical of all Stags and some slight attention to the seals would probably fix it.

The quiet engine felt a bit tight and this seems to be confirmed by the acceleration figures which, even allowing for the losses of the automatic gearbox, are somewhat down on what Triumph claim as typical. Rear wheel traction is good and that, too, lessens initial acceleration because even by holding the car on the brakes and letting the lot go all at once it isn't possible to spin the back wheels and use them as a clutch when taking off. Thus the 0-50 time of 7.8 seconds compares with Triumph's claimed time of 7.0 for the manual and against our 0-70 of 14.0 it has 12.5. Knowing, I am sure that its figures would be correct for a fully run-in manual car.

And if it is true that the engine was still tight, then the petrol consumption figures are very good for a 3-litre automatic with eight cylinders, because some fairly hectic motoring produced an all-over consumption of 20 mpg while high-speed cruising was returning 27. Fully run in and treated gently, it should do a genuine 30 mpg. If we take 25 as a conservative figure, the 14 gallon petrol tank gives a fail-safe range of about 340 miles, which is just about right.

Big tank means small boot, though, but since the rear seats are only suitable for medium-length trips if occupied by adults, the couple nipping off to Alice Springs for a suspect weekend will have ample room for all their toothbrushes and associated gear.

In fact, the rear seats aren't too bad and certainly suitable for children up to the age of about 16. They are much more comfortable than the usual 2-plus-2 rear seats and lack more in width than in legroom.

The front seats have a long range of adjustments but even when they are fully back, with a considerable angle of recline, there is still an acceptable amount of backseat space. The steering wheel helps here by being adjustably mounted. A straight-arm position comes naturally — indeed, is almost imposed upon the driver and it is a great pity that all cars aren't made thus so that people would have to sit correctly even without the application of commonsense. But even the wheel-huggers will be happy with the four inches of adjustment axially, plus two inches vertically.

Big pedals are slightly offset to the right but very easy to use and the brake is wide enough for occasional touches by the left foot when the mood takes you at traffic lights. A lot of thought has gone into the control layout and although some initial learning is required, especially when it comes to familiarisation with the minor instruments peppered around the very pleasant and tasteful wooden fascia, they've done a pretty good job.

All-round vision is good because there is none of this up-swept cow-hip or wedge nonsense to keep down the price of the glass, and the seat is fairly high, too. The halogen headlights are magnificent, giving a clear white beam which suggests really heavy copper wiring (many cars have a 1½-volt drop at the headlamps because of thin wiring).

The body feels rigid and rattle-free and although it is apparently an open car with an attached roof, there is that massive roll-over T-bar contributing a lot of strength. But it is rather difficult to understand why there is a single central leg instead of twin ones at each side which would not only make it stronger still, but give the upper edges of the doors something more substantial to shut against and probably stop the wind-hiss referred to earlier.

It is only when you come to the suspension that there is any real evidence of the car being a cousin to the Triumph 2000. There are McPherson struts at the front and effective but not over-refined semi-trailing arms at the rear. The spring settings are relatively soft so that you get considerable straight-line comfort coupled with good stability except when the wind is very gusty (even then, there is nothing really worth complaining about). **68▶**

wheels road test
technical details

TRIUMPH STAG

MAKE	TRIUMPH
MODEL	STAG
BODY TYPE	2 plus 2
PRICE	$8048
OPTIONS	Hardtop
COLOR	Brown
MILEAGE START	1570
MILEAGE FINISH	1830
WEIGHT	3000 lb

FUEL CONSUMPTION:

Overall	20 mpg
Cruising	27 mpg

TEST CONDITIONS:

Weather	Dry, blustery
Surface	New asphalt
Load	Two People
Fuel	Super

SPEEDOMETER ERROR:

Indicated mph	30	40	50	60	70	80	90	100
Actual mph	30	40	50	59	68	78	88	97

ACCELERATION (through gears):

0-30 mph	4.0 sec
0-40 mph	5.7 sec
0-50 mph	7.8 sec
0-60 mph	10.3 sec
0-70 mph	14.0 sec
0-80 mph	18.4 sec
0-90 mph	24.7 sec
0-100 mph	34.2 sec

	1st gear	2nd gear	3rd gear
20-40 mph	3.0 sec	5.1 sec	—
30-50 mph	3.7 sec	5.2 sec	—
40-60 mph	—	5.3 sec	—
50-70 mph	—	5.9 sec	7.7 sec

STANDING QUARTER MILE:

Fastest run	17.5 sec
Average all runs	17.7 sec

BRAKING:

From 30 mph to 0	(9.4 m) 31 ft

PERFORMANCE

Piston speed at max bhp	(709 m/min) 2327 ft/min
Top gear mph per 1000 rpm	(31.6 kph) 19.8 mph
Engine rpm at max speed	5800
Lbs per net bhp (power-to-weight)	20.7

MAXIMUM SPEEDS:

Fastest run	(186.6 kph) 116 mph
Average of all runs	(183.4 kph) 114 mph
Speedometer indication, fastest run	(191.5 kph) 119 mph

IN GEARS:

1st	(86.8 kph) 54 mph (6500 rpm)
2nd	(143.2 kph) 89 mph (6500 rpm)
3rd	(183.4 kph) 114 mph (5800 rpm)

Graph labels: 2nd 89 mph / STANDING ¼ MILE 17.7 / 1st 54 mph / TRIUMPH STAG / TOP SPEED 114 mph / ACCELERATION THROUGH GEARS WITH CHANGE POINTS / MPH / ELAPSED TIME IN SECONDS

SPECIFICATIONS

ENGINE:

Cylinders	V8
Bore and stroke	(86 mm x 64.5 mm) 3.385 in. x 2.539 in.
Cubic capacity	(2997 cc) 182.9 cu in.
Compression ratio	8.8 to 1
Valves	ohc
Carburettor	Two Stromberg
Fuel pump	Mechanical
Oil filter	Full flow
Power at rpm	145 bhp at 5500 rpm
Torque at rpm	170 lb/ft at 3500 rpm

TRANSMISSION:

Type	Borg Warner automatic
Gear lever location	Floor

RATIO:

	Direct	Overall	mph per 1000 rpm	(kph)
1st	2.39:1	8.85:1	8.3	(13.2)
2nd	1.45:1	5.37:1	13.6	(21.7)
3rd	1.0:1	3.7:1	19.8	(31.6)
Final drive	3.7:1			

CHASSIS AND RUNNING GEAR:

Construction	Unitary
Suspension front	McPherson Strut
Suspension rear	Semi-trailing arms
Shock absorbers	Telescopic rear
Steering type	Adwest rack and pinion
Turns l to l	4
Turning circle	(10.2 m) 33 ft 6 in.
Steering wheel diameter	16 in.
Brakes type	Disc front, drum rear
Dimensions	10-5/8 in. dia front, 9 in. x 2¼ in. drums rear

DIMENSIONS:

Wheelbase	(2540 mm) 100 in.
Track front	(1352 mm) 53¼ in.
Track rear	(1362 mm) 53-5/8 in.
Length	(4420 mm) 14 ft 5¾ in.
Width	(1612 mm) 5 ft 3½ in.
Height	(1258 mm) 4 ft 1½ in.
Fuel tank capacity	(63.5 litres) 14 gal

TYRES:

Size	185 HR 14 Radial
Pressures	26 psi front/30 psi rear
Make on test car	Michelin XAS

GROUND CLEARANCE:

Registered	(11.4 cm) 4½ in.

WHEELS, November, 1972

66▶

On the other hand, despite its wide track, the Stag rolls an amount which would be little for a sedan but a lot for a sports car. The effect is minimised by a good grip offered by the seats and you have to be motoring in a fairly extreme fashion to be bothered by roll. Radial-ply thump is well damped out by the suspension mountings and you can hammer the Stag fast over rough surfaces at speeds limited only by the driver's courage.

In general, the speed limit seems to be whatever the car will do in the circumstances and cruising at over 100 mph would be a safe and sensible way to proceed even though some do-gooders will undoubtedly disagree. But then, it has always been the way of the mob to decry whatever it doesn't understand. Engine and road noise are very subdued and if it weren't for the hiss, the radio volume correct for 40 mph would still be right for 100, and you never have to raise your voice to converse.

Cornering, braking and acceleration adhesion is splendid, even on damp roads, and the Stag can be hustled through bends very rapidly and safely once you have become used to two factors.

One of these is the roll already mentioned, but you can cope with that once you realise that the car cocks up a certain extent and then goes no further. The other is the standard-fitting Adwest rack-and-pinion power steering coupled with four turns lock-to-lock (a power-steering Ford Falcon has 2½).

The initial reaction to this steering is to say that it destroys the feel, and stump off after having slammed the door behind you. But it isn't really so — there is quite a lot of feel and you just have to learn to be more fairy-fingered with it in the initial stages. I have heard it described as "too insensitive" but, after sampling it for some time, I disagree and would put any lack of sensitivity down to pilot error.

Confirmation of this can be obtained quite easily by taking the car up to its surprisingly high cornering limits when the understeer slowly and predictably changes to oversteer. You can feel it happening and, more important, you can feel a front wheel that is thinking of going for a slide on a tight slippery bend almost before it happens. In short, the steering is

in keeping with the general character of the car and to condemn it is to miss the whole point of the Stag.

And, praise be, it has the screen wipers mounted the correct way for driving on the left of the road so that they clean right up to the very top corner of the screen. The car undoubtedly looks at its best with the lid taken off and we leave you with a final word from the Triumph brochure: "With the hood down and rollover bar exposed, it takes on a wicked, hot-blooded look".

Well, they said it, not me . . . *

Two Saab 99/Triumph Dolomite engines make one Triumph Stag V8. Performance is subdued and further restricted by automatic transmission but smoothness is never questioned.

WHEELS, November, 1972

Hard-top to soft-top in 1 min. 36 sec. L. to r.: hard-top fitted; top off, hood down showing roll-over structure (42 sec.); erecting the previously hidden hood (54 sec.); soft-top erect.

43▶

alloy manifolding, the angled plugs accessible with the right tool, as is the dip-stick, which showed that the sump had lost none of its eight pints of oil in more than 1,100 miles. Oil changes are scheduled very 6,000 miles and there are no greasing chores. Visibility forward is good but reversing is less easy.

I tried to like this Triumph Stag, to please Lord Stokes of Leyland, T.D., D.L., LL.D., D.TECH., D.SC., C.ENG., F.I.MECH.E., M.S.A.E. It needs better steering, power or otherwise (say ZF), a better gearbox, for those who do not specify the automatic transmission, and more poke—

like Eartha Kitt's Englishman, the Stag takes time to get going. (The makers quote a 0-to-60-m.p.h. acceleration time of 9.5 sec. and one journalist got 9.9 sec. but mine is closer to the average figure.) Given these changes, and a more easily erected top, the Stag could be a great success, for although its engine isn't quite as silky as I anticipated, vibration being felt through the gear-lever, the Stag is a very nice-looking 2+2 coupé/convertible, reasonably priced at £2,173 (as tested) for an eight-cylinder car having (save the mark!) power-assisted steering, electric windows, a concealed hood and Italian styling.—W. B.

13,000

Mile Long Term Triumph

STAG...

63 ▶

duced mpg. In this context, the fuel filler is a constant source of irritation and waste. It blows back on every possible occasion and will never accept normal pump delivery.

The developers have managed to design reliability and most of the pinka-pinka out of the blinking units for the direction indicators. At each service they have been 'looked at', but have yet to work regularly or properly. The trouble is that you can be booked by the police for this. It's in the regulations.

The circle of warning lamps is carefully positioned on the panel behind the driver's left hand and forearm to make it hard to see. Triumph's service people hit on an effective way to cure a persistent wrong red warning of radiator overheating. They disconnected it. The fuel gauge continues to read ⅜ full when empty, but now we are used to this. An 8 per cent optimistic error on the speedo is too much. The odometer and trip mileage, on the other hand, are very accurate.

We are on our third Trico washer bottle. They keep splitting where the holding bracket cuts. Fortunately, it still leaves you with nearly half a bottle of liquid. We had exactly the same trouble in our Jensen FF last year. Must get around to designing a new bracket; filing the sharp edges of the one we have is not enough. The only other recurrent trouble has been with the doors and door-locks. They tend to drop, get loose, lock themselves when slammed, or catch their inside trim on the fixed rubber sealing strips.

Being a very early Stag from an unhappy production line, it is not surprising perhaps that there was a fair amount of work to be done or redone after running in and again after the Swiss journey. The biggest inconvenience was the time taken to deal with faults in body fittings, instruments and the transmission indicator which came off. The car went in for its first check on 10 February and came out on the 12th with just the mechanical bits attended to. It went in again on 16 February for "3 days" but was still waiting for parts on 26 February. Triumph's mechanical and body servicing people in London seem to be pleasant, overworked and optimistic. When planning car

usage, it may be best to add a fair margin to their time estimates for completion of work.

Of the attention under warranty, the most serious trouble was a flooding carburettor, caused we were told by a punctured diaphragm. In the course of a short drive the air filter box slowly filled with petrol and made the mixture hopelessly rich. No-one likes to have hot petrol swilling around above the cylinder blocks but this was obviously an isolated fault in one of the pair of Strombergs. Otherwise the Stag engine has been very reliable and uses hardly any oil. It has been drained and refilled at 6,000 and 12,000-mile services and has otherwise taken only about 1 pint per 1,000 miles. It is a sure starter if you give it time. Both hot and cold, however, it needs several seconds of turning before it bites. It also needs half choke for two or three miles on a cold morning before it will pull and even then, it occasionally stalls. The radiator never seems to need topping up.

Fuel consumption is now consistent for given circumstances. Around cities it gives 18.5 mpg. Long, fast journeys go up to 19.5 mpg and the best leisurely journey average we recorded last summer was 23.0 mpg. The manual Stags seem to do about 1½ mpg better.

Michelin XAS handed tyres are fitted and these we changed round as recommended at 6,000 miles. Adhesion on wet roads became noticeably poor at 12,500 miles with between 1½ and 2 mm tread remaining, so at 13,000 we changed them for new ones. The spare has not been used. These new tyres have been the only sizeable expense in the first year.

Turning to practical aspects of design details, that battery mounting accessibility will have to be improved. Take the power steering pump off to lift out the battery? Inevitably there are shorts and sparks as you struggle to put a spanner on the terminal clamp bolts.

A forward-opening bonnet is right; a self-supporting one is best. If you must have a stay, we think it should be placed the same side as the dip-stick and washer-bottle.

Next, a look at the sort of conveniences and comforts which you grow to appreciate, or otherwise, when you live with a car. We have approved seat comfort and forward view and now add the following plus points: all-round look-out with hard top fitted, good ventilation and heating, handy secondary controls—dipper, flasher, wiper, washer and horn on stalks round the steering wheel. The glove-locker is rather small but in compensation there are: a shelf, two small pockets in the doors and two more bigger ones at the back. There are also little trays in the scuttle-top on the passenger side and in front of the gear selector.

The boot is, at best, of big sports car or small coupé capacity. It's shallowness and the incur-

sion of the hinges are the points of criticism. You can carry two suitcases side by side and quite a lot of small and soft things around and on top.

The folding hood was fitted as an afterthought last summer and the "folding" was a misnomer to start with since it would not go down properly. Having been persuaded to do so, over a period of half an hour, it never rose again until seen to by the body service people. We hope to be able to report faultless folding next spring.

With the exception of the battery, everything is reasonably accessible for the help-yourself man. Replacing the dip stick, when you eventually find the hole, you have to take care to push it right home. Garage-men mostly don't, so you risk overfilling.

At night the Stag is pretty good; no nasty reflections, excellent full beams and clean, not too abrupt cut off. With a full load, the tail goes down and the lamp beams up, causing hard words and embarrassment. We have not felt the need for spot lamps, particularly since the not entirely good regulations forbid the use of a single offside lamp in fog. It is not easy to read the main instruments at night, but you soon learn that 30 mph is just past 9 o'clock, 70 mph at 12 and peak rpm at 3 o'clock.

At present we have a Smiths' radio and cartridge player fitted, with a pair of speakers tucked in above the rear pockets. This equipment gives adequate two-speaker stereo; two more speakers would be better. The standard single speaker for radio (central front and temporarily disconnected) gives good, clear volume. For comparison, we also have a portable Smiths' tape recorder-cassette player wired in. This gives facilities for alternative music, or for dictation, or will record direct from the radio. Finally, we have a Readycall FM radio-telephone, which at present gives us Greater London coverage only, and goes off at 8 pm.. and weekends. You have your own call-up signal and there is private conversation both ways. Quality of reception is usually good and free from interference but there are a few areas of weak reception. No sound is heard when the set is on until you call, or are called.

As with all *Autocar's* long-term test cars, one man is in charge, but all drive the Stag from time to time. The concensus of opinion is definitely favourable. It is a nice car with a satisfying touch of elegance and spirit. Now that Triumph have been able to deliver some few thousands of them at home and abroad, we are beginning to hear from owners who agree.

Sometimes we are only too ready to sell our long-term test cars as soon as we can. We hope to keep the Stag for at least a second year. Draw your own conclusions. □

Petrol pipe clamped in such a way that it rubs through on an adjacent bolt head. Here it has been twisted round to show the puncture. Air filter box has been removed

COST and LIFE of EXPENDABLE ITEMS

Item	Life in Miles	Cost per 10,000 Miles
		£ p.
One gallon of 4-star fuel average cost today 35p	19.2	182.00
One pint of top-up oil, average cost today 17p	1,000	1.70
Front disc brake pads (set of 4)	6,500	8.00
Rear brake linings (set of 4)	15,000	4.10
Michelin XAS tyres (front pair)	12,000	23.50
Michelin XAS tyres (rear pair)	12,000	23.50
Service (main interval and actual costs incurred)	6,000	35.44
Total		278.24
Approx. standing charges per year		
Depreciation		150.00
Insurance		58.45
Tax		25.00
Total		**511.69**

Appox. cost per mile = 5.1p

Road Impressions

The Triumph Stag

WHEN I tried the Triumph Stag as a new car, way back in 1970, I was disappointed with several aspects of the car. It has since had time for development, although it remains basically unchanged, so I thought I had better try it again, because it is an interesting concept – a very good-looking sporting car of two-seater size but with room for two more occupants should this be required, a good arrangement of hood when the neat hard-top is not in use, and a very refined vee-eight 3-litre overhead-camshaft power unit.

The British Leyland Press Office complied very readily with my suggestion and so, after a day which had embraced 1930 Bentley and 1973 BMW motoring, I found myself heading for home in a Pimento red Stag with chestnut vinyl upholstery which you could have fooled me was real leather. It was shod with Avon tubeless radial tyres with those smooth sidewalls that reminded me for a moment of the special track covers of the Brooklands days.

There is no need to describe this Stag in detail, because the specification has not altered since we did this fairly fully in the issue of October 1970. It is amusing that the very complete leather—bound Stag hand-book quotes nut-tightening torques but omits any reference to power output. This the catalogue gives as 146 b.h.p. at 5,700 r.p.m. and the red-area of the tachometer begins at 6,500 r.p.m., although only in some pretty brisk driving did I have to take the revs. that high.

For some reason the Stag prompts journalists to photograph it with the appropriate animal

STAG MEETS STAG. One of our contemporaries drove a Stag into Europe to try to photograph the animal with the Triumph, so we are rather pleased that this picture was taken economically without driving far from London.

beside it. My friend Philip Turner of a weekly contemporary once had this irresistible urge and I believe went far into Europe to try to satisfy it, but had to admit defeat. So I had been amused to learn that, before I took over the car, one of the MOTOR SPORT photographers had secured the picture which heads this article without going much more than about 20 miles from the London office. . . .

My initial impressions of the Stag were as unfortunate as before. The power-assisted rack-and-pinion steering is far too light and the weaving effect of what seemed to be too-hard independent rear suspension constitutes handling which does not appeal at all. This is a pity, because the steering is very high geared $2\frac{5}{8}$th.-turns, lock-to-lock, from a very small racing-type wheel, with a really small turning circle. On longer acquaintance with the car I got accustomed to the lack of feel, the "in-built over-steer", at the wheel but this and the dodgy running damns the Stag in my view. Admittedly the steering is consistent, which that on the 1970 test-car was not. And Rolls-Royce Silver Shadow drivers have a similar light control to put up with. So perhaps there are Stag owners who do not regard their cars as sufficiently sporting to warrent better control characteristics. There is now only a faint sound from the power assistance via its belt-driven pump, but it is the end-product which distresses me.

That apart, the Triumph Stag is a nice motor-car. It has much of the tradition of the older sports-cars about it, but with all the very smooth power delivery and excellent bottom-end torque to be expected of a multi-cylinder engine of nearly 3-litres capacity. This adds up to very real and readily delivered performance. The ride is on the hard side, but comfortable, the gears are changed by a long lever with considerable across-the-gate movement, but one which functions very nicely, reverse easily obtained by slapping the lever to the right between the 3rd and top-gear positions. Its knob contains the switch for the overdrive, labelled IN and OUT, a selection which could not be more convenient. The hand brake lies between the front seats but its hefty hand-grip needed a good pull to make it hold. In torrential rain, no water entered car or boot.

The disc-drum servo brakes are efficient. The engine has a healthy exhaust note but with the electric windows up, there is scarcely any sound, either when accelerating or cruising fast – a veritable Rolls-Royce among sporting cars.

The V8 Triumph Stag has handsome lines.

Instruments – m.p.h./k.p.h., trip/total 140 m.p.h., speedometer, clock, heat, volts and fuel-level gauges, and tachometer – are set on a walnut veneer dash, all on the driver's side, and have been neatly recalibrated, with new green night-time illumination. The eight warning lights are in the grouped Triumph circular cluster, there is a variety of fresh-air vents, and twin stalks control the lamps, horn, turn indicators, two-speed wipers, etc. There are elaborate arrangements for heating and ventilation, including knob-wound half-windows and openable side windows, and refinements include the essential Triplex Hotline heated rear window, height-adjustment for the front seats, adjustable steering column, red lamps in the doors, boot illumination, lockable flush-fitting fuel filler, excellent door locks, etc. Before the front passenger are a generous-size lockable glove box and stowage shelf, and elastic-topped pockets provide extra stowage space. Altogether, then, this Triumph Stag is a very well-appointed and well-contrived car, with good door locks, stainless steel body mouldings and screen surround, etc. It has anti-dazzle visors not always found on soft-top cars and for safety in open form there is the T-shaped roll-over bar. Recent mods. include the smaller steering wheel, a rest for the clutch foot, the option of tinted glass, o/d as standard, and automatic transmission for a modest extra cost.

Realising that 25 years ago I road-tested an Allard in N. Wales and that it had a V8 engine of 3.6-litres but with side valves, and that the Stag has an o.h.c. V8 power unit of all but 3-litres, I set off to cover much of the same terrain. Alas, crawling holiday traffic has increased tenfold and what with congestion in Dolgellau and flooded roads outside this busy town, I had to cut out some of the route. However, the Stag did ascend and descend Bwlch-y-Groes, which anyway is child's play to a modern car, but the track away from Lake Vyrnwy on which I had got the Allard stuck (MOTOR SPORT, June, 1948) proved elusive.

One likely track petered out hundreds of feet above the road with a sheer drop on the right, calling for some careful reversing, and I am inclined to think that the decently-surfaced but narrow route to Bala was the one we had used previously, when as a rough track it caused us some mild adventure.

These excursions proved that the Stag has ample clearance under its twin exhaust pipes and plenty of controllable power. With judicious use of overdrive I got 20.5 m.p.g. of four-star petrol and no oil was needed after 600 miles. By the time that long day's driving was over I had almost come to accept the lack of feel in the steering and the odd running of the independent rear suspension. It is commendable that British Leyland offer multi-cylinder vee engines in Jaguar, Daimler, Rover and Triumph cars. I do not like the handling of the Stag or of the Rover 3500 V8, so I am hoping that the new MG V8, which eschews i.r.s. and a De Dion rear axle for a beam back axle, may suit me better. It is interesting to note that the price of the M.G.-B V8 GT at £2,294 compares favourably with that of the Stag, which sells for £2,615 in soft-top form, or £2,720 with soft-top and detachable hard-top; it should be remembered that this includes a well-designed hood which stows away efficiently and four Lucas halogen headlamps. I have yet to try the new M.G., but anticipate that this effectively two-seater, permanently closed coupe, will appeal to a more sporting driver than the Stag: the two V8 models should complement each other in British Leyland's extensive range. – W.B.

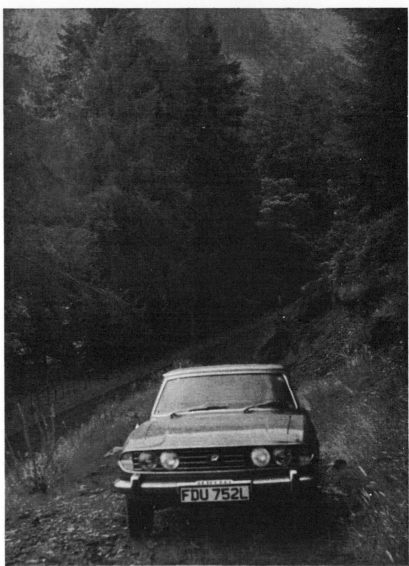

Stag in stalking country.

TRIUMPH STAG
27,000 mile report

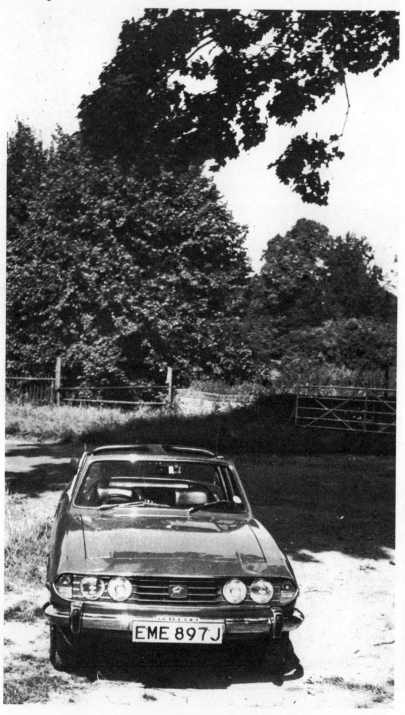
EME 897J

AUTOCAR 13 September 1973

When we wrote our first long-term test in February last year, Stags were still scarce. We had bought our red automatic in December 1970 — one of the first off the line — and it had covered its first 13,000 miles in 13 months. Now, after nearly three years, it has done more than twice that mileage and continues to be a pleasant and usually well-behaved car.

STAGS SEEM to be gregarious. Someone buys one and within a few months there are half a dozen in the immediate neighbourhood. Now, there are at least six others operating within a quarter of a mile of our Stag's garage in Surrey. Not infrequently, we are approached by complete strangers, "Oh, you've got a Stag! What do you think of it?" And there is an air of these cars being rather unknown and exciting. To the extent that they are 2+2 convertibles of modest overall size and cost, and with lively performance, they are still quite exclusive. There is little to compete or compare directly with them.

Once you drive V8, you are reluctant to go back to a six or a four unless it is very good and responsive — which usually means expensive too. In our previous test report, we asked for more zip from the Triumph V8 without loss of its attractive gentleness. By raising the compression ratio from 8.8 to 9.25, in common with that of the Dolomite, the makers have now taken a first step and provided a fraction more performance for those occasions when you will want to press on. Our old Stag is still good for 110 mph and will cover a standing ¼-mile in 18 seconds; and of course the manual cars are a bit quicker.

We chose automatic transmission because of the high proportion of our day-to-day driving which has to be done in built-up areas and heavy traffic. In these conditions, the overall average mpg had remained very steady at 19.3. Out on the open roads we usually manage 21 mpg.

The long warm-up period, in cold weather, and the prolonged use of choke that goes with it, seems to affect the fuel consumption more than with most cars. This may be one of the causes of the otherwise unexplained improvement in consumption for the period April to August this year for which our records show 21.6 mpg overall.

Last month we had the first signs of electric pump trouble — an occasional flurry of ticking but no fuel to the carburettors. Without doing anything about it, fuel would eventually flow again. Soon this changed to continuous, fast ticking at all times and low pressure delivery to the carburettors. To forestall trouble we fitted a replacement pump and all is well again. This is not a difficult job, the pump being accessible behind the side lining of the boot, which is "attached" by self tappers (only one of each registers with a hole in the car structure).

We have had no regrets about going automatic, in spite of the slightly higher fuel consumption. If we want to hurry, we use the central selector like a manual shift and go up into the high 5,000s of revs, which the engine willingly gives. In traffic the almost continuous use of a clutch can be very tiring and we are glad to be spared it.

After prolonged driving in traffic, the engine is sometimes hesitant and needs to clear its throat for a mile or so but it never actually misfires or "loses" plugs (except as described later) and a short spell on the open road makes it crisp again. The engine always starts, however frosty the night. In fact, like so many V8s, any reluctance to start — or re-start — comes when it is very hot, then it seems best to put the accelerator on the floor until it fires.

In our first assessment of this car we listed the large number of items of equipment which are included in the standard specification. One of these is the power-assisted steering. This takes a little time to get used to because of the lightness and very quick response, yet we now say again that it is first class and can be a real safety factor if sudden avoiding action or skid correction should be necessary. The reduction in steering wheel diameter by one inch on current production cars is a sensible change.

Another feature we continue to appreciate is the 2-way adjustment of the steering column — up and down on angle, as well as in and out. This, together with a 3-way seat adjustment, means that almost everyone can get comfortable and on long journeys alter their sitting and arm positions slightly if they begin to feel "seized up". For the over six-footers with long bodies, the head room even in front is inadequate unless they are prepared to angle the seat back and recline a little. Owing to the catch knobs on the upper outside edge of the front seats colliding with the hood-frame boxes, the recline of the front seats is limited. Someone forced one of our seats back to about a 45 deg. angle, thereby dislodging the knob from the metal-strip lever and this in turn gashed the trim material.

How has the Stag come out under the wear and tear headings? So far as the "original sin" is concerned, it has never packed up and left us stranded. It came near to doing so on one occasion and this in fact was the only serious trouble we have had. Previously, we had found that every few thousand miles, minor clunks and clonks had developed in the suspension and transmission. A check around the underneath revealed various loose attachments and sloppy bushes. Nothing dangerous; just some unwanted movement.

Having read that Stags tow well we fitted a Witter Mongoose tow-ball (20,866 miles) and shortly afterwards towed a 14cwt trailer for some 200 miles. A little later we took delivery of an Eccles Amethyst caravan from Newmarket and towed it to Farnborough and back. On both occasions the car did in fact tow very well but a few weeks later there developed more noises in the suspension. It was 40 miles later before this could be checked and on the way to our garage there were ominous signs of final-drive trouble, difficult to describe in words if you have not experienced them. Backing into our parking bay produced dental crunches which lead us to put the Stag on to a transporter to Triumph's service depot at Acton. This was at 22,213 miles. Some weeks later the car emerged in good running order but the invoice shook us somewhat. While the labour charges seemed fair enough, the £101 for two half shafts and another £69.50 for the diff. seemed pretty steep. Equivalent shafts for the Granada cost only £35.70 each with CV joint while for a Jaguar XJ12 with Hooke joints you pay only £15.61 each. Not until you get to high quality imported cars like the 280 Mercedes do you get to a figure like £62 per shaft and joint.

One day, an excited gent flagged us down and shouted "Some-one's stuffed a rag up your pipe and it's on fire!" We had in fact noticed that the stuffing was coming out of one of the end silencers which was both corroded and eroded quite badly. Two miles later another chap tapped on the window

Our Stag in open form. The current hardtop version now includes the hood which was formerly an extra

and said "Gorrabirdsnestinyerpipe mate!" To please him we stuffed the glass fibre back, tidied up the jagged end of the outer case and it is still in use but looking tatty, as the picture shows.

Triumph admit to early hood folding trouble. The majority of Stags seem to keep their hard tops all the year round. Some owners, if they looked in the hood box, might well be surprised to find it empty, as we originally were. Our hood, an optional extra, was fitted after purchase and we have become reasonably adept at getting it up and down, now that we know the sequence of actions must be correct and that it is really a job for two people working together. The hood and its seals are a poor fit and one result is that the wind noise is considerable above about 60 mph. Even so, it has proved to be waterproof and reasonably draught-free and has not suffered any appreciable damage or rubbing while stowed away through three winters. The car has been running open for most of four months of the year. The front-seat occupants find it cosy and free from wind buffeting.

Among the few minor troubles experienced has been the reluctance of the starter to engage for two short periods. A clean-up of the contacts and connections more or less

Not a bird's nest up the exhaust pipe but the glass-fibre stuffing coming out of the badly corroded tailpipe silencer

cured this problem, and a new battery fitted after 25 months also helped. The battery mounting is highly inconvenient and you almost need to "get a man in" to remove the battery from its tray.

Courtesy light switches and door latches have needed occasional attention and the outer trim strip carrying the rubber seal for the passenger side window blew out completely. Fortunately we were able to retrieve it undamaged but were not able to refit it because the clips were strained. The whole window now rattles but probably for different co-incidental reasons.

Earlier this year we ran into a spell of rough running and misfiring. The car went in for service — plugs, points and so on — and came out no better. "Like tennis elbow" the garage man said, after a second attempt, "There's nothing actually wrong, it'll work off". And later: "Give it good burst down the motorway". Being interpreted, this meant "We don't know what the trouble is and would prefer not to have any more bother with this car".

A few days later, after the burst down the motorway, the engine was positively limping and stalled at most traffic lights. It seemed to pull in bursts, if you could work the speed up. So we earmarked the next Saturday morning for personal attention at home. We went through the ignition from end to end and were satisfied that all plugs sparked. Each cylinder had proper compression and the mixture supply was apparently normal. Then we got a clue.

TRIUMPH STAG

With the engine set to idle, as best it could on four or five cylinders, we pulled off number 1 plug lead and found it ran better. With number 2 off, it ran better still. Could we have the leads crossed? We checked this and the answer was no. One and two cylinders, at the front of each block, fire consecutively (order: 1,2,7,8,4,5,6,3).

Continuing with our elimination process, we took number 3 lead off but the engine shook once and stopped, so that one was doing some work! With 3 lead back on we tried 7 off and this had no appreciable effect on running. Now we understood. We took off the distributor, cleaned the inside very carefully and examined it in a bright light and there

they were: a tiny jagged line of hair-cracks, linking contacts 1, 2 and 7. Our spark had been jumping along these hair-cracks, sometimes firing the plug, sometimes not, and sometimes firing one of the plugs at the wrong time. The faulty distributor cap moulding was disconnected and the local Lucas agent produced a replacement off the shelf for £2.36. With the new one fitted, the engine burst instantly into smooth and healthy life — and has not looked back since then.

Stag headlamps, quartz halogen, are very good but there is one snag. If the car is

Left: A feature of the Stag is the padded roll-over bar. In spite of its sporting looks the car is a four seater with a reasonable boot

Below: Persistent misfiring which professional garage attention failed to cure was finally traced to a hairline crack in the distributor cap between contacts 1, 2 and 7

carrying four people or heavy luggage, or both, the tail goes down and the lamp beams go up — to the irritation of approaching drivers and the embarrassment of Stag owners. Except to set them so that they have only a limited range when driving solo, we have not found a solution. Some other British models have a similar problem.

So far as regular check-ups are concerned, oil consumption can be almost forgotten, still being negligible, and the power steering reservoir which originally needed frequent topping up, now remains level. The radiator also remains full.

The paint work and plate are standing up fairly well with the exception of two nasty blisters of rust adjacent to the trim shield, one on the nose, the other on the tail. We have cleared these two spots and inhibited them with Naval Jelly and after touching them up they are now just visible but no longer unsightly.

The spare wheel and tools are kept under the boot floor which is detachable, and has a loose carpet on top. The little plastic fasteners meant to hold the floor panel are brittle and some have snapped. Although still quite presentable, the carpet does not stay flat but the floor section remains in place. The size of the boot is marginal for journeys. With careful arrangement, two suitcases and other soft packages can be accommodated.

Those are some of the hard facts of Stag ownership. The list of significant trouble after 26,000 miles is shorter than average — which is a reflection on the reliability of too many modern cars. Since pride and pleasure of ownership are so important, we must record that the family enjoy the car; those who drive like driving it, all approve of its handy size and light controls and appreciate the convenience of electrically-powered windows. Next year we may well buy a replacement Stag embodying the several small improvements which are the outcome of three years' experience and development. □

Improvements embodied in current Stags

1. Clearer instrument markings.
2. Brighter instrument lighting.
3. Provision for head-rests on front seats.
4. Smaller diameter steering wheel.
5. Intermittent wiper action.
6. Rest for driver's left foot.
7. Extra courtesy lamp on roll-over bar.
8. Under-bonnet arrangements tidied up.
9. Overdrive as a standard fitting on manual cars.
10. Stronger bumper mountings.
11. Flame resistant trim materials.
12. Tail panel and sills painted matt black.
13. Double coach line added at waist level.
14. New options.
15. Special cast alloy wheels.
16. Laminated windscreen and Sundym glass.

Stags are still in short supply and a wait of three to six months for delivery must be expected. In 1971 home market deliveries were 2,136, as compared with 1,551 for export. Last year, the figures rose to 3,262 at home but dropped to 967 abroad, many overseas orders having been lost because customers got tired of waiting and went elsewhere. Stag sales appear to have suffered considerably from a series of production hold-ups but at home the selective demand seems likely to continue, assuming that the model survives British Leyland's future rationalization plans. The proportion of women owners appears to be higher than average and there may be something to learn from this about the qualities they appreciate. □

STAG

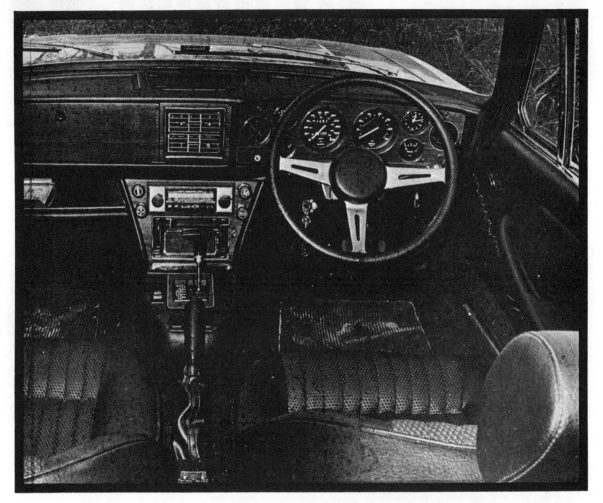

85 ▶

Perhaps it could be fitted with 'air' as standard equipment, but Leyland Australia do not consider the factory job capable of offsetting Aussie temperatures to their complete satisfaction, so they bring in Stags without air conditioning and recommend certain local companies to fit an integrated system for between $600 and $700. That's pretty good, considering you get a local unit which can cope with the climate, and, it's fully-integrated.

There are no dramatic changes to the standard equipment levels on Stag, except that the next shipment of cars will feature the nifty mag wheels as standard equipment rather than as an option.

Leyland Australia report that between 450 and 500 Stags have been delivered to Australian owners over the past five years and expect to sell more than 400 in the next year — so that's a good indication of the increasing popularity of this fine English touring car.

You'll gather we liked it, and we did.

The Stag does everything it's supposed to and is a smart, sophisticated machine — we just hope Leyland Australia is keeping a close eye on demand, because we think it will skyrocket as this relatively mysterious stranger makes more new friends down under. **Ⓗ**

COST SCHEDULE

Make/Model: . Triumph Stag Automatic

Pricing (basic): $10,210
    (as tested): $10,414

Options (prices):
Alloy wheels: $185
Stereo cassette/radio: $199

Registration: $153.15

Insurance Category: 4
Rates quoted below are for drivers over 25 with 60 percent no-claim bonus and where the car is under hire-purchase. This is the minimum premium level — decreasing rates of experience and lower age groups may have varying excesses and possible premium loadings.
Non-tariff: $341
Tariff: $377
N.R.M.A.: .... $410 (Group 8)

Warranty: .... 12 months or 20,000 km

Service:
Initial service is free. This covers the first 1500 km and includes inspection and adjustments. Oil used is charged for.

Other Services:
Lubrication and maintenance services every 5000 km. Parts and labour is charged.

Spare Parts:
(recommended cost breakdown)
Disc Pads (set of four): $27.84
Muffler (front): $32.00
Muffler (rear): $41.95
Windscreen: ... $37.20, $119 laminated
Shock Absorbers: Front: .$46.20 (strut)
    Rear: $23.50
Headlamp Assembly: $46.00
Taillamp Assembly: $17.00
Bumpers: Front: `.` $162.00
    Rear: $70.00
Front Guard: $104.00

ROAD TEST Triumph Stag

The Stag is at its best either fully open or with the beautifully made hard-top in position. Removing or replacing the top, however, is a trial of strength

FOR : very well finished and equipped ; nice controls and instruments ; smooth, automatic transmission ; good ride ; enjoyable to drive
AGAINST : limited luggage and passenger space ; seats too flat ; hood difficult to erect ; hardtop too heavy

The predictable success of the Stag has resulted in a year's waiting list for Triumph's top-of-the-range model. This test of the latest automatic indicates that detail improvements have bettered an already good car, so the delays are unlikely to improve.

Some (subjective) improvements like the quieter and smoother engine and the tauter handling can only be explained by detail developments, perhaps better production, as there have been no design changes to account for them. Improvements that have been made include a reduction in assistance for the power steering to give the driver more "feel"; the inclusion of a divided braking system; an intermittent wipe facility; optional head restraints ; flame retardant material for the trim; and optional alloy wheels. Modifications have also been made to the folding mechanism for the hood, and the silencing system, and rationalisation has made the combustion chambers and pistons the same as those of the Dolomite. This has resulted in an insignifi-

cant increase in horsepower o 1 bhp, and a reduction i torque of 3 lb ft. Visual altera tions include matt black stone resistant paint on the sills and rear panel, and side stripes.

The Stag's alloy-headed V8— yet to be used in any other Bri tish Leyland vehicle—is based o two Dolomite engines pu together, but with a shorte stroke giving a capacity o 2997 cc rather than 3708 cc When we first tested the car we thought the engine was les smooth than it ought to be for V8. Now we withdraw that obser vation as that of the latest ca was very smooth indeed, an made very little clatter; th restrained burble from the ex haust is rather pleasing.

With its tiny power increas and lower overall gearing the acceleration of the automatic i almost identical to that of th manual we tested before, an there is nothing to be gained b using the manual hold and hang ing on to the gears. But wherea the manual car (on which over drive is now standard) will wine

Above: the sumptuous seats lack thigh support despite the facility of a built-in cushion tilt. Top right: a smaller diameter wheel and less assistance give more feel to the steering. Below left: the built-in roll cage not only offers protection but stiffens the framework as well. Below right: entry to the rear is awkward and headroom limited. The seat, however, is comfortable

Above: the fan-boosted swivel vents in the centre are effective, unlike the ram operated side ones. Below: the stalk controls are excellent

The gearchange is sited too far forward, all other controls are well placed

The comprehensive instrumentation is easy to read and well-sited. We query the fitting of a battery condition meter in preference to an oil pressure gauge

up to well over 120 mph in o/d top, the automatic managed no more than 112.4 mph for a lap at MIRA, and 116.8 mph on the most favourable flying quarter mile. Even so, the automatic would be a comfortable cruiser at more than 100 mph were it not for considerable wind noise.

Fuel consumption is also affected by the automatic trans-'mission, the touring consumption deteriorating by as much as 4 mpg. Even so, the overall value of 18.9 mpg is not bad considering the performance and how hard we drove the car. With its 9.25:1 compression ratio, the Stag feeds on four-star fuel without pinking.

An American-style "T" shift controls the Borg-Warner 35 gearbox. Its dog-leg change pattern is precise, but the positions are unnecessarily close. Moreover, the selection guide is set for LHD models and therefore is at times masked by the lever itself. One virtue of the dog-leg pattern is that it prevents inadvertent selection of neutral, a move that's all too easy on many other automatics.

Automatic changes both up and down the gearbox are very smooth on part throttle, but can be quite jerky under full acceleration. The kickdown is also very responsive at mid-range speeds, but is reluctant to select first on

the move even at 5 mph.

Perhaps the most significant improvement is to the steering. A smaller diameter wheel and a reduction in the amount of assistance has resulted in much better response and feel. You can now use the performance with much more confidence, though some say the steering is still too light.

Understeer is the predominant handling characteristic, though such was the adhesion of the fat Avon radials on our car that the breakaway point was very high indeed. Over bumpy surfaces the car is less tidy, with traces of lurch and diagonal pitch, and it is on these occasions that still more feel to the steering would be appreciated. Under most conditions, however, the car is very well mannered and can be thrown into corners in perfect safety. A slight wriggle after powering out of a turn suggests that there is still a trace of spline lock-up in the driveshafts, though this quirk is far less pronounced than it was on earlier cars.

Another fault, perhaps peculiar to our test car, was slight sponginess in the brakes, the powerful servo-assisted disc/drum set-up needing an occasional pump to restore full efficiency.

Large catches set into the side of the seats release the backrests for access to the rear. This would be less of a scramble if the whole

MOTOR week ending October 27 1973

MOTOR ROAD TEST No 53/73 • TRIUMPH STAG

PERFORMANCE

CONDITIONS
Weather	Dry, wind 4-15 mph
Temperature	58-66 F
Barometer	29.8 in. Hg
Surface	Dry tarmac

MAXIMUM SPEEDS
	mph	kph
Banked circuit	112.4	180.9
Best ¼ mile	116.8	187.9
Terminal speeds:		
at ¼ mile	66	106
at kilometre	83	134
Speed in gears (at 6500 rpm).		
1st	55	89
2nd	89	143

ACCELERATION FROM REST
mph	sec	kph	sec
0-30	3.6	0-40	2.9
0-40	5.2	0-60	4.7
0-50	7.5	0-80	7.3
0-60	9.9	0-100	10.4
0-70	12.8	0-120	14.5
0-80	17.0	0-140	20.3
0-90	22.4	0-160	29.2
0-100	30.2		
Stand'g ¼	17.6	Stand'g km	32.2

ACCELERATION IN KICK-DOWN
mph	sec	kph	sec
30-50	3.9	40-60	1.8
40-60	4.7	60-80	2.6
50-70	5.3	80-100	3.1
60-80	7.1	100-120	4.1
70-90	9.6	120-140	5.8
80-100	13.2	140-160	8.9

FUEL CONSUMPTION
Touring*   21.7 mpg
     13.0 litres/100 km

Overall	18.9 mpg	
	15.0 litres/100 km	
Fuel grade	98 octane (RM)	
	4 star rating	
Tank capacity	12.75 galls	
	57.9 litres	
Max range	276 miles	
	— km	
Test distance	2119 miles	
	3409 km	

* Consumption midway between 30 mph and maximum less 5 per for acceleration.

SPEEDOMETER (mph)
Speedo	30	40	50	60	70	80	90	100
True mph	30	41	52	62½	72	82½	93	104

Distance recorder: accurate.

WEIGHT
	cwt	kg
Unladen weight*	24.7	1254.8
Weight as tested	28.4	1442.8

* With fuel for approx 50 miles.

Performance tests carried out by Motor's staff at the Motor Industry Research Association proving ground, Lindley.

GENERAL SPECIFICATION

ENGINE
Cylinders	V8 (90°)
Capacity	2997 cc (182.9 cu in.)
Bore/stroke	86/64.5 mm (3.38/2.53 in.)
Cooling	Water
Block	Cast iron
Head	Aluminium alloy
Valves	2-ohc
Valve timing	
inlet opens	16° btdc
inlet closes	56° abdc
ex opens	56° bbdc
ex closes	16° atdc
Compression	9.25 : 1
Carburetter	Two Stromberg CDS (E) V
Bearings	5 main
Fuel pump	Electrical
Max power	146 bhp (DIN) at 5700 rpm
Max torque	167 lb ft (DIN) at 3500 rpm

TRANSMISSION
Type	Borg Warner type 35 automatic
Internal ratios and mph/100 rpm	
Top	1.00 : 1/20.0
2nd	1.45 : 1/13.7
1st	2.39 : 1/8.4
Rev	2.09 : 1
Final drive	Hypoid bevel 3.70 : 1

BODY/CHASSIS
Construction	Unitary all steel
Protection	Phosphated by 7-stage process

SUSPENSION
Front	Independent by Mac-Pherson struts, coil springs, telescopic dampers, anti-roll bar
Rear	Independent by semi-trailing arms, coil springs and telescopic dampers

STEERING
Type	Rack and pinion
Assistance	Yes
Toe-in	⅛-¼ in.
Camber	1° positive ± 1°
Castor	2 ± 1°
King pin	10½° ± 1°
Rear toe-in	0-⅛ in.

BRAKES
Type	Disc/drum
Servo	Yes
Circuits	Yes
Rear valve	No
Adjustment	Self-adjusting

WHEELS
Type	Steel 5J
Tyres	185 HR14 radial
Pressures	26 F; 30 R

ELECTRICAL
Battery	12 volt, 56 ah
Polarity	Negative earth
Generator	Alternator
Fuses	12
Headlights	4 x 5¾ Quartz Halogen

COMPARISONS

	Capacity cc	Price £	Max mph	0-60 sec	30-50* sec	Overall mpg	Touring mpg	Length ft in	Width ft in	Weight cwt	Boot cu ft
Triumph Stag	2997	2685	112.4	9.9	3.9	18.9	21.7	14 6.75	5 3.5	24.7	3.6
Reliant Scimitar GTE	2994	2517	—	8.7	7.6	21.7	28.2	14 2.25	5 5	22.8	—
Alfa Romeo 2000 GTV	1962	2689	115.3	8.9	10.9	20.8	26.9	13 4.5	5 2.5	20.2	6.8†
Datsun 240Z	2392	2690	125.1	8.3	9.0	25.7	31.2	13 7	5 4	20.3	11.4
Lotus Elan +2S 130	1558	2789	121.0	7.7	8.5	21.0	26.1	14 0.5	5 3.5	16.8	4.2†
MGB GT V8	3528	2309	125.3	7.7	6.2	19.8	25.7	12 9	5 0	21.2	6.6
Opel Commodore Coupe GS	2490	2800	106.8	12.0	4.7	17.1	21.3	15 0	5 7.5	24.3	11.3

*kickdown for Stag and Commodore   †measured with boxes not cases

Make : Triumph
Model : Stag
Makers : British Leyland (Triumph) Ltd, Coventry England
Price : £2303.0 plus £191.92 car tax plus £249.49 VAT equals £2744.41. Automatic transmission £45.29 (in lieu of overdrive), Sundym glass £45.29, alloy wheels £68.52; total as tested equals £2903.51

seat tilted forward. Once you are installed in the back, headroom beneath the hood or hardtop is limited, and the backrest is a little upright. For short journeys, however, there is sufficient room for two adults.

Boot space is very limited, but there is excellent stowage for oddments, with map pockets in the front doors and the back of the seats, handy trays to the side of the rear seats, as well as a parcel shelf and glovebox in the facia and a flat area on the console ahead of the gearlever.

The driving position is very good and can be adjusted to suit all shapes and sizes. The steering column, for instance, can be altered for reach and rake and a handle on the front of the seat alters the tilt of the cushion, though we found the range of adjustment insufficient and the cushion always too flat and lacking in thigh support. The backrests will recline fully.

A large brake pedal allows for left- or right-foot braking, but some of our testers complained that both pedals were offset too far to the right. A rare and welcome refinement is a footrest for the left foot.

The traditional Triumph fingertip controls now include parking lights and electric washers, as well as the newly added intermittent wipe facility. The instruments are unchanged apart from a slightly restyled calibration.

Though Triumph say no alterations have been made to the suspension, the ride seemed better than before. It can become a little turbulent on poor secondary roads, where it feels underdamped, but unlike so many cars that are comfortable at speed the Stag has an excellent town ride.

Ram pressure through the eyeball face vents is poor but output can be supplemented by the opening quarterlights and the fanboosted swivel vents in the centre of the facia. Overall, the heating anr ventilating system is good. our only complaint being heater tends to bleed too much air from the ventilation system.

Road noise was always subdued on this car and engine and exhaust noise have both been cut down, so it is only wind noise that breaks the peace. When the car is open or fitted with the well-sealed hardtop, wind noise is tolerable, but it is very loud with the hood up.

The Stag's equipment can only be described as lavish. Fittings include a clock, map, reversing and parking lights, heated rear window set into the hardtop.

Although the hood and hardtop have been improved, erection of both is still a trial of strength. Fixing the rear hood catch in place calls for much struggling and the hardtop, though beautifully made, requires two strong men to manhandle it on and off.

This test of the updated Stag reaffirms our initial impression that the car is not only unique in character and a highly desirable property, but that the standard of finish makes it a world-beater at the price.

10,000 MILES ON TRIUMPH STAG

by C. John French

This originally started off as a Running Report requested by the Editor (whom God preserve) when I had completed 7000 miles in the Mark 2 Stag. However, with the privilege he shares with the opposite sex of changing his mind at short notice, it appeared that 7000 miles was too far for a Running Report (and rightly so for a gentleman advancing in years), so I threw away the deathless prose I had already submitted and started again, when the car had completed 10,000 miles which apparently makes this a long-term test.

Before proceeding farther, you should know that this report is contributed by the Publishing Director of this highly reliable journal, and not by one of those blasé sophisticated young men who are usually responsible for such affairs. This means, of course, that the views expressed are those of an individual whose journalistic talents are generally confined to judging others, and who is at last free to show his knowledge and skill as a tester and journalist.

The reason for selecting the Stag as my personal car can be traced to the Road Test in Motor in September 1973. I borrowed the test car one evening and with the hood down, motored home to delectable sunny Surrey, and for the first time in many, many years, asked my ever-loving wife if she would care for a blow in the car after dinner. Not being a violent man, she took my meaning immediately and we actually went driving for pleasure in the fresh air in what had almost ceased to exist—a Grand Touring car. Regular readers may remember that the French Blue road test car had Borg-Warner automatic transmission and it was this version, with the addition of a hard top, that Henlys delivered in January 1974. In its hard top role, the car looks very distinguished indeed to my eyes.

The car, driven exclusively by me, has now done just over 10,000 miles, and has proved a source of considerable pleasure from the moment it arrived. It was also regarded with considerable interest, not to say envy, by the rest of the staff and the great British motoring public. Only recently did a gentleman (obviously) say there was only one thing wrong with it; that it was in my and not his possession.

I remember now that the Editor did ask me for some facts and I have kept a meticulous record of the car's behaviour.

For the first six months of its life I left the hard top on and used the car mainly for commuting 34 miles a day. During this period the only faults were a failed bulb on the automatic console and the flasher unit, both replaced at the first free service. Since then the car has given yeoman service.

The automatic transmission and the power steering take most of the fatigue out of commuting in London, and the acceleration on kick-down has I think surprised various other enterprising motorists, left astern at very short notice. The change up in automatic drive with your foot hard down on the accelerator takes place at 40 mph from first to second, and at 70 mph into top; such full throttle changes are marked by a distinct jerk through. Driven normally, the changes are almost imperceptible but in 30 mph zones one has to lift off gently to engage top, which the box is reluctant to do under 40 mph.

During the petrol shortage I was forced on to a 3-star (91 octane) petrol but I could not detect pinking nor any other trouble. I stayed on 3-star in the interests of economy for some time but for high-speed touring (100 mph or more) abroad, there was always the fear of detonation which you couldn't hear, so I now use 4-star again.

Going to Le Mans through France I did notice that the temperature after the first hour was moving nearer to the red danger area, but as I had been holding 6000 rpm on 3-star petrol for some time, perhaps that's not so surprising.

The oil consumption has been negligible—in 10,000 miles, apart from the two service oil changes, it has consumed only 2½ pints. The petrol consumption remains fairly constant between 17-19 mpg when used only in London, but improves to 22-25 mpg on other longer journeys. The average mpg for 10,000 miles is 19.2 which, considering the high town mileage, seems to me very reasonable and

is almost the same as the overall figure of our original road test car. Some of these figures were obtained while the hard top was in position and although I thought they would improve with it off, this has not proved the case—probably the extra drag offsets the lighter weight.

This leads me into a very interesting (and in retrospect amusing) saga—the removal of the hard top and the erection of the hood. Taking the hard top off requires two people but is not too difficult. However, the emergence of the hood for the first time is an altogether different matter.

Carefully following the instructions in the handbook and with the aid of two strong men, we were able to erect it in the manner prescribed—ie engage the front catch pins and after releasing the spring-loaded catches at each side of the frame, then snap (splendid word) the rear plunger into the body catch. Being determined to do things alone, I then lowered the hood again, and with the aforementioned help, not only raised it again but lowered it too. The evening being sunny, I motored home open-aired.

Now, at this time I was living alone (my wife having departed on one of her numerous holidays) and having read the nasty weather forecast for the following day, I decided that the hood must be

Continued on page

	Long term test Stag	Road test Stag
MAXIMUM SPEED		
Lap	115.2	112.4
Best quarter mile	120.0	116.8
ACCELERATION		
0-30	4.8	3.6
0-40	6.8	5.2
0-50	9.8	7.5
0-60	12.2	9.9
0-70	15.3	12.8
0-80	19.5	17.0
0-90	26.4	22.4
0-100	34.7	30.2
Standing quarter	18.7	17.6
Standing km	33.2	32.2
ACCELERATION IN KICK-DOWN		
30-50	5.0	3.9
40-60	5.4	4.7
50-70	5.5	5.3
60-80	7.3	7.1
70-90	11.1	9.6
80-100	15.2	13.2
FUEL CONSUMPTION		
Overall		18.9
Touring	22.1	21.7

Fuel consumption

Tyre wear

O/S front & rear
N/S rear
N/S front
Legal minimum

Fuel consumption graph shows the benefits of obeying the 70 mph limit. Tyre wear graph reveals remarkably low tyre wear for a car of this type

Unique as a Grand Tourer? The Stag in picturesque surroundings with its top in place. Left: the car's dual personality symbolised by its driver's selection of headgear. Below right: tasting the open air delights on the way to Le Mans

The Stag's "very distinguished" profile with hard top in place. It requires two to remove the top, a conversion which had no noticeable effect on the fuel consumption

erected – by myself. I keep reminding myself to tell the manufacturers that unless you are a professional strongman, it is unlikely that the hood can be erected alone except by engaging the *rear* catch first and *then* dealing with the front catches where one can exert some leverage.

At one period whilst trying to follow their instructions, I was standing on a kitchen stool with sweat pouring off me and an evil look on my face, stamping with my foot, endeavouring to engage the rear catch but completely without success. Having gone through their drill four times, I then tried the method I have outlined, that is to engage the rear catch *first* and the front one *last*. The whole operation was then completed in two minutes. The neighbours continue, as before, to regard me strangely as they pass, and mutter "something to do with publishing, I believe".

It is a very efficient hood and there have been no noticeable draughts or leaks in heavy rain. On my particular car, I did for a time experience minor difficulty in engaging one of the tonneau catches which house the hood, but Henlys have now adjusted the cable and it all works very well. In fact the hood is so easily raised and lowered when you know how, that at Le Mans this year, in lovely weather, we lowered the hood to travel from the hotel to the track and then popped it back on in a trice. There is a picture of the car outside the Hotel des Hunaudieres on the Mulsanne Straight which shows how pleasant an open car can be on such occasions (and in fact makes me feel restless to get back).

The pleasure of open-air motoring has another benefit not immediately obvious: you are not tempted to drive very fast because the exhilaration is quite enough at 70 mph. At speeds above this, the buffeting around the back of the neck becomes uncomfortable.

The suspension is firm but not harsh, and improves with a full load. When pushed into a corner, using the power to help the car round, an unwanted kick-down change can cause oversteer, but one

soon allows for this and there always seems to be an ample reserve of adhesion on the Michelin XAS radials, when entering one of those corners which appears as though it will never end. Nevertheless, the rear-end does rock when going really fast through winding main-road turns.

The power-assisted brakes, discs at the front and self-adjusting drums at the back, have performed very well. I wore out a set of front pads in the first 3500 miles but a harder set of replacement Ferodos are still wearing well.

One word of warning. I thought I'd read the handbook thoroughly but overlooked the manufacturer's instruction not to raise or lower the electrically operated windows without the engine running. Consequently I left myself with a flat battery at the Lygon Arms, Broadway, and I would like to thank the garage there who started me with jump leads and would not accept a fee.

When the Stag was delivered I had fitted a Lucas audio LS120 push-button radio, described in full in *Motor*, June 19, 1974; as it has proved very satisfactory, I agree

with the assessment of it in that issue.

In a long motoring life one has many experiences. I remember in my very first car, a pre-war Standard 10, managing a complete spin on ice, finishing up still proceeding in the right direction. In an Austin utility during the war I had a slight collision with an excessively large steam locomotive during the blackout on the docks at Marseilles. I have been rolled over by an over-enthusiastic French chauffeur in a Delage sedanca-de-ville (on the only hairpin on the pass from Marseilles to Toulon with a ditch instead of a precipice). Inevitably, I suppose I was likely to have a fire sometime as well, and it happened at 9,300 miles in the Stag – a burning moment to remind you how important it is to have a fire extinguisher.

The fire was caused by the positive lead from the battery chafing on the pipe feeding the power steering pump. On a run back from Brighton, I noticed that the engine appeared to be running hot so I opened the bonnet lid and had quite a nasty turn – about 4-5 inches of the positive lead was white hot with a small flame from the smouldering insulation. Amazingly

a small hole had also been rubbed in the oil pipe and with the admission of the air by raising the lid, I suddenly had flames a foot high.

Fortunately I had in the boot an absolutely splendid device called the Tyrenfire extinguisher marketed by East London Hydraulics Ltd., Tyre Division, 46 Spurstowe Road, Hackney, London E8. This is a CO_2 extinguisher so easy to operate that I read the instructions on the top as I ran from the boot back to the engine. By a simple turn of the nozzle top, the fire was immediately extinguished; turning the nozzle in the opposite direction stopped the flow of CO_2, leaving an ample charge still available. Fortunately, the incidental damage was virtually nil. This extinguisher can be easily re-charged and can also be used for inflating flat tyres and is a very worthwhile investment at £7 to £9 according to size.

I notice that on the latest Stag there is a clip on the positive lead to prevent any movement; in their repair to the electrics of my car, Henlys taped the lead up to save me from burning before my time.

With 4-star petrol at its present 54p per gallon, it would cost £274.11 for 10,000 miles for the fuel, to use the Stag as I have done, mainly in urban areas, probably 25 per cent cheaper in the country.

Summing up, I'd like to dwell on the effect the Stag has had on me, which amuses my friends – I have grown my hair longer, wear more extraordinary ties and racy hats and generally behave as though I have shed 20 years, which can only mean that I am enjoying the car immensely. One does not look out of place in the commuter stream and can out-dash the coxiest of county show gentry when desired – in all, a very pleasing dual purpose Grand Touring car. It is also very pleasant to motor to the office on fine mornings with the hood down – it gives one the impression of proceeding on a day of fun instead of the usual nose-to-the-grindstone stuff.

If permitted, I will give you more information of the Stag's progress at a later mileage.

STAG-SWEET

AND FLEET

STYLISHLY individual and sophisticated in personality the Triumph Stag is a true gentleman's sporting carriage. It's also well-mannered, comfortable, thoroughly British, and we loved it.

RIGHT: It's not what you'd call a large boot, but for two people touring there is ample accommodation behind the front seats to supplement the boot. Note carpeted finish and large toolkit.
BELOW: Handling is stable and predictable, but the power steering has a slightly dead feel at speeds over 110km/h. The optional mags and wide track give Stag a wide stance on the road.

T RIUMPH'S Stag is still a relative mystery to many Australians — the car was in dramatically short supply at its introduction in July 1970. There were hardly enough for Brits with the ready cash, let alone the Aussie export market.

With its current $10,000-plus pricetag here, it's a safe bet Stags will retain their mystique, and exclusivity. It has been in relatively popular demand, but now with a new thrust by Leyland Australia, aimed at the top end of the luxury market, this car and a number of other luxury Leyland cars will be seen more often on Australian roads. The Stag *is* a *luxury* car — in the truest sense of the word — it costs a

lot of money, it's basically only a two-plus-two and consequently it's a luxury to be able to own one. It's not quite as self-indulgent as some touring coupes, there's ample accommodation for four over short distances, but it is really an excellent piece of luxury *personal* transport.

The styling caused mixed reactions during our test period. Some said it was dated, some said it was confused and awkward and many drooled over is Michelotti-inspired lines.

The big styling points of the car are its lift-off hardtop and the massive integrated roll-bar. Everything else is basically the same as the current Triumph sedans. The hardware is

identical, as is the mechanical layout, the only real difference being the V8 engine.

The 2997cc V8 powerplant was built exclusively for the Stag. Basically it is two Dolomite four cylinder engines arranged at 90degrees. The output (109kW) is adequate to push the car along at respectable touring speeds, with plenty in reserve. The test car ran down the standing 400m under 18seconds and that's quite impressive.

In Drive the excellent Borg-Warner 35 auto transmission changes up at 62km/h and 105km/h and this was quite acceptable. The ratios might not look very sporting at first glance, but in practice the gearbox ratios are well-matched to the V8's stepless torque curve. There is nothing we would like changed in this regard. Although sporting buffs would probably prefer the four-speed manual

◄——— *Although Stag comes complete with a lift-off hardtop we conducted most of this test with the top removed. As an open car the Stag was delightful, with noticeable lack of buffeting and wind roar. The car's forte is highway cruising and at constant touring speeds Stag can return up to 25mpg.*

STAG

gearbox, we enjoyed using the BW box in typically sporty conditions.

When British Leyland introduced the Stag they endowed it with a "British enthusiast drives across Europe" image and heavily promoted the car's ability to cruise swiftly and easily along continental autobahns and mountain passes. Indeed the Stag handles such conditions with ease and comfort and for that express purpose it is a delight.

The handling is precise and predictable, although the power steering can give a slightly 'dead' feel under certain circumstances. It is nowhere near as good as the system which BL use on the Jaguar XJ sedans. We doubt whether the Stag really needs power steering, but the unit fitted at present could do with some serious attention if Triumph claim to offer pin-sharp response.

The all-independent suspension front McPherson struts/rear trailing arms is supple and positive. The ride was comfortable and yet the driver has ample control when he calls on the car to perform quickly over twisty territory. For a nose-heavy car the Stag is quite surprising in its reaction. Most times it understeers, but tends to become neutral quite quickly. It will oversteer in certain circumstances, but it's not in the least vicious. It is a feature of the Stag's rear suspension design that the tail should eventually break away with ultimate cornering pressures, but a gentle squeeze on the throttle makes the tail settle down nicely and allows the driver to power smoothly out of the corner.

The Stag is reasonably stable, but can be affected by heavy side gusts. Wet weather driving requires a little more concentration and we warn that there shouldn't be too much uncontrolled squeezing of the throttle in greasy conditions. In the wet the tail simply breaks away and the Stag is quite a handful when you lose it.

At first the ride felt a little too firm, but combined with the excellent front seats we decided after a short while that the Stag is a great long distance touring car in the typical British manner.

The brakes on the test car were a little disappointing, but overseas reports tend to confirm that braking is not the Stag's forte. The brakes work well enough, but we encountered lock-up on a number of occasions during test, and the deceleration rates were what we'd expect, but nothing to write home about. Pedal pressures were moderate, but the brake efficiency 'went-off' rather quickly and the brakes got very 'wiffy' shortly after our five maximum stops from 100km/h.

We believe the test car would have performed better with a harder pad material, but say again that the brakes performed alright, we just felt that a car with this performance potential should have a more effective set of stoppers. The handbrake was just so-so.

The driving position is very good, for short or tall drivers. The seats offer a wide range of adjustment and are very comfortable. The relationship of seats to wheel, dash and windshield is excellent. The steering column is adjustable for rake and the leather-bound wheel was pleasant to use. The column controls are normal Triumph hardware and convenient in operation. The remainder of the dashboard controls were quite

LEFT: Stag's V8 is a totally unique engine — it is used only in the Triumph sporty car. The 2997cc engine puts out a healthy 109kW, but returns a welcome 25mpg. ABOVE: Optional on the test car, but standard on the newer models, the racy five-spoke mags give the car a stable footing for sporty driving.

ROAD TEST DATA & SPECIFICATIONS

Manufacturer: .. British Leyland Motor Corporation, Coventry, UK
Make/Model: .... Triumph Stag
Body type: .... 2-door convertible
Test car supplied by: .... BLMC, Coventry

ENGINE
Location: .... Front
Cylinders: .... Eight, 90degree vee-formation
Bore & Stroke: .... 86mm x 64.5mm
Capacity: 2997cc
Compression: .... 9.25 to 1
Aspiration: .... Twin Stromberg 175CDS carburettors
Fuel pump: .... Electric SU
Fuel recommended: .... Maximum octane (90 plus)
Valve gear: .... SOHC
Maximum power: .... 108.8Kw @ 5700rpm
Maximum torque: .... 226.4Nm @ 3500rpm

TRANSMISSION
Type/locations: ..... Borg-Warner 35 automatic transmission, T-bar shift
Driving wheels: .... Rear

Gear	Direct Ratio
1st	2.390
2nd	1.450
3rd	1.000
Final drive	3.7 to 1

SUSPENSION
Front suspension: .... Independent by McPherson struts with anti roll ba
Rear suspension: .... Independent by Semi-trailing arms, co spring
Shock absorbers: .... Telescopi
Wheels: .... 5.5J x 14 4 Stu
Tyres: .... 185 x 1

STEERING
Type: .... Rack and pinion, power assisted, adjustabl
Turns lock to lock: .... 2.
Wheel diameter: 36.2cr
Turning circle: 10.4r

BRAKES
Front: .... Disc. Diameter: 26.8cr
Rear: .... Drum. Diameter: 22.9cr
Servo assistance: .... Standar

DIMENSIONS AND WEIGHT
Wheelbase: 254.0cr
Overall length: 442.0cr
width: 161.2cr
height: 125.8cr
Track, front: 133.7cr
rear: 134.6cr
Ground clearance: 10.2cr
Kerb weight: 1265k

well-placed and the electric window switches very handy — they're located at the trailing edge of the centre console, adjacent to the handbrake.

The transmission shifter is also stock Triumph and features a stepped gate, it works okay, but the quadrant lighting is poor at night.

The ventilation is exceptionally good (especially with the roof off) and we were surprised that a European design could be so adequate for Australian conditions. The dashboard centre and side vents give a good flow of air and direction control is simple. The heater controls are well-placed and easy to operate. The quarter windows in the doors are operated by a knurled rotary knob and supplement the fresh air supply.

Also impressive is the quietness of the Stag. The motor is smooth and mechanically quiet, and wind noise is apparent, but not offensive. There was some flutter around the upper A-pillar, but a lot of that had more to do with carefully re-fitting the hardtop in its proper position.

The hardtop removal and replacement is definitely a two-person operation, but the actual fitting

system is quite simple, once you get used to carefully lining-up the hardtop locking slots and getting everything square before dropping it into place. We can't in all honesty say it was draught and water-free. The test car's hardtop leaked and allowed wind to whistle around the occupant's ears, but we are assured this was a particular fault with the test car and has now been rectified and should not be seen as a chronic complaint.

The soft-top hides under a well-designed panel which runs around the rear of the passenger compartment. The auxiliary soft-top is a great idea and we were very impressed with the quality of the top and the simplicity of raising and lowering it.

Back seat comfort (actually comfort isn't the right word) is marginal, and it's not a long distance pew by any regards. However it has pleasant seat cushions and backrest and for short distances (and short people) it is entirely adequate.

It's our opinion the Stag really is a *grand tourer* — it's auto travel in the grand, luxurious manner. The Stag is stylish and comfortable and completes

its duties without fuss and bother.

It is a practical car in many respects. The rubber-lined recess on the top of the dashboard is great for cigarette packets, a ball-point pen, roadmap or the like. The glovebox is large and well-placed and the doors feature handy (and capacious) map pockets. The controls are very handy and *driving* the car is not a difficult task at all.

The unique integrated rollbar is finished in zip-on vinyl and of course became part of the design due to US crash regulations. It serves another purpose, increasing the rigidity of the body structure — always a problem with open cars. By using this concept BL engineers were able to cut down weight appreciably, the Stag weighs a neat 1265kg, giving a good power to weight ratio of 11.6kg/kW.

Despite its high pricetag we believe the Stag has a definite future in Australia. Its suspension seems to cope pretty well with the various road surfaces and it's reasonably economical. It's comfortable and offers the luxury car buyer everything he would want and because of its styling it has a unique appeal. 75▶

ABOVE LEFT: The pedals are a good size and well-located. The rubber pads are big enough for the driver not to make a mistake when he wants to stop in a hurry. CENTRE: Access to the rear seat is good, but it's definitely a short-distance affair. RIGHT: General finish is a very high standard and the car is very comfortable over most surfaces. As a high-speed touring machine it is smooth and swift.

CAPACITIES AND EQUIPMENT

Fuel tank:	64litres
Cooling system:	10.4litres
Engine sump:	4.5litres
Battery:	12V 56AH
Alternator:	Lucas 45A

PERFORMANCE

FUEL CONSUMPTION

	Litres/100km	(MPG)
Average for test:	14.1	(20.2)
Best recorded:	13.9	(20.7)
Possible best (under optimum conditions):	11.1	(25)

ACCELERATION

	Drive	Held
40km/h	2.7	2.7
60km/h	4.5	4.5
80km/h	7.0	6.9s
100km/h	10.4	10.6s
110km/h	12.1	11.9s
120km/h	14.0	13.7s
130km/h	18.7	18.6s

OVERTAKING TIMES (holding gears)

km/h	2nd	Drive
0-70	3.9	3.8
0-80	2.9	2.9

60-100	5.8	5.8
80-100	3.7	3.7
100-130		7.9

STANDING 400M

Average:	17.8
Best Run:	17.6

SPEEDS IN GEARS

	Drive	Held	rpm
1st	62	110	6000
2nd	105	150	6000
3rd		188	5600

BRAKING

Three maximum stops from 50km/h:

Stop	G-force	Pedal pressure (kg)	Distance (M)
1	.84	20	11.7
2	.77	38	12.8
3	.94	20	10.4

Five maximum stops from 100 km/h:

Stop	G-force	Pedal pressure (kg)	Distance (M)
1	.80	20	49
2	.75	15	52
3	.89	15	44
4	.87	18	45
5	.96	20	41

SPEEDO CORRECTIONS

Indicated:	60	80	100	110
Actual:	62	83	105	116

20 000 MILES ON TRIUMPH STAG

" Motor's " Publishing Director, John French, continues the tale of his widely travelled two plus two

It seems a far cry from *Motor* w/e September 21, 1974 when I reported on the progress at 10,000 miles of my Triumph Stag on long-term test. For a start 4-star petrol costs were then calculated at 54p per gallon, now the price is 73p.

The second 10,000 miles confirms my original opinion of the car as one of considerable attraction, particularly in appearance, and with a distinct character and temperament. On the opposite page you will find a "Service Diary" item relating to a bearing failure which the engine

sustained shortly after the 10,000 mile report. Apart from this incident which, at the time, caused me some considerable alarums and excursions as I was en route from the Parish Show to Spain for a holiday, the car had performed admirably.

At the time of the 10,000 mile report I said that the Borg-Warner automatic box was "lazy," ie that it showed a reluctance to change up or down gently. As the car was still under warranty a gentle carp at Borg-Warner via Triumph has caused them to bend their skills to this

problem and the gearbox now provides a smooth upwards change under both steady and fierce acceleration.

An annoying clonk now occurs only when proceeding in Drive and the box in intermediate gear, though when lifting off, the box will change into top at much too low a speed, with a jerk. This occurs only in town driving and usually where there is a short distance between corners. With a little foresight you can engage "hold" in intermediate until the second corner is rounded.

The Michelin XAS radials are unchanged and look good for at least another 8,000-10,000 miles (30,000 miles—not bad for such a car). The power-assisted brakes continue to serve excellently, though I am on my third set of disc pads. Regular readers will remember that the original ones were too soft and had to be replaced at 3000 miles; the harder second set were replaced at just over 18,000 miles. This means that the second set lasted for 15,000 miles and the linings for the rear drum brakes remain unchanged but will probably need replacing at the next service, coming up within the next month.

On my return from France in October I replaced the hood with the hardtop for winter usage without difficulty; again it has proved draught-free and rainproof. Having reached the allegedly good weather period in

the United Kingdom only recently (on May 1) I once again removed the hardtop to its place in the garage and the hood has emerged from the tonneau, still in first class condition. It is put up and down without trouble to suit the vagaries of our changeable climate and creates remarkably little extra noise. In the last report I commented on the buffeting which occurred with the hood down at high speeds but since then I've found this is reduced if the side windows are lowered.

Apart from the normal service changes, oil consumption is negligible. The engine and ride are commendably smooth and the lines of the body, in my view, have not dated in the five years since the car's introduction. It still elicits admiration—the attendant at the local supermarket car park says he sells it regularly at least four times a week. The average mpg including a large percentage of driving in town, with very few long journeys to assist, has averaged 19.1 mpg but on a recent run to Thruxton and back it averaged 22.5 mpg.

The front adjustable seats have provided comfort for all shapes and sizes of passengers but other than for children—or two small adults—the rear seats are uncomfortable. As I commented in the previous report, a load in the back does improve the ride though. No major replacements

SERVICE DIARY

STAG-GER

The two pictures (below) show how a combination of minor faults can have dramatic effects. The car was a Stag (see story opposite) which had always shown a slight increase in temperature at sustained high cruising speeds. While still under guarantee it received dealer attention to cure a noisy timing chain, but on re-assembly it was alleged subsequently to have been incorrectly re-timed—but only slightly.

During routine servicing a new oil filter of proprietary manufacture was fitted, recommended for use in the Stag (many others had been fitted in previous Stags without causing any trouble) although BLMC pointed out later

Damage to a replacement oil filter on the staff Stag led to failure of two big ends . . . .

. . . which in turn caused two pistons to hit the valves, as the indents testify

that these particular filters were not on *their* recommended list.

The sequence of events leading up to the failure of two big ends causing the pistons to hit the valves appears to have been as follows. A minor rise in temperature, no doubt aided by the re-timing error, was accentuated when the car had been cruised for approximately 100 miles on the Autoroute du Sud at between 90-100 miles per hour. The pressure of the overheated oil damaged the top of the filter element and the sealing gasket, as the picture shows. A series of foreign bodies arriving at the bearings caused the trouble, but fortunately the rise in temperature was spotted in time before even more expensive damage was done.

Fram, who manufactured the filter, had had no similar experience in four years of manufacture. But at the time of the correspondence (last February), stated that even one failure such as this was unacceptable to them. Pending a re-design they withdrew this filter from their catalogue for Stag application—a commendable act on their part.

Finally, Triumph traced the minor overheating to a slight casting obstruction in a water-flow channel, the removal of which has effected a cure.

FLAT

Four minutes flat (if you'll pardon the pun) to fix a puncture—and the cost? 88p, which I think is expensive.

It was all done properly, too. When the source of the puncture was discovered the tyre was removed from the wheel, a clearance hole made, a dab of adhesive stuck on the inside, and a mushroom-headed plug pulled through. The tyre was then replaced on the rim, inflated, the protruding end of the plug was cut off (as shown) and the wheel was placed in a tray of water to check for leaks.

Of course, you could say that you pay for such service, but against that the repairers (a tyre factor, not a garage) had the wheel for 48 hours. I reckon these people must make quite a

Are the tyre people charging too much for fitting and repairs?

good living: the firm in question employs two fitters, both of them fully occupied: at 10 repairs to the hour it means £9 per hour per man, or £72 a day.

On one occasion I saw a Triumph drive in: it was jacked up, all the wheels were fitted with new tyres, the wheels replaced and the driver was away 35 minutes later. Now, with new tyres at (say) £11 each, or £55 the five, and remembering that the factor works at about 33⅓ per cent discount, that gives him just over £18 for about half an hour's work. And alignment and balancing are extra. . . .

BANG

With so much tight street parking these days it is quite common to see a car reversing into a spot, and then see the car behind give a shudder—occasionally accompanied by the tinkle of glass. Yet for some very strange reason the drivers seldom look fore or aft to see if they have done any damage to their own or the other car. They must know they have hit, yet they walk away quite nonchalantly.

I for one now know where so many of these little dings and dents on wings and bumpers come from: recently, after one of these performances (you can't call them accidents) I checked the two cars. I was amused to find that the offending driver had come off considerably worse, for what she hadn't realised was that the 3.4 Jaguar she had reversed into was fitted with a towing bracket!

As a matter of interest I measured the height of various bumpers from the ground to the top of the bumper bar. The figures were:

Austin 1800	16½in
Ford Corsair	19in
Ford Cortina	23in
Hillman Hunter	21in
Austin Maxi	18in
Singer Gazelle	16in
Austin Mini	16in
Jaguar 3.4	16in
Triumph Herald	19½in

All measurements are with the vehicle unladen.

Four of the cars had towing brackets standing 4-4½in proud of the bumper, three of them had reversing lamps broken, again because they protruded beyond the bumper, and none had overriders.

have been required—only the occasional bulb for stop lights but nothing more, and there is no sign of deterioration through rust or corrosion on the chromium plating.

I have rectified one minor irritation. The plug leads from the cylinder bank on the opposite side to the distributor pass over the rocker box and are meant to be held clear by a plastic gate which is not tall enough. The leads, therefore, were being gently cooked as the rocker box warmed up, giving off a hot plastic odour, now cured by lifting the leads higher and taping them to the bulkhead.

The performance, alas, can no longer be used legally in the higher speed range but the acceleration is still lively and at the present legal maximum the engine is so smooth and under-stressed that it feels it could go on forever.

The Stag still gives me considerable pleasure not only to drive but to look at, and it will be a pity if in BLMC's rationalisation programme this body shape should disappear.

Summing up, despite the service errors which caused the engine failure in France, I took the Stag to Le Mans and went on from there to Spain. As I intend to continue with it as my personal transport, and if the Editor so desires, I may be able to give you a further year's history at this time in 1976.

Buying Secondhand

Triumph Stag

THE SHAPE of the Triumph Stag is essentially the work of the Italian stylist Michelotti, who was of course responsible for the looks of several other Triumphs before. It was conceived in 1966 (before the birth of British Leyland) as a sports-coupé using the Triumph 2000 floor-pan and drive. Several notable changes occurred whilst the idea was still on paper, including a shortening of the wheelbase, a new nose and tail — which Triumph liked enough to incorporate on the 2000 (and 2.5PI) to make the longer Mk.2 versions (before the Stag was announced) — and the substitution of a 90-degree vee-8 version of the single ohc engine Triumph supplied originally to Saab for the 99. Originally the swept volume of the new engine was to have been 2½ litres, but this was increased to 3.0 with a slightly bigger bore but much shorter stroke than the Saab unit, giving very over-square dimensions — 86x64.5mm, 2,997 c.c.

The Stag is of course a luxury sports-car, with all of the comforts of a good 2 + 2 saloon, provided that you don't ride in the back, for any great distance at any rate. It bears some resemblances to the same sort of cars produced by Mercedes-Benz at the time, including a hefty steel detachable hard top (you need at least a strong friend to help you remove it) or convertible soft top. Since Triumph were original-enough thinkers to fit an elaborate forward-braced roll-protection bar (principally to meet expected American safety requirements), it is a little puzzling that they didn't evolve the steel folding roof that we still need as the answer to the wind-noise and thief-proofing weaknesses of the fabric soft top. The inside is handsomely equipped, with Triumph's idea of a wooden facia, very convenient fingertip controls for major accessories, electric lifts for the windows, and manual or Borg-Warner type 35 three-speed automatic transmission. Overdrive was an option at first. Clutch and brakes were bigger than on the 2.5PI, whilst the suspension — MacPherson strut front, semi-trailing arm independent at the back — was similar to the Triumph saloons, though with different rates for the coil springs. The 2.5PI gearbox had a higher first gear, but the final drive ratio (3.7) was set midway between the 2000 and 2.5PI ones (4.1 and 3.45 respectively), which, going by our Road Test of 30 July 1970, gave the car a slightly low-geared top and a reasonably long overdrive — though judging by the fact that maximum speed was achieved in overdrive (115 mean, 117 best against direct top's 113 mph) it could usefully be longer still.

The engine looked a quite advanced design, with a cast iron block and light alloy heads, each with single overhead camshafts driven by chains rather than exposed belts, a two-plane crank-shaft, a jack-shaft and skew-gear-driven water pump in mid-block, and wedge-shaped combustion chambers fed by two SU-principle Stromberg carburettors inside the vee. Triumph took some trouble to make the unit easy to work on; you can for example remove the cam-shafts without disturbing the sprockets.

It developed a claimed 145 bhp at 5,500 rpm (the 2.5PI six produced 142 bhp in TR6 guise) and maximum torque, appreciably more than the 2.5PI, was 170 lb. ft. 3,500 rpm. Overhead camshafts, especially at and before the Stag's 1970

Stag could be had manual or automatic, with hard or soft top. The soft top version had a rigid roll-over bar for safety (above). V8 engine fitted easily under bonnet (below) and facia was well equipped and of high quality (bottom) with a full range of instruments and face-level ventilation.

Performance data

Road Tested in Autocar of	Stag manual (O/d) 10 June 1971	Stag auto 10 June 1971
Mean max speed (mph)	116	112
Acceleration (sec)		
0-30	3.5	4.1
0-40	5.1	5.8
0-50	7.1	7.9
0-60	9.3	10.4
0-70	12.7	14.2
0-80	16.5	18.6
0-90	21.8	24.9
0-100	29.2	34.5
Standing ¼-mile (sec	18.2	17.9
Top gear		
10-30	—	—
20-40	10.8	—
30-50	11.1	—
40-60	11.3	—
50-70	11.6	—
60-80	13.2	8.6
70-90	16.1	9.9
80-100	21.9	14.8
Overall mpg	20.6	17.2
Typical mpg	25	20
Dimensions		
Length	14ft 5¾in	
Width	5ft 3½in	
height	4ft 3½in	
kerb weight (cwt)	25.1 (25.3 auto)	

launch, were usually expected to bring, amongst other things, a better top end to an engine's performance, but as with the Dolomite engine from which the Stag one is derived, this was not so on this car. Smoothness and a pleasant if not at all exceptional spread of power were its best characteristics; there was none of the quite exciting urge high up of the 2.5PI. Certainly a little of that impression is due to the extra weight of the Stag (which is 2½cwt heavier than the saloon), but the rest is the fault of the engine which never felt as eager as its size and specification declared it ought to be.

Triumph's not very subtle power-assisted steering was standard. It was (and remains) entirely satisfactory for most users, being light and quite "quick" in a car which doesn't roll too much ordinarily and which has reasonably good roadholding. Its failings when compared with other systems were a lack of any feel and a curious and highly distinctive "notch" effect at the straight-ahead position. Turning the rather large steering wheel (adjustable though in both tilt and telescope senses) either side was accompanied by a noticeable — if small — increase in effort needed, so that at first one tended to steer a little jerkily. Ultimate roadholding is limited by the inevitable camber-change effects caused by fact that semi-trailing arms are not pure trailing arms.

What to look for

Having been around for only a relatively short time, and also since Triumph seem to have learnt more than some other makers about avoiding it, rust and body rot do not seem to have been noted so far. Details like fittings may have deteriorated superficially, but we have not heard of any serious cases of decay on the Stag to date. That doesn't mean of course that such troubles may start to appear at any time, so a proper inspection both on top and underneath for rust is still very worthwhile; the best protected of cars will deteriorate fast if it has suffered crash damage which hasn't been repaired properly. The same applies to stone damage at both the front and behind wheels; sills can suffer in the hands of the show-off and the clumsy.

The suspension has a good reputation amongst dealers too. The usual wear of pivots occurs, but not to any unusual extent; test for this in the usual way, by shaking each wheel sideways whilst a helper keeps the brakes on — if there is play, a bush may need replacing; if there is play with the brakes off, then suspect a wheel bearing.

A peculiarity common to any of the Triumphs using semi-trailing arm rear suspension is a curious lurch sideways from the back when you go from drive to neutral or over-run — during a gearchange for instance. It doesn't always happen, but when it does it is caused by the splines of the telescopic drive shafts sticking and then freeing, thereby locking, then releasing the rear suspension. Ball splines avoid this problem, but they are much more expensive than the Stag's plain splines. Triumph have always told us that this is a lubricating problem that should not arise, though they admit that it sometimes does. It isn't a thing to worry about however.

The gearbox has a reputation for synchromesh that wears out, and a strong weakness for gearlever buzzes after a lot of use. Cases are reported of a metallic ping from the propellor shaft rear companion flange where it couples to the quill shaft of the differential, due to looseness. But no one we spoke to mentioned any true unreliability of the transmission. Final drives have a good reputation.

The power steering can leak, but to no greater extent than on any other power-steered car. Inspect the gaiters on the rack for signs of oil leaks. Oddly, several dealers told us that repairing power steering (with new seals and so on) has always proved rather unsatisfactory, though they find it hard to explain why.

Brakes troubles are rare. The hold of the convertible can leak and if it has not been used for a long time can prove very awkward indeed to erect. Once one has managed to lift the weighty hard

Boot was large, with a wide opening (above); folding the aft section of the soft top was somewhat complicated (right) but back seat was quite roomy despite the width swallowed up by seat well, which meant no proper elbow rests (bottom). Thick roll-over bar supported belts and housed interior lights.

top (which comes with a heated rear glass) into place, the clips securing it (very like the similarly excellent ones on the Mercedes 280 SL) should work well.

The engine of the Stag has, at any rate in older cars, proved to be the great weakness, to such an extent that there is a tendency to christen the car the "Triumph Snag." Aluminium alloy heads are ideal things in theory, but if they are not designed or made correctly, they can give a disproportionate amount of trouble. The Stag heads have a bad reputation for warping in service, often at only around 25,000 miles, thereby blowing gaskets which if they are not dealt with quickly can all too easily lead to damaged head faces needing skim-

ming if they are to be rescued. The trouble is that there is very little meat to be skimmed; up to 0.010in. is officially allowed for removal (one dealer told us he had got away with 0.020in. but did so unhappily), but this isn't always enough of course. Corrosion is another problem if whoever maintains the car has not used a corrosion-inhibiting coolant as he should have done. Head bolts then seize as they have done on many aluminium engines in the past. New heads each cost well over £200.

On earlier models there was a history of oil pressure bothers leading to crank journal wear, but

Left: Hard top could be detached but was massive affair needing two men to lift off or replace; the process took some time.

this has reportedly been cured. Triumph themselves say that the head troubles are a thing of the past too, but any prospective buyer must feel some disquiet knowing that there is at least one London-based firm who, we are told, will fit you a Rover vee-8 in place of the Stag unit. And he may also be aware that all the indications are that Leyland rationalisation will almost certainly mean the dropping of (at any rate) the engine in favour of the Rover engine. A pity, because if properly developed both the engine and less so the car could be made into something much more positively successful. ☐

Milestones and chassis identification

	Chassis No.
June 1970: 2+2 convertible/hard top based on Triumph 2000/2.5PI introduced, with new vee-engine based on four-cylinder design first seen sold to Saab (later in Triumph's Dolomite and derivatives). Distinctive anti-crash bar provided. Power steering, electric windows standard. Overdrive for manual box and Borg-Warner automatic transmission and air conditioning optional. Detachable hard top version, with soft top as extra.	2 BW
October 1972: Overdrive on manual version standard	—
February 1973: Matt black sills and tail panel, re-styled instruments, courtesy lamp in roll bar	20001
January 1974: Hazard warning and seat belt warning lamps fitted	31153
March 1975: Air conditioning option dropped	—
January 1976: Alloy wheels, tinted glass and laminated screen now standard	40793

MOTOR week ending October 6, 1979

To say the Stag

99▶ . . . came about by accident is a gross over-simplification, but if it hadn't been for the friendship between two men it might have been a totally different animal. Mike McCarthy talked to Harry Webster, formerly Chief Engineer at Triumph

HARRY WEBSTER first met Giovanni Michelotti back in 1957, when the Italian stylist was working for the coachbuilder Vignale: he was responsible for the facelift of the Standard Vanguard, a model which in fact became known as the Vignale Vanguard.

"I used to go and see 'Micho' every other weekend or so for, oh; five or six years or more . . . My missus used to play hell with me . . . I used to set sail (after the races) from Coventry to London, fly to Paris, then change and fly on to Turin — it was the only way I could get there on a Saturday. I used to work with him, often on Saturday night and certainly on Sunday, then set off home on Monday morning — there's a direct flight back: it was very convenient . . .

"'Micho's' first major job was the Herald, and he went on to design most of what was to become the Triumph range — Spitfires, Vitesses, GT6s, and so on . . ."

Having completed the Triumph 2000 and 1300, Michelotti asked Harry if he could have a 2000 chassis for a one-off show special. "These styling boys, they're proud fellows, they always want to show you what they can do, show off a bit . . . Anyway, he asked me for a 2000 chassis so that he could put a one-off body on it and put it in the Turin show that year(1966 — MM).

"I agreed to let him have the chassis, but on one condition — that if we liked it we would pay him for it and take it back to Coventry . . ."

It was on one of his trips to Italy that Harry saw what Michelotti had done. He had created a smooth, sleek convertible featuring a wide, horizontal grille behind which hid the headlights (fronted by electrically-operated flaps), wire wheels and a sharply cut off tail again with wide horizontal tail-lights, which echoed the shape of the grille particularly at the edges where the side lamps came to a point. Interestingly enough one feature that was to make the production car so distinctive didn't appear on the prototype

— the T-bar over the passenger compartment.

"Well, when I went to see it, I liked it, took it back, and set the wheels in motion for production . . ."

The other major difference between the prototype and the production car was the engine. As first envisaged, the Stag was to be equipped with the 2.5 litre fuel-injected straight six engine from the TR and 2.5PI. However, in 1963 a clever Triumph engineer, Lewis Dawtrey, had drawn up a report, proposing Triumph's future engine plans. It boiled down to basically two: a slant-four, originally of 1500 cc but capable of enlargement to 2 litres, and by "ordering in" the other half of the four cylinders, a V-8. When Spen King, now Deputy Chairman, BL Technology, took over as Chief Engineer at Triumph after Harry's appointment to the Austin-Morris division following the Leyland/BMC merger, he, too, liked the car but felt it could take a lot more power: he therefore delayed the introduction of the car until the V8 was ready. This put the weight up slightly, and, though the six (since the car was basically a 2000) slotted straight in, the engine bay had to be widened to take the V8. This led to a lot more modifications until eventually there were very few (if any) common body parts between the Stag and the big Triumph saloons. And it also meant that the car didn't see the light of day until 1970.

The T-bar was another story again. "After 'Micho' finished the prototype we made some hand-built prototypes ourselves — and suffered from the most enormous scuttle-shake! Oh boy, it was horrid! You almost had to try and catch the steering wheel, if you know what I mean! The torsional stiffness of the body had gone to hell, of course, and the only way to get it back was to join up the A and B posts (*the structural members fore and aft of the door — MM*) with a good torsional box across the top, and that's exactly what the T-bar does". So it wasn't just brought in to help with roll-over

regulations or for styling? "Oh no! Of course it helped with the roll-over conditions, but it's very much part of the structure, I can assure you!".

Were there many other problems? "Not while I was in charge, remembering it was to have the six cylinder engine — after all most of the suspension, engine, transmission and so on had been sorted in the saloon. One of the interesting problems was the convertible top: it had to disappear completely into a bin behind the seats with a lid on so that we could fit the hard top. The way the hood folded gave us some headaches . . ."

So the Stag came about because Harry liked what Michelotti had done

Above: Harry Webster (on the left) with his successor at Triumph, Spen King. They were responsible for the birth of the Stag.

Left: the Stag as envisaged by Michelotti, *sans* T-bar and side ornamentation but with wire wheels and hidden headlights

— but what was the rationale behind the car? "Triumph realised back then that we couldn't compete with the big boys — we had to find a niche or market gap to fill, and that was where the Stag came in. It was aimed at the "young executive", someone who'd gone through the motor bike/sports car/family and family saloon, and wanted something different, something sporty but with creature comforts. Hell, I wanted one myself at the time!"

Then the surprise of the day: "I'm getting one myself, actually. My wife wants me to have one when I retire — something to play about with . . ."

How's that for confidence in your own product?

Little deer . . . ■ Proud owners of Triumph Stags may like to know that a model of their car, to 1/43rd scale, is available.

Long Term Report

Triumph Stag (24,000 miles)

Multi-point Stag

By Maurice A. Smith

STAGS HAVE CARVED a definite niche for themsleves in the diminishing list of out-of-the-ordinary British models. Whether it is the niche originally foreseen for them is open to question. The fortunes of the model have swung around as a result mainly of external influences by no means peculiar to Stags. They came on to the market late in June 1970 at what now sounds a very modest price of between £2,000 and £2,500 according to equipment and extras. Now you have to pay nearly £6,000 for the same thing which seems expensive.

On seeing their first Stag some people said "ah, a big TR" which Stags are not, and they went on to complain about handling and performance shortcomings by 3-litre sports car standards. The jumble of speed limits, high petrol costs, road congestion and anti-motoring propaganda in the intervening 6½ years have taken some of the steam out of performance appeal and the majority of those who operate Stags found, and still find, the

acceleration, speed and handling very adequate. Whether Triumph knew they were introducing a car which would also have real woman appeal is another question to be considered. Certainly it is a very popular "wife's car" for those who can afford it.

What a pity that British Leyland did their too familiar trick of introducing an attractive new model and then failing to produce them. Very many sales in Europe and the UK were lost through failure to deliver or even to quote a firm delivery date, and now it is too late since the production days of Stags must be numbered.

Turning from the general to the particular, I have heard of a few Stags that have "blown up" Cylinder head gaskets, bearings, pistons, even a broken rod have been mentioned as causes. Looking closely at these, it seems more than coincidental that a few of the owners have been the sort of "out-to-prove-something" drivers who might be expected to blow up cars and put rods through crankcase sides. Let's say it is just good

luck that our two Stags have stayed together, the second one now on 26,000 miles, remaining sweet and responsive and always starting at the second short churn, whether sun-baked or ice-covered.

Oil consumption is negligible but the oil looks dirty by the time a change is due. The pressure water cooling system needs topping up most months and one wonders where the water goes. Like Jaguars and sometimes other large cars such as Rolls-Royces and Mercedes, the Stag has a steamy exhaust most of the time, said by some to be owed to condensation in long and elaborate exhaust systems. I wonder whether the suspect Stag cylinder head gaskets are allowing slight seepage of water into the cylinders. Would this occur more when the engine is hot or when cold? Such small quantities, if they exist, do not show up in the oil or on the plugs.

It seems likely that failure to check water level or notice symptoms of shortage may have led to the engine overheating reported by a few owners. If water

is short the heater matrix goes cold before the temperature gauge gives any indication of abnormal temperature. Overheating is first indicated when idling or crawling in thick traffic and there is a return towards normal as soon as the engine and water pump are revved up. This may not be noticed by a driver concentrating on the traffic and obscuring the gauge with his left hand on the steering wheel. It is cured when the expansion bottle is replenished.

Talking about climatic extremes, the Stag's heater will really cook you if you want it to and can include plenty of face level cold air while your legs are being toasted. Full air conditioning was an option on early models but was not well regarded. Last summer in Britain was a real Stag summer and the soft top was folded away in its neat flush fitting box for months on end. The soft top has a zip round its rear window allowing it to fold open and flat. The rear quarters are blind and special care is needed when moving into and across traffic lanes.

The detachable hard top comes

as near to being a coupé conversion for the winter as you can hope for and includes a heated rear window which plugs itself in when the hard top is attached. Extractor rear quarter lights are fitted.

Like Harold Wilson I have said it before and I will say it again; the worst sin on the part of one's car is to pack up suddenly and leave you stranded. There are degrees of sin depending on where, when and how it does it. Our Stag sinned a little bit. Petrol starvation leading to momentary instances of cutting out gave a hint of trouble to come. I chose not to take the hint at once and did not pull into the next Leyland garage. As a result while I was driving into London to get service on the following day, the electric petrol pump in the boot finally died and left me stranded on the Albert Embankment. I had to be towed in and the replacement unit cost £16.50. Otherwise we have enjoyed over 24,000 miles in 2½ years without any trouble of note. The car has had regular services more or less at the specified times, there have been a few minor adjustments and bulb re-placements.

The most expensive trouble to date was with the alternator which wore down its brushes last August at 22,580 miles, causing minor internal damage by the time the red no-charge warning light came on. Strictly speaking this might have been anticipated and a check made at the 18,000 miles service. In addition a repair rather than a replacement alternator should have been possible except that there is a built-in regulator which suffered and there was the time out of use to be considered if a repair were to be made. The cost of new parts, plus labour charges was a reasonable £22.54 from Autocar Electrical, who are good friends but in no way connected with *Autocar* magazine.

At the very beginning of August

(21,036 miles) a minor but illegal fault ocurred — you have guessed it, electrics again. The indicator flasher unit became sluggish and sometimes gave up all together. A replacement for this small sealed unit cost £5.40 trade price. Perhaps they are gold plated. The battery is still good and very seldom needs topping up.

Checking back on the maintence records I see a note of eight new sparking plugs at 16,098 miles. This could have waited until the 18,000 mile service but the earlier time was convenient for sparing the car. Otherwise the entries are routine.

There are lots of good points about this Stag, some already mentioned in two earlier stories but worth summarising in what might be a final report on this particular car (although we don't plan to sell it yet). First there is the high degree of comfort in the broad sense, owed to good quality, properly shaped seats with three modes of adjustment and in addition to the two-way adjustable steering column. The very effective heating and fresh air supply have already been mentioned. Forward view is above average and aided in rain by the two speed and intermittent wipers which sweep full arcs, the

blade on the driver's side being articulated to move parallel to the screen pillar and wipe the last sector. Head room is adequate for people up to about 5ft 10 in but limited for those over 6ft. It always amuses me to watch an "anti" chap

of 6ft. proving his point that he cannot sit in a Stag at all and then next day another "pro" chap of similar size proving that he can tuck in perfectly comfortably with a bit of careful seat adjustment. As my aunty used to say "there is none so blind as those who do not want to see".

Touches of convenience and class are provided by screw-opening front quarter-lights (or ashtrays as some might say) and electrically operated windows — which reminds me that the mechanism on the driver's side is getting a bit lumpy in operation, which may be ominous.

The original Michelin tyres are still fitted having been rotated corner to corner when scuffing was becoming obvious on the outside

treads of the front wheels. Stags have a good lock and light, power-assisted steering so drivers tended to turn abruptly when manoeuvring — as tyre squeal on dry tarmac or ruts in gravel drives indicate. Long tyre life must be owed in part to the big wheels which of course carry more rubber than small ones as well as having a larger footprint on the road.

If I can afford eight (or more) cylinders I shall continue to do so. The smoothness, the idling, the starting, even the exhaust note are, or should be, that bit better than with a four or six. Thinking of exhausts, here is another good feature of the later Stags: To date there have been no leaks or rattles and no section has needed replacement in 2½ years.

Above. The roll-over bars do not detract from the open car feeling, and front seat passengers are well protected from wind buffeting. Above right. Comfortable, three-way adjustable seats with good shoulder support and compact head restraint. Just enough room at the back (right) to call it an occasional four seater, and reasonably easy to climb in

Long Term Report
Triumph Stag

Pictures may indicate that this long-term car has non-standard brushed nylon covered seats "borrowed" from the Triumph saloon line and not usually fitted to open models. I have preferred sitting on this material having experienced the alternative vinyl on my earlier Stag, and it has stood up well. It is more prone to picking up dirt and fluff but has not been difficult to brush clean. Another non-standard feature on this Stag is the black air dam under the nose. It was fitted ex-TR6 for four reasons; to improve appearance (the Stag nose appearing too high); to improve top speeds by reducing drag; to reduce front-end lift and improve directional stability at high speeds (Stags get lighter in front at around 100 mph or over and are then more susceptible to gusts, having little keel surface); to try to increase air flow through the radiator and engine compartment (Stags have been known to overheat in extreme conditions, particularly if towing a trailer). The first point is a matter of opinion, the other three seem to have been modestly effective. Some 3-5 mph higher than average top speed was recorded when the car was fully run in at about 12,000 miles. The 123 mph best figures indicated should be about 116 mph true. This compares with the *Autotest* Stag automatic maximum of 112 mph.

Luxury fittings obviously cost money and when included as standard items cumulatively account in part not only for the attraction but also the high price of the Stag today. Steering column adjustment, opening quarter lights, electric windows, three-speed wipers with articulated blade — these have already been mentioned. Some other details are the indicator repeaters on the sides of the front wings; the powerful twin halogen headlamps, viscous fan coupling; lockable flush petrol filler cap; red door-open warning

Maximum speeds						
Gear	**mph**		**kph**		**rpm**	
	LT	RT	LT	RT	LT	RT
Top (mean)	115	112	185	180	5,750	5,660
(best)	117	113	188	182	5,850	5,710
Inter	89	89	143	143	6,500	6,500
Low	54	54	87	87	6,500	6,500

Acceleration				
True mph	**Time (sec)**		**Speedo mph**	
	LT	RT	LT	RT
30	4.2	4.1	31	29
40	6.0	5.8	41	39
50	8.1	7.9	52	50
60	10.7	10.4	62	61
70	14.7	14.2	73	72
80	19.2	18.6	84	84
90	25.7	24.9	94	95
100	35.7	34.5	105	107

Standing ¼-mile: LT 18.3 sec 77 mph; RT 17.9 sec 78 mph
kilometre: LT 33.7 sec 97 mph; RT 32.6 sec 98 mph

mph	Top		Inter		Low	
	LT	RT	RT	LT	LT	RT
10-30	—	—	—	—	3.1	3.0
20-40	—	—	—	—	3.2	3.0
30-50	—	—	—	—	3.8	3.7
40-60	—	—	5.5	5.3	—	—
50-70	—	—	6.1	5.9	—	—
60-80	8.9	8.6	7.6	7.4	—	—
70-90	10.2	9.9	—	—	—	—
80-100	15.3	14.8	—	—	—	—

Consumption	
Overall mpg: LT	20.8 (13.6 litres/100km)
RT	17.2 (16.4 litres/100km)

Note: "RT" denotes performance figures for Triumph Stag Automatic tested in Autocar of 10 June 1971

lamps in the arm rests; dipping day/night interior mirror; thick rubber inlays in the bumper over-riders and framed front number plate; and independent boot lamp and an electric clock which continues to keep good time.

What would I now want included if there were to be a Mk 3 Stag, assuming that only details could be changed at this late stage in its life? In no special order, I would change

the design and position of the segmented warning lamps dial which I find ugly and usually obscured by the driver's left hand. The upper seat belt attachments (or guides) are dreadful. They cause the straps to rub the seat back; they tangle and jam and seldom take up tension.

The rear head room in the hard top is too limited and if even another inch could be found it would be valuable. The soft top could do with transparent quarter panels for better rear vision. The styling strips along the side of the Mk 2 car should be replaced by proper rubbing strips with rubber inlays. A second filler cap on the port side would often be convenient. The plastic clips intended to hold down the floor panel of the boot are miserable fragile little objects which should be improved.

I would expect that with some better dampers the initial harshness, often felt when the car is rolling over coarse road surfaces, could now be improved. This is not to be regarded as a serious shortcoming and the ride in general is very comfortable and quiet.

There are no complaints about the way paintwork, trim and carpets are standing up, and so far there are no rust pocks like the two or three which came through the paintwork on our first Stag. In fact, after a clean and polish the car can still look practically new.

Good, low mileage secondhand Stags can now be had for between £3,000-£4,000. This may sound a lot but compared with other cars of a broadly similar type — 3000 Capri, Scimitar, Datsun 260Z — and including lesser models bought new in this price range, they are well worth considering. In my experience Stags will provide very pleasing and versatile driving with, of course, the additional rare pleasure for those that want it, of open-car motoring. □

Left. Engine compartment keeps pretty clean and the equipment is accessible. Above, a battery mounting in the nose is inaccessible but cool. It seldom needs topping up. Power steering pump may need to move before battery can be removed, but luckily this has not yet been necessary

Left. The hard top gives closed car comfort but there is some extra wind noise from the screen top joint. Below. Four-way adjustment of the steering column. in-out and up-down

Above. Specially fitted TR6 air dam, which apparently brings aerodynamic advantages

Below. The official Witter tow attachment is convenient but prominent. Not the solid bumper section

Cost of ownership

Running costs	Life in Miles	Cost per 10,000 miles £
One gallon of 4-star, average cost today 80p	19.2	416.66
One pint of top-up oil, average cost today 38p	4,000	0.95
Front disc brake pads (set of 4)	35,000	2.54
Rear brake linings (set of 4)	16,780	5.88
tyres (front pair)	30,000	9.56
tyres (rear pair)	30,000	9.56
Service (main interval and actual cost incurred)	6,000	22.99
†Repairs		47.54
Total		515.68
Running cost per mile:	**5.1p**	
Approx. standing charges per year		
Insurance		89.50
Tax		40.00
Depreciation		
Price when new (less soft top and radio)		£3,158.00
Trade in cash value (approx)		£2,800.00
Typical advertised price (current)		£3,250.00
Total cost per mile (based on cash value)	**10.0p**	

'Insurance cost is for 60 year old driver, living in Surrey

†Repair costs include alternator, fuel pump, indicator flasher unit, bulbs and one wiper blade.

Specification

Engine: 9 deg V8, 86×64.5mm (3.39×2.54in.), 2,997 c.c. (182.9 cu.in.); CR 9.3 to 1; ohc; 2×Stromberg carbs, 146 bhp (DIN) at 3,500 rpm; max torque 167 lb.ft. (23.1 mkg) at 3,500 rpm.

Transmission: Front engine, rear drive. Automatic, overall ratios 3.70-8.51, 5.37-12.36, 8.84-20.40 rev 7.73-17.80. Top gear mph/1,000 rpm 19.8.

Suspension: ifs, MacPherson struts, lower links, telescopic dampers, anti-roll bar. Rear, independent, semi-trailing arms, coil springs, telescopic dampers. Steering, rack and pinion (power assisted).

Brakes: hydraulic dual circuit (servo), 10.6in. front discs, 9.0×2¾in. rear drums.

Dimensions: Wheelbase, 8ft 4in. (254 cm); front track 4ft 4¼in (133 cm), rear track 4ft 5in. (135 cm). Overall length, 14ft 5¾in. (441 cm), width 5ft 3½in. (161 cm), height 4ft 1½in. (126 cm). Turning circle 34ft (10.4 m). Unladen weight 2,720 lb (1,235 kg). Max payload 1,000 lb (454 kg).

Others: Tyres 185HR-14 in.; 5½in. rims; Fuel 12¾ gal (58 litres); service interval 6,000 miles. Warranty period 12 months/unlimited mileage.

SUV 443N

Golden Oldie

Stag at bay . . .

. . . no longer. Only two years after its demise, (hastened by its engine's fragile reputation), the Stag is now a star ascendant among cars worth keeping, as Roger Bell explains

"DON'T BE AFRAID to boot it!" Tony Hart's invitation to have a blast in his five-year-old car certainly helped to restore confidence in the machinery. Tales of woe from other owners over the years had seriously undermined the reputation and

respectability of the Triumph Stag, which ranks as one of Leyland's more endearing misfits, superb in concept but found wanting a little in execution, development and perhaps glamour. Its Michelotti body, conceived in the early 'sixties, was not the most eye-catching of Italian jobs, though it clothed what on paper was a very respectable, even exciting, running gear. Ironically, the engine that helped to make the Stag the undeniably appealing car that it was (and still is) also accounts for its reputation as an expensive liability — which, as we shall see, is not altogether justified.

The 3-litre V8, in simple terms a doubled-up Dolomite "four", was designed and developed for the Stag and an up-market 3-litre version of the 2.5 saloon before BL's rationalisation programme was in full swing with its axe. It was a *fait accompli* that Leyland could have chopped but elected to live with, though with the ex-Buick Rover V8 also in the stable, Triumph's offering, despite being on paper a more modern and attractive design with its overhead cam valvegear, was a luxury they could have done without. Had Leyland foreseen the problems that were to dog the engine in service, no doubt they *would* have abandoned it at a very late stage, and shoe-horned the Rover V8 into the Stag instead. Yes, it does fit, as the engine swappers have proved. So does the straight-six Triumph and Ford's

V6, both of which are now also powering a number of Stags that blew their original engines. Not having driven any of these hybrids, I must take the word of Stag specialist and purist Tony Hart that they are expensive and inferior alternatives to the real thing. And the real thing when it's in good shape is a very pleasing and potent piece of machinery, as *Motor*'s original 1970 road test underlines. Even with a test weight approaching 1½ tons, the original press car accelerated to 60 mph from rest in 9.7 sec and lapped MIRA at 117 mph, reaching well over 120 mph on the fastest section of the course. Tony Hart's car felt every bit as quick as the automatic *Motor* tested in 1973, which did 112 mph and was only a fifth of a second slower to 60 mph. Of the two, the six-speed manual is surely the more attractive, though, its long-legged overdrive top giving over 24 mph/1000 rpm and therefore very relaxed and economical cruising — almost 30 mpg at 70 mph. Tony Hart reckons to get 20 mpg overall from his automatic, while some of his customers claim over 26 mpg from gently driven manual versions.

The Stag was born in 1970 as a luxury grand tourer with particularly sophisticated headgear — open, closed or ragtop — and it wasn't until after production had ceased two years ago that many people began to appreciate just how attractive it was in concept and character. Ignoring supercar

Comfortable cockpit was an excellent blend of modern ergonomics with traditional style

The compact 3-litre alloy-head overhead cam V8 fits with room to spare in the engine bay

£10,000, though half that amount will buy a good '76/77 car, and £1,500 an early example. A few years ago, old Stags were such bad news in the trade you could hardly give them away: like the NSU RO80, many an otherwise sound car with a duff engine was sold for little more than scrap value.

It was just such a sick car that kindled Tony Hart's interest in the model a few years back, since when his Hart Racing Services in Britannia Rd, London SW6 has become Britain's largest Stag specialist. To underline his faith in the car, Tony not only drives one on the road but is now campaigning a wide-wheeled modsport version which, even with a standard engine (there's a 250 bhp tweaked one on the way) has already raised a few eyebrows. As two thirds of the 26,000 Stags that Triumph produced remained in Britain — the car was not a great export success, which was disappointing, as it seemed just right for sunny American climes — there are plenty around to receive his expert attention. And, more to the point, plenty on the market for buyers to choose from.

Jeremy Sinek has described the nature of the engine problems on page 70, so I won't go into it all here. It all sounds and looks a bit alarming, but Hart claims that the use of a good quality anti-freeze with the right inhibitor to prevent corrosion, and flushing out the whole system once a year — particularly the radiator to unclog

it — are the only precautions necessary to prevent these chronic disorders. He also strongly recommends changing the oil and filter every 3,000 miles and checking the timing chain every 25,000: once they start to zizz, there's a danger of jumping a tooth which is sufficient to cause destructive encounters of the eight-fold kind between valves and pistons. And if you've had the heads off for any reason, Hart recommends torquing them down to 60 lb ft instead of the recommended 55, then re-torquing them immediately after the engine has been warmed to full running temperature, rather than after the recommended 500 miles.

What you mustn't do in a Stag is to attempt — as the previous owner of Tony Hart's car apparently did — to make it to the next garage if there are any signs, from whatever cause, of overheating. With an iron-headed engine you might make it without serious consequences. In the Triumph, with its very heat-sensitive alloy heads and lubrication system, you won't. If you're buying a Stag, .ncidentally, a rattly engine does not necessarily indicate imminent bearing failure: it could simply be a loose timing chain which, provided it doesn't jump first and self destruct the innards, is probably not as serious as it sounds. Check that the radiator is as hot at the bottom as it is at the top: if it's not, there's something amiss with the circulation and the expensive damage may

continued over

Mercedes, the prices of which are out of sight, there is nothing on the market now that comes anywhere close, which is why young, low-mileage Stags can command very high prices. Rumour has it that a few T-registered cars, the last of the new stock, have actually changed hands for around

MOTOR week ending October 6, 1979

already have been done. Check, too, that the radiator thermostat hasn't been removed to mask some chronic cooling problem, and make sure that the oil pressure light is connected. Leave well alone if it's not.

Apart from the engine, which can give long and reliable service provided it is properly maintained, Tony Hart contends that the Stag has no other major weaknesses, though it's important to keep the rear axle breather clear. Clogging here can cause the oil to overheat and escape, with the consequent danger of seizure. Although you need to watch for corrosion over the front wheelarches and rear wing/sill joints, rust is not a serious problem. The bodywork of Tony Hart's car, an N-registered automatic with 45,000 miles on the clock, was generally in good shape despite a few rust blemishes.

To drive, his Stag was much as I remembered, with a number of endearing qualities and a few innate flaws too. Start-up was prompt and apart from a lumpy idle, the engine ran smoothly and cleanly up to the red line at 6500 rpm with a characteristic burble that has always seemed a little more pronounced than on other V8s. Something to do with the exhaust it seems. Despite its fairly high weight of 26 cwt with the hardtop in place, and a relatively modest output which remained at 145 bhp throughout the car's production run, the performance is satisfyingly brisk, though the Borg Warner 35 automatic gearbox of this car had seen better days. It thumped fiercely when engaging gear, and seemed a little reluctant to shift into top when pottering around town.

The power steering (which all Stags had) has the same sort of feel as that of the Rover SD1s — quick in response and accurate with it, though a little lacking in feel. On non-standard 205 section tyres, the cornering powers of Tony Hart's car are very high, though on fast bends there's a discernible loss of composure and enough diagonal pitching to wobble your head uncomfortably. Although the car nose dives under braking, and squats when you accelerate hard, just as it always did, there was no evidence of the twitching off line when you changed gear or throttled back, behaviour that we criticised in the road tests. We always put this irritating characteristic down to spline lock (an unlock) in the drive-shafts, but Tony Hart says it can be cured by replacing the rubber suspension bushes with harder nylon ones. The slightly soft, sloppy and clonky behaviour of the

suspension, as well as the rather agitated high-speed ride, are typical characteristics, the slight pull to the left in the steering, and an off-centre wheel, minor irritations hopefully peculiar to this five-year-old. The brakes were strong and true, though the pedal was a little spongy.

Even by current standards — in fact especially by current plasticky standards — the interior gets high marks. Triumph really did have a knack of embracing a modern control layout in a traditional British setting, represented by generous areas of attractive matt-finish wood. Real timber at that. Aesthetically and ergonomically, it is an excellent arrangement, with a neat, readable and comprehensive set of instruments supported by Triumph's all-systems-go cluster of warning lights, handy fingertip switchgear, and efficient heating and ventilation. A nice steering wheel that's adjustable for reach and rake helps to achieve a comfortable driving position, though Tony Hart's car reminded me of two gripes of old — the seat cushion is too flat and the transmission bulge forces your left leg to rest on it awkwardly. The pedals are also offset to the right for the same reason. Even so, the Stag is a comfortable, relaxing and pleasant car to drive as well as to ride in — provided you're in the front. The back seat is very cramped for adults. Refinement, though, is marred by excessive wind noise — a problem that was never developed out of the car — even with the heavy but totally weatherproof hardtop in place. It's a two-man job to remove, incidentally, so you can't slip it off with every break in the clouds. For me, the car is at its excellent best as an open sunshine tourer.

Like so many interesting, up-market cars, third and fourth-hand Stags were often bought by people who could not really afford to run and maintain them properly. However, Tony Hart is now aware of changing trends in ownership. Stags are definitely becoming respectable again, even rather desirable. A number of his customers are well-heeled enthusiasts who could no doubt afford more expensive modern machinery but prefer instead to run a Stag because of its investment value and appealing concept, and to have it professionally attended to by a specialist who not only understands the car but shares their love for it. Hart, who sees 25 to 30 Stags through his large and well-equipped premises every week, offers a range of routine services, as well as major repair and restoration work. He can be contacted on 01-731 3287.

Broken harts

Jeremy Sinek attempts to sort the fact from the fiction about what went wrong with the Stag, and why

TO USE a culinary simile, the Triumph Stag was an exotic dish with top-quality basic ingredients, which went somewhat awry when it came to the herbs and spices of its technical execution. But make no mistake: the Stag had — and second-hand examples still do have — all the makings of a dish fit for kings.

For a start, it looks distinctive, with styling by an Italian coachbuilder (Michelotti) that's recognisably from the Triumph stable, yet stylishly different from the 2000/2500 saloons from whose floorplan and running gear the Stag was developed. In its concept — as a civilised convertible with two plus two accommodation — the Stag was near flawless.

Under the skin, its all-independent suspension layout has much in common with those adopted by certain teutonic thoroughbreds, with MacPherson struts at the front and semi-trailing arms at the rear; but the steering has the theoretical superiority of a rack and pinion mechanism. Transmission-wise, the choice was between a three-speed automatic, or a four-speed manual with overdrive.

So far, the technicalities follow Triumph's big-saloon practice, and as originally conceived the Stag would probably have also had the same straight-six engine. When it finally appeared, though, it was with an all-new overhead cam three-litre V8, and in the event this engine's greater capacity and power necessitated many detail changes to the saloon's running gear: the gearbox was uprated, and so were the final drive gears; it was felt that bigger brakes were needed, and that in turn meant the adoption of 14-inch instead of 13-inch wheels.

It was that engine, though, that on paper was the source of much of the Stag's appeal, but which in practice was also the cause of nearly all its problems.

On the face of it there was no reason why the Stag's V8 should have proved troublesome in service: there was nothing over-ambitious about its design, nor was it in a particularly high state of tune. The two cylinder banks are set at 90 deg in a cast iron block incorporating a crankcase which extends well below the crankshaft centre-line, with bore/stroke dimensions of 86×64.5 mm giving a swept volume of 2,997 cc.

Separate single-roller chains are driven by separate sprockets on the nose of the crankshaft, and each operates a single overhead camshaft in each alloy cross-flow cylinder head. The inverted valves, in wedge-shaped combustion chambers, are operated by the cams via

Left: A Hart digit points out the kind of corrosion that was the source of the troubles on many engines

Left; note the water pump, mounted high and off-centre between cylinder banks, which didn't provide even distribution of water between the two banks

inverted bucket type tappets, with adjustment by hardened steel shims.

Skew gears on a jackshaft, driven by one of the timing chains, drive the ancillaries — the oil pump, distributor and water pump. The latter is of the impeller type, and is mounted vertically between the banks where it also directs water through the inlet manifold, on which are mounted a pair of Stromberg 175CDS carburetters. On a compression ratio of 8.8:1 the engine produces a useful but conservative 145 bhp (net) at 5,500 rpm, and 170 lb ft of torque at 3,500 rpm.

It shouldn't have added up to a fragile and temperamental unit, but such it has proved to be.

One weakness was in the timing chains, which wear rapidly and become noisy, often requiring replacement every 25 to 30 thousand miles — a problem that might well have been avoided with twin-roller chains.

Then there was a brief period when crankshaft bearings wore out prematurely, a consequence of a (temporary) machining problem which resulted in the wrong surface finish on the crankshaft journals. Premature wear could also occur as a consequence of poor maintenance, or if the engine (and hence, the oil) was running too hot as a consequence of cooling problems.

Everyone I've talked to, including some who were involved in the development of the engine, are agreed that it was various aspects of the cooling system that, in an interlinked sort of way, were the main problem areas.

It does seem that the design of the cooling system was somewhat marginal in several respects, any one of which could initiate problems which would in turn reduce the safety margin in other areas; but it's difficult to pinpoint any single root cause, or to define a specific sequence of events.

What *does* seem clear is as follows: on the Stag engine — as with most V8 engines having a single water pump — water flow between the cylinder banks is delicately balanced and easily upset; that Stag engines need more care in assembly than most, which the garages that repaired them (or even the workers who originally assembled them?) were not always able to provide, leading to poor gasket sealing and continuing problems for owners who had spent hundreds of pounds on repairs; and that some of the anti-freeze/inhibitors used didn't always work as well as they should have, allowing corrosion that affected gasket sealing and

water circulation.

What it boils down to (ouch) is that the Stag's is an engine that can't simply be thrown together after an overhaul, nor is it one that can be neglected in daily use, or small problems can develop into major ones. You only need to lose a little bit of water, from a leaking hose for example, for the water level to drop below that of the high-mounted water pump and hence cease to circulate; or a poorly sealing head gasket (provoked, perhaps, by careless assembly, or by corrosion), could allow combustion gases to interfere with the delicately balanced flow through one bank of cylinders, cause localised overheating (which might well not register on the water temperature gauge) and if it went on long enough the head could warp. Then the gasket leaks could get worse and in

extreme cases cause total loss of water at speed and a badly cooked engine.

Even if things didn't quite reach that stage, the heads would usually have to come off for skimming or even replacement, and sometimes that would be easier said than done, corrosion around the studs making it near-impossible to get the head off at all.

Then again, choked radiators (a common ailment arising out of corrosion deposits) could lead to poor circulation and excessively high running temperatures, which means overheated oil, ineffective lubrication, and big-end failures.

If it all begins to sound pretty hopeless, then take heart (ouch); Tony Hart has got the answer — but you've read all about that in the preceding Golden Oldie feature.

91 ▶

For peace of mind, many Stag owners have opted for the transplant route. Above is a Rover V8 conversion, as effected by C. J. Hutton Automotive Services, 142A East St. Epsom. A similar conversion is available from V8 Conversions, Oak Farm, Green Street Green, Orpington, Kent; or a d-i-y kit is available from Dawson Stag Conversions, details from Ashtead (Surrey) 76991. Alternatively, you can have the Ford V6 fitted by Hurley Motor Engineering, 10-16 Arbury Ave, Foleshill, Coventry, or fit it yourself using Hurley's kit

The specialists

Hart racing

Jonathan Wood *went to see a company that specialises in nothing but Triumph Stags*

IT seems amazing that a British production car that only went out of production two years ago has already achieved collectable status. Yet just this has happened to the controversial Triumph Stag, some 25,000 having been built between 1970 and 1977.

Now Stag owners can benefit from a garage well situated in Central London that specialises in nothing but, and they've never been busier! Hart Racing Services of 73-77 Brittania Road, Fulham, London S.W.6 (01-731 3287-9) probably deals with about 100 Stags a month and this includes the 1974 editorial example.

Anthony Hart told me that he got into the Stag business almost by accident. He had initially been involved in the preparation of historic racing cars, Aston Martins, Ferraris and the like. Then a friend of his purchased a Stag with a noisy timing chain. Unfortunately the engine went bang before Anthony could get to it so he fitted a replacement short motor. This was followed up by another example with similar problems and an advertisement in *Exchange and Mart* did the rest. Soon Anthony had outgrown his cramped Hammersmith premises and in May of 1978 moved to his present address.

The Stag, says Anthony, is a reliable enough car providing it is serviced regularly, the prescribed intervals being every three months or 3000 miles. Another vital task that must be carried out at 25,000 is the fitting of new timing chains. This costs about £100 but if you leave them, the timing jumps (the reason for the aforementioned "bang") and the valves meet up with the pistons and the outcome could set you back about £900. The old chains tend to stretch unduly probably because they have single rather than double links. He keeps a rather grisly "Black Museum" on his counter of pistons with pieces of valve embedded in them to show what happens when the chain is left for too long. Other important points relating to the running of the Stag include stopping the moment it boils and using anti-freeze with an aluminium inhibitor. If the latter action isn't adherred to the water passages in the head start to corrode and before you know where you are you're loosing coolant. In view of the fact that engine problems can occur if the unit isn't regularly ministered to, HRS have a department that reconditions the 3 litre V8 on the premises. You can therefore buy exchange cylinder heads for £140 each, short motors are £255 while complete exchange engines are £595.

Although Hart Racing Services no longer prepare customers cars for competition, the name being an inheritance from the days when Anthony was involved in historic car racing, the company does have its own racing Stag that first appeared this season in the Modsport championship. He has made two appearances this year and next year it is planned to campaign the car in the BRSCC championship round. The garage also sports a pick up truck which is, of course, a converted Stag although this is a customised effort and something of a head turner.

At present the Stag spares situation isn't too bad but HRS are sensibly stockpiling parts, both new and secondhand for the days when they'll be harder to come by. It certainly seems that the time won't be too far off when they start regularly restoring Stags. For interest in the model is such that HRS have recently received examples from Belgium and Switzerland that have to be "sorted". Other services are to include special gaskets to resurrect overskimmed cylinder heads and blank main bearing caps which they say will "smooth up your big end".

It seems that HRS is going to be kept busy for many years to come. Clearly British Leyland's loss is Anthony Hart's gain!

Stop Press! If you want to join the Stag Owners Club write to June Armstrong at HRS. ●

Top, Stag engines being re-built at HRS. Middle, Stags at Bay. Below, part of the extensive stores. Bottom left, top, a warning of using the wrong anti freeze in heads on left, note corroded water passages and (below) maladies that can strike Stag engines.

TRIUMPH STAG

TRIUMPH STAG 1970-1980

A total of 28 articles develops the Stag story
from its introduction in 1970. Included are
ten road tests and a comparison test v. the
Reliant Scimitar. Other articles deal with
10,000, 13,000, 20,000 and 24,000 mile
reports, touring, buying a secondhand
vehicle, and a piece covering the Stag
specialists Hart Racing Services.
   100 Large Pages.

TRIUMPH STAG Collection No. 1
(1970-1984)

Some 17 articles from the UK, US and
Australia trace the Stag from its launch
in 1970. 2 comparison tests, a service test,
4 road tests and 2 restropsective articles
follow the Stag through its production.
Other articles cover the car's initial
introduction, engineering details and
specifications.
   70 Large Pages.

These soft-bound volumes in the 'Brooklands Books' series consist of reprints of original road test
reports and other stories that appeared in leading motoring journals during the periods concerned.
Fully illustrated with photographs and cut-away drawings, the articles contain road impressions, per-
formance figures, specifications, etc. NONE OF THE ARTICLES APPEARS IN MORE THAN ONE
BOOK. Sources include Autocar, Autosport, Car, Cars & Car Conversions, Car & Driver, Car Craft,
Classic & Sportscar, Modern Motor, Motor, Motor Manual, Motor Racing, Motor Sport, Practical Classics,
Road Test, Road & Track, Sports Car Graphic, Sports Car World and Wheels.

From specialist booksellers or, in case of difficulty, direct from the distributors:
BROOKLANDS BOOK DISTRIBUTION, 'HOLMERISE', SEVEN HILLS ROAD,
COBHAM, SURREY KT11 1ES, ENGLAND. Telephone: Cobham (09326) 5051
MOTORBOOKS INTERNATIONAL, OSCEOLA, WISCONSIN 54020, USA.
Telephone: 715 294 3345 & 800 826 6600

Give your St

Hart Racing Services know their way to a Stag's heart — everything from a quick pick-me-up to a full overhaul.

The equipment we employ and the experience we've gained makes us the people to see to give your Stag more tractable performance and more driving pleasure.

Our normal stock includes full or short reconditioned engines, cylinder heads, gearboxes, differentials, driveshafts, distributors and power steering racks — in short, everything a Stag could want.

What's more, our special 'HRS' parts include blank main bearing caps, extra large radiators and special gaskets to resurrect overskimmed cylinder heads. Also in stock are stainless steel exhaust systems guaranteed for the life of the car.

Apart from our huge stock of new parts, we also buy and sell used parts.

We can also offer the same service for the Dolomite and TR7.

BRITAIN'S GENUINE STAG SPECIALISTS

g new Hart!

TIMES HAVE CHANGED...

... Triumph of the Stag

Times have changed. The Triumph Stag should have been a winner from the first! Today, the Stag has left its troublesome reputation far behind. It is now a highly collectable car enjoyed by thousands of enthusiasts.

Offering power, style and versatility, the Stag brings many rewards to the discerning owner. This Grand Tourer's popularity is underlined by the growth of the Stag Owners'

Club. With a membership of over 4,000 SOC is now the largest single-model enthusiasts club in the U.K.

SOC members benefit from:

*Nationwide discounts on spares
*Special insurance terms
*A 50-page plus monthly magazine
*Technical advice/support
*Local/national events

**Find out more about a unique club.
For membership details send a large S.A.E. to:
Stag Owners' Club
Warmlake Estate,
Sutton Valence, Maidstone Road,
Maidstone, Kent ME17 3LP.**